Family Sins
&
OTHER STORIES

Family Sins

&

OTHER STORIES

WILLIAM TREVOR

VIKING

VIKING
Published by the Penguin Group
Viking Penguin, a division of Penguin Books USA Inc.,
40 West 23rd Street, New York, New York 10010, U.S.A.
Penguin Books Ltd, 27 Wrights Lane, London W8 5TZ, England
Penguin Books Australia Ltd, Ringwood, Victoria, Australia
Penguin Books Canada Ltd, 2801 John Street,
Markham, Ontario, Canada L3R 1B4
Penguin Books (N.Z.) Ltd, 182–190 Wairau Road,
Auckland 10, New Zealand

Penguin Books Ltd, Registered Offices:
Harmondsworth, Middlesex, England

First American Edition
Published in 1990 by Viking Penguin,
a division of Penguin Books USA Inc.

1   3   5   7   9   10   8   6   4   2

"Events at Drimaghleen," "Honeymoon in Tramore," "The Printmaker,"
and "A Husband's Return" first appeared in *Grand Street*; "Family Sins,"
"The Third Party," "A Trinity," and "Kathleen's Field" in *The New Yorker*;
"In Love with Ariadne" in *Harper's*; "Children of the Headmaster" in *The
Spectator* and "August Saturday" in *Woman's Journal*.

LIBRARY OF CONGRESS CATALOGING IN PUBLICATION DATA
Trevor, William, 1928–
Family sins & other stories / William Trevor.
p.   cm.
ISBN 0–670–83257–X
I. Title.   II. Title: Family sins and other stories.
PR6070.R4F36   1990
823'.914– dc20   89-40645

Printed in the United States of America

CONTENTS

Family Sins

&

OTHER STORIES

Events at Drimaghleen

Nothing as appalling had happened before at Drimaghleen; its people had never been as shocked. They'd had their share of distress, like any people; there were memories of dramatic occurrences; stories from a more distant past were told. In the 1880s a woman known as the Captain's wife had run away with a hunchbacked pedlar. In 1798 there'd been resistance in the hills and fighting in Drimaghleen itself. During the Troubles a local man had been executed in a field by the Black and Tans. But no story, and no long memory, could match the horror of the tragedy that awaited the people of Drimaghleen on May 22nd, 1985, a Wednesday morning.

The McDowds, that morning, awoke in their farmhouse and began the day as they always did, McDowd pulling on his shirt and trousers and lifting down a black overcoat from the pegs beside the kitchen door. He fastened it with a length of string which he kept in one of its pockets, found his socks in his gum-boots and went out with his two sheep-dogs to drive the cows in for milking. His wife washed herself, put the kettle on the stove, and knocked on her daughter's door. 'Maureen!' she called. 'Come on now, Maureen!'

It was not unusual that Maureen failed to reply. Mrs McDowd re-entered her bedroom, stepped out of her night-dress and dressed herself. 'Get up out of that, Maureen!' she shouted, banging again on her daughter's door. 'Are you sick?' she enquired, puzzled now by the lack of movement

(9)

from within the room: always at this second rousing Maureen yawned or spoke. 'Maureen!' she shouted again, and then opened the door.

McDowd, calling in the cattle, was aware that there had been something wrong in the yard as he'd passed through it, but an early-morning torpor hindered the progression of his thoughts when he endeavoured to establish what it was. His wife's voice shouting across the field at him, and his daughter's name used repeatedly in the information that was being inadequately conveyed to him, jolted him into an awareness that what had been wrong was that Maureen's bicycle had not been leaning against the kitchen window-sill. 'Maureen hasn't come back,' his wife repeated again when he was close enough to hear her. 'She's not been in her bed.'

The cows were milked because no matter what the reason for Maureen's absence they had to be. The breakfast was placed on the kitchen table because no good would come of not taking food. McDowd, in silence, ate with an appetite that was unaffected; his wife consumed less than usual. 'We will drive over,' he said when they had finished, anger thickening his voice.

She nodded. She'd known as soon as she'd seen the un-used bed that they would have to do something. They could not just wait for a letter to arrive, or a telegram, or whatever it was their daughter had planned. They would drive over to the house where Lancy Butler lived with his mother, the house to which their daughter had cycled the evening be-fore. They did not share the thought that possessed both of them: that their daughter had taken the law into her own hands and gone off with Lancy Butler, a spoilt and useless man.

McDowd was a tallish, spare man of sixty-two, his face almost gaunt, grey hair ragged on his head. His wife, two years younger, was thin also, with gnarled features and the hands of a woman who all her life had worked in the fields. They did not say much to one another, and never had; but they did not quarrel either. On the farm, discussion was rarely apt, there being no profit in it; it followed naturally that grounds for disagreement were limited. Five children had been born to the McDowds; Maureen was the youngest and the only one who had remained at home. Without a show of celebration, for that was not the family way, her twenty-fifth birthday had passed by a month ago.

'Put your decent trousers on,' Mrs McDowd urged. 'You can't go like that.'

'I'm all right the way I am.'

She knew he would not be persuaded and did not try, but instead hurried back to her bedroom to change her shoes. At least he wouldn't drive over in the overcoat with the string round it: that was only for getting the cows in from the field when the mornings were cold. He'd taken it off before he'd sat down to his breakfast and there would be no cause to put it on again. She covered up her own old skirt and jumper with her waterproof.

'The little bitch,' he said in the car, and she said nothing.

They both felt the same, anxious and cross at the same time, not wanting to believe the apparent truth. Their daughter had ungratefully deceived them: again in silence the thought was shared while he drove the four miles to the Butlers' house. When they turned off the tarred road into a lane, already passing between the Butlers' fields, they heard the dog barking. The window of the Volkswagen on Mrs McDowd's side wouldn't wind up, due to a defect that had developed a month ago: the shrill barking easily carried above the rattle of the engine.

That was that, they thought, listening to the dog. Maureen and Lancy had gone the night before, and Mrs Butler couldn't manage the cows on her own. No wonder the old dog was beside himself. Bitterly, McDowd called his daughter a bitch again, though only to himself. Lancy Butler, he thought, my God! Lancy Butler would lead her a dance, and lead her astray, and lead her down into the gutters of some town. He'd warned her a thousand times about Lancy Butler. He'd told her the kind of fool he was.

'His father was a decent man,' he said, breaking at last the long silence. 'Never touched a drop.'

'The old mother ruined him.'

It wouldn't last long, they both thought. Lancy Butler might marry her, or he might wriggle out of it. But however it turned out she'd be back in six months' time or at any rate a year's. There'd probably be a baby to bring up.

The car turned into the yard, and neither McDowd nor his wife immediately saw their daughter lying beside the pump. For the first few moments of their arrival their attention was claimed by the distressed dog, a black and white sheepdog like their own two. Dust had risen from beneath the Volkswagen's wheels and was still thick in the air as they stepped from the car. The dog was running wildly across a corner of the yard, back and forth, and back and forth again. The dog's gone mad, Mrs McDowd thought, something's after affecting it. Then she saw her daughter's body lying by the pump, and a yard or so away her daughter's bicycle lying on its side, as if she had fallen from it. Beside the bicycle were two dead rabbits.

'My God,' McDowd said, and his wife knew from his voice that he hadn't seen his daughter yet but was looking at something else. He had walked to another part of the yard, where the dog was. He had gone there instinctively, to try to calm the animal.

She knelt down, whispering to Maureen, thinking in her confusion that her daughter had just this minute fallen off her bicycle. But Maureen's face was as cold as stone, and her flesh had already stiffened. Mrs McDowd screamed, and then she was aware that she was lying down herself, clasping Maureen's dead body. A moment later she was aware that her husband was weeping piteously, unable to control himself, that he was kneeling down, his hands on the body also.

Mrs McDowd did not remember rising to her feet, or finding the energy and the will to do so. 'Don't go over there,' she heard her husband saying to her, and saw him wiping at his eyes with the arm of his jersey. But he didn't try to stop her when she went to where the dog was; he remained on his knees beside their daughter, calling out to her between his sobs, asking her not to be dead.

The dog was crouched in a doorway, not barking any more. A yard or so away Mrs Butler lay with one of her legs twisted under her, blood on the ground already turned brown, a pool of it still scarlet. Looking down at her, Mrs McDowd thought with abrupt lucidity: Maureen did not fall off her bicycle. She went back to where her daughter lay and behind the two tin barrels that stood by the pump she saw the body of Lancy Butler, and on the ground not far from it the shotgun that must have blown off Mrs Butler's face.

*

O'Kelly of the Garda arrived at a swift conclusion. Old Mrs Butler had been as adamant as the McDowds in her opposition to the match that her son and Maureen McDowd had planned for themselves. And there was more to it than that: Mrs Butler had been obsessively possessive, hiding from no one her determination that no other woman should ever take her son away from her. Lancy was her only child, the single one to survive years of miscarrying. His father had died when Lancy was only two years old, leaving mother and child to lead a lonely life on a farm that was remote. O'Kelly knew that Mrs Butler had been reputed to be strange in the head, and given to furious jealousies where Lancy was concerned. In the kind of rage that people who'd known her were familiar with she had shot her son's sweetheart rather than suffer the theft of him. He had wrenched the shotgun from her and by accident or otherwise it had exploded. A weak man at the best of times, he had turned it upon himself rather than face the reality of what had happened. This deduction, borne out by the details in the yard, satisfied O'Kelly of the Garda; the people of Drimaghleen arrived themselves at the same conclusion. 'It was always trouble,' McDowd said on the day of the funerals. 'The minute she went out with Lancy Butler it was trouble written down for poor Maureen.'

Drimaghleen was a townland, with nothing to mark it except a crossroads that was known as Drimaghleen Crossroads. The modest farms that comprised it, each of thirty or so acres, were scattered among bogland, one separated from the next by several miles, as the McDowds' and the Butlers' were. The village of Kilmona was where the people of Drimaghleen went to mass, and where they confessed to Father Sallins. The children of the farms went to school in the small town of Mountcroe, driven each morning in a yellow bus that drove them back to the end of their lanes or farm tracks in the afternoon. Milk churns were collected in much the same way by the creamery lorry. Bread and groceries were bought in the village; fresh meat in Mountcroe. When the men of Drimaghleen got drunk they did so in Mountcroe, never in the village, although often they took a few bottles of stout there, in the bar beside the grocery counter. Hardware and clothes were bought in Mountcroe, which had had a cinema called the Abbey Picture House until the advent of television closed it in the early 1960s. Drimaghleen, Kilmona and Mountcroe formed a world that bounded the lives of the people of the Drimaghleen farms. Rarely was there occasion to venture beyond it to the facilities of a town that was larger—unless the purpose happened to be a search for work or the first step on the way to exile.

The children of the McDowds, whose search for such work had taken them far from the townland, returned heartbroken for their sister's mass. All four of them came, two with husbands, one with a wife, one on her own. The weddings which had taken place had been the last family occasions, two of them in Kilmona, the third in distant Skibbereen, the home of the girl whom the McDowds' son had married a year ago. That wedding was on their minds at Maureen's mass—the long journey there had been in the Volkswagen, the night they had spent in Eldon's Hotel, the farewells the next day. Not in the wildest horror of a nightmare could any of the McDowds have guessed the nature of the occasion destined to bring them together next.

After the funeral the family returned to the farm. The younger McDowds had known of Maureen's and Lancy Butler's attachment, and of their parents' opposition to it. They had known as well of Mrs Butler's possessive affection for her son, having grown up with stories of this maternal eccentricity, and having witnessed Lancy himself, as a child and as a boy, affected by her indulgence. 'Oh, it can wait, Lancy, it can wait,' she would say a dozen times an hour, referring to some necessary chore on the farm. 'Ah, sure, we won't bother with school today,' she had said before that, when Lancy had complained of a difficulty he was experiencing with the seven-times table or Brother Martin's twenty weekend spellings. The people of Drimaghleen used to wonder whether the farm or Lancy would suffer more in the end.

'What did she see in him?' Mrs McDowd mused sadly at the funeral meal. 'Will anyone ever tell me what she saw in him?'

They shook their heads. The cheeks of all of them were still smeared with the tears they had shed at the service. Conversation was difficult.

'We will never recover from it,' the father said, with finality in his voice. It was all that could be said, it was all they knew with certainty: for as long as the older McDowds remained in this farmhouse—which would be until their own deaths—the vicious, ugly tragedy would haunt them. They knew that if Maureen had been knocked from her bicycle by a passing motor-car they could have borne her death with greater fortitude; or if she had died of an illness, or been the victim of incurable disease. The knife that turned in their pain was their memory of the Butlers' farm-yard, the barking dog running back and forth, the three still bodies. There was nothing but the waste of a life to contemplate, and the cruelty of chance—for why should it have been simple, pretty Maureen whose fate it was to become mixed up with so peculiar a couple as that mother and son? There were other girls in the neighbourhood—underhand girls and girls of doubtful character—who somehow more readily belonged with the Butlers: anyone would tell you that.

'Why don't you drive over and see us?' one of the daughters invited. 'Can't we persuade you?'

Her father stared into the table without trying to reply. It was unnecessary to say that a drive of such a distance could only be contemplated when there was a wedding or a funeral. Such journeys had not been undertaken during Maureen's lifetime, when she might have looked after the farm for a day; in no way could they be considered now. Mrs McDowd tried to smile, making an effort to acknowledge the concern that had inspired the suggestion, but no smile came.

*

Being of a nature that might interest strangers, the deaths were reported in the newspapers. They were mentioned on the radio, and on the television news. Then everything became quiet again at Drimaghleen, and in the village and in the town. People wrote letters to the McDowds, expressing their sorrow. People came to see them but did not stay long. 'I am always there,' Father Sallins said. 'Kilmona 23. You have only to summon me. Or call up at the rectory.'

The McDowds didn't. They watched the summer going by, taking in their hay during the warm spell in June, keeping an eye on the field of potatoes and the ripening barley.

It began to rain more than usual; they worried about the barley.

'Excuse me,' a man said in the yard one afternoon in October. 'Are you Mr McDowd?'

McDowd said he was, shouting at the dogs to behave themselves. The stranger would be a traveller in fertilisers, he said to himself, a replacement for Donoghue, who had been coming to the farm for years. Then he realised that it was the wrong time of year for Donoghue.

'Would it be possible to have a word, Mr McDowd?'

McDowd's scrawny features slowly puckered; slowly he frowned. He lifted a hand and scratched at his grey, ragged hair, which was a way he had when he wished to disguise bewilderment. Part of his countryman's wiliness was that he preferred outsiders not to know, or deduce, what was occurring in his mind.

'A word?' he said.

'Could we maybe step inside, sir?'

McDowd saw no reason to step inside his own house with this man. The visitor was florid-faced, untidily dressed in dark corduroy trousers and a gabardine jacket. His hair was long and black, and grew coarsely down the sides of his face in two brushlike panels. He had a city voice; it wasn't difficult to guess he came from Dublin.

'What d'you want with me?'

'I was sorry to hear that thing about your daughter, Mr McDowd. That was a terrible business.'

'It's over and done with.'

'It is, sir. Over and done with.'

The red bonnet of a car edged its way into the yard. McDowd watched it, reminded of some cautious animal by the slow, creeping movement, the engine purring so lightly you could hardly hear it. When the car stopped by the milking shed nobody got out of it, but McDowd could see a figure wearing sun-glasses at the wheel. This was a woman, with black hair also, smoking a cigarette.

(17)

'It could be to your advantage, Mr McDowd.'

'What could be? Does that car belong to you?'

'We drove down to see you, sir. That lady's a friend of mine, a colleague by the name of Hetty Fortune.'

The woman stepped out of the car. She was taller than the man, with a sombre face and blue trousers that matched her blue shirt. She dropped her cigarette on to the ground and carefully stubbed it out with the toe of her shoe. As slowly as she had driven the car she walked across the yard to where the two men were standing. The dogs growled at her, but she took no notice. 'I'm Hetty Fortune,' she said in an English accent.

'I didn't tell you my own name, Mr McDowd,' the man said. 'It's Jeremiah Tyler.'

'I hope Jeremiah has offered you our condolences, Mr McDowd. I hope both you and your wife will accept our deepest sympathy.'

'What do you want here?'

'We've been over at the Butlers' place, Mr McDowd. We spent a long time there. We've been talking to a few people. Could we talk to you, d'you think?'

'Are you the newspapers?'

'In a manner of speaking. Yes, in a manner of speaking we represent the media. And I'm perfectly sure,' the woman added hastily, 'you've had more than enough of all that. I believe you'll find what we have to say to you is different, Mr McDowd.'

'The wife and myself have nothing to say to the newspapers. We didn't say anything at the time, and we have nothing to say since. I have things to do about the place.'

'Mr McDowd, would you be good enough to give us five minutes of your time? Five minutes in your kitchen, talking to yourself and your wife? Would you give us an opportunity to explain?'

Attracted by the sound by voices, Mrs McDowd came

(18)

out of the house. She stood in the doorway, not quite emerging from the kitchen porch, regarding the strangers even more distrustfully than her husband had. She didn't say anything when the woman approached her and held out a hand which she was obliged to shake.

'We are sorry to obtrude on your grief, Mrs McDowd. Mr Tyler and I have been keen to make that clear to your husband.'

Mrs McDowd did not acknowledge this. She didn't like the look of the sombre-faced woman or her unkempt companion. There was a seediness about him, a quality that city people seemed often to exude if they weren't smartly attired. The woman wasn't seedy but you could see she was insincere from the way her mouth was. You could hear the insincerity when she spoke.

'The full truth has not been established, Mrs McDowd. It is that that we would like to discuss with you.'

'I've told you no,' McDowd said. 'I've told them to go away,' he said to his wife.

Mrs McDowd's eyes stared at the woman's sun-glasses. She remained where she was, not quite coming into the yard. The man said:

'Would it break the ice if I took a snap? Would you mind that, sir? If I was to take a few snaps of yourself and the wife?'

He had spoken out of turn. A shadow of anger passed over the woman's face. The fingers of her left hand moved in an irritated wriggle. She said quickly:

'That's not necessary at this stage.'

'We've got to get the pictures, Hetty,' the man mumbled, hushing the words beneath his breath so that the McDowds wouldn't hear. But they guessed the nature of his protest, for it showed in his pink face. The woman snapped something at him.

'If you don't leave us alone we'll have to get the Guards,' McDowd said. 'You're trespassing on this land.'

'Is it fair on your daughter's memory that the truth should be hidden, Mr McDowd?'

'Another thing is, those dogs can be fierce if they want to be.'

'It isn't hidden,' Mrs McDowd said. 'We all know what happened. Detectives worked it out, but sure anyone could have told them.'

'No, Mrs McDowd, nothing was properly worked out at all. That's what I'm saying to you. The surface was scarcely disturbed. What seemed to be the truth wasn't.'

McDowd told his wife to lock the door. They would drive over to Mountcroe and get a Guard to come back with them. 'We don't want any truck with you,' he harshly informed their visitors. 'If the dogs eat the limbs off you after we've gone don't say it wasn't mentioned.'

Unmoved by these threats, her voice losing none of its confidence, the woman said that what was available was something in the region of three thousand pounds. 'For a conversation of brief duration you would naturally have to be correctly reimbursed. Already we have taken up your working time, and of course we're not happy about that. The photograph mentioned by Mr Tyler would naturallly have the attachment of a fee. We're talking at the end of the day of something above a round three thousand.'

Afterwards the McDowds remembered that moment. They remembered the feeling they shared, that this was no kind of trick, that the money spoken of would be honestly paid. They remembered thinking that the sum was large, that they could do with thirty pounds never mind three thousand. Rain had destroyed the barley; they missed their daughter's help on the farm; the tragedy had aged and weakened them. If three thousand pounds could come out of it, they'd maybe think of selling up and buying a bungalow.

'Let them in,' McDowd said, and his wife led the way into the kitchen.

EVENTS AT DRIMAGHLEEN

*

The scene of the mystery is repeated all over rural Ireland. From Cork to Cavan, from Roscommon to Rosslare you will come across small, tucked-away farms like the Butlers' and the McDowds'. Maureen McDowd had been gentle-natured and gentle-tempered. The sins of sloth and greed had not been hers; her parents called her a perfect daughter, close to a saint. A photograph, taken when Maureen McDowd was five, showed a smiling, freckled child; another showed her in her First Communion dress; a third, taken at the wedding of her brother, was of a healthy-looking girl, her face creased up in laughter, a cup of tea in her right hand. There was a photograph of her mother and father, standing in their kitchen. Italicised beneath it was the information that it had been taken by Jeremiah Tyler. *The Saint of Drimaghleen*, Hetty Fortune had written, *never once missed mass in all her twenty-five years.*

The story was told in fashionably faded pictures. 'You know our Sunday supplement?' Hetty Fortune had said in the McDowds' kitchen, but they hadn't: newspapers from England had never played a part in their lives. They read the *Sunday Independent* themselves.

The Butlers' yard was brownly bleak in the pages of the supplement; the pump had acquired a quality not ordinarily noticed. A bicycle similar to Maureen's had been placed on the ground, a sheepdog similar to the Butlers' nosed about the doors of the cowshed. But the absence of the three bodies in the photographed yard, the dust still rising where the bicycle had fallen, the sniffing dog, lent the composition an eerie quality—horror conveyed without horror's presence. 'You used a local man?' the supplement's assistant editor enquired, and when informed that Jeremiah Tyler was a Dublin man he requested that a note be kept of the photographer's particulars.

The Gardai—in particular Superintendent O'Kelly—saw

(21)

only what was convenient to see. Of the three bodies that lay that morning in the May sunshine they chose that of Lancy Butler to become the victim of their sluggish imagination. Mrs Butler, answering her notoriously uncontrollable jealousy, shot her son's sweetheart rather than have him marry her. Her son, so Superintendent O'Kelly infers from no circumstantial evidence whatsoever, wrenched the shotgun out of her hands and fired on her in furious confusion. He then, within seconds, took his own life. The shotgun bore the fingerprints of all three victims: what O'Kelly has signally failed to explain is why this should be so. Why should the Butlers' shotgun bear the fingerprints of Maureen McDowd? O'Kelly declares that 'in the natural course of events' Maureen McDowd would have handled the shotgun, being a frequent visitor to the farm. Frequent visitors, in our experience, do not, 'in the natural course of events' or otherwise, meddle with a household's firearms. The Superintendent hedges the issue because he is himself bewildered. The shotgun was used for keeping down rabbits, he states, knowing that the shotgun's previous deployment by the Butlers is neither here nor there. He mentions rabbits because he still can offer no reasonable explanation why Maureen McDowd should ever have handled the death weapon. The fingerprints of all three victims were blurred and 'difficult', and had been found on several different areas of the weapon. Take it or leave it is what the Superintendent is saying. And wearily he is saying: Does it matter?

We maintain it does matter. We maintain that this extraordinary crime—following, as it does, hard on the heels of the renowed Kerry Babies mystery, and the Flynn case—has not been investigated, but callously shelved. The people of Drimaghleen will tell you everything that O'Kelly laboured over in his reports: the two accounts are identical. Everyone knows that Lancy Butler's mother was a sharp-tongued, possessive woman. Everyone knows that Lancy was a ne'er-do-well. Everyone knows that Maureen McDowd was a deeply religious girl. Naturally it was the mother who sought to end an intru-

sion she could not bear. Naturally it was slow, stupid Lancy who didn't pause to think what the consequences would be after he'd turned the gun on his mother. Naturally it was he who could think of no more imaginative way out of his dilemma than to join the two women who had dominated his life.

The scenario that neither O'Kelly nor the Butlers' neighbours paused to consider is a vastly different one. A letter, apparently—and astonishingly—overlooked by the police, was discovered behind the drawer of a table which was once part of the furniture of Lancy Butler's bedroom and which was sold in the general auction after the tragedy—land, farmhouse and contents having by this time become the property of Allied Irish Banks, who held the mortgage on the Butlers' possessions. This letter, written by Maureen McDowd a week before the tragedy, reads:

'Dear Lancy, Unless she stops I can't see any chance of marrying you. I want to, Lancy, but she never can let us alone. What would it be like for me in your place, and if I didn't come to you where would we be able to go because you know my father wouldn't accept you here. She has ruined the chance we had, Lancy, she'll never let go of you. I am always cycling over to face her insults and the way she has of looking at me. I think we have reached the end of it.'

This being a direct admission by Maureen McDowd that conclusion in the romance had been arrived at, why would the perceptive Mrs Butler—a woman who was said to 'know your thoughts before you knew them yourself'—decide to kill Lancy's girl? And the more the mental make-up of that old woman is dwelt upon the more absurd it seems that she would have destroyed everything she had by committing a wholly unnecessary murder. Mrs Butler was not the kind to act blindly, in the fury of the moment. Her jealousy and the anger that protected it smouldered cruelly within her, always present, never varying.

(23)

But Maureen McDowd—young, impetuous, bitterly deprived of the man she loved—a saint by nature and possessing a saint's fervour, on that fatal evening made up for all the sins she had ever resisted. Hell hath no fury like a woman scorned —except perhaps a woman unfairly defeated. The old woman turned the screw, aware that victory was in sight. The insults and 'the way of looking' became more open and more arrogant; Mrs Butler wanted Maureen McDowd out, she wanted her gone for ever, never to dare to return.

It is known that Lancy Butler found two rabbits in his snares that night. It is known that he and Maureen often made the rounds of the snares when she visited him in the evenings. He would ride her bicycle to the field where they were, Maureen sitting side-saddle on the carrier at the back. Lancy had no bicycle of his own. It is our deduction that the reason the shotgun bore Maureen's fingerprints is because they had gone on a shooting expedition as well and when they returned to the yard she was carrying both the shotgun and the snared rabbits. It is known that Maureen McDowd wept shortly before her death. In the fields, as they stalked their prey, Lancy comforted her but Maureen knew that never again would they walk here together, that never again would she come over to see him in the evening. The hatred his mother bore her, and Lancy's weakness, had combined to destroy what most of all she wanted. Mrs Butler was standing in the yard shouting her usual abuse and Maureen shot her. The rabbits fell to the ground as she jumped off the bicycle, and her unexpectedly sudden movement caused the bicycle itself, and Lancy on it, to turn over. He called out to her when it was too late, and she realised she could never have him now. She blamed him for never once standing up to his mother, for never making it easier. If she couldn't have this weak man whom she so passionately loved no one else would either. She shot her lover, knowing that within seconds she must take her own life too. And that, of course, she did.

There was more about Maureen. In the pages of the

colour supplement Mrs McDowd said her daughter had been a helpful child. Her father said she'd been his special child. When she was small she used to go out with him to the fields, watching how he planted the seed-potatoes. Later on, she would carry out his tea to him, and later still she would assist with whatever task he was engaged in. Father Sallins gave it as his opinion that she had been specially chosen. A nun at the convent in Mountcroe remembered her with lasting affection.

O'Kelly fell prey to this local feeling. Whether they knew what they were doing or not, the people of Drimaghleen were protecting the memory of Maureen McDowd, and the Superintendent went along with the tide. She was a local girl of unblemished virtue, who had been 'specially chosen'. Had he publicly arrived at any other conclusion Superintendent O'Kelly might never safely have set foot in the neighbourhood of Drimaghleen again, nor the village of Kilmona, nor the town of Mountcroe. The Irish do not easily forgive the purloining of their latter-day saints.

*

'I wanted to tell you this stuff had been written,' Father Sallins said. 'I wanted it to be myself that informed you before you'd get a shock from hearing it elsewhere.'

He'd driven over specially. As soon as the story in the paper had been brought to his own notice he'd felt it his duty to sit down with the McDowds. In his own opinion, what had been printed was nearly as bad as the tragedy itself, his whole parish maligned, a police superintendent made out to be no better than the criminals he daily pursued. He'd read the thing through twice; he'd looked at the photographs in astonishment. Hetty Fortune and Jeremiah Tyler had come to see him, but he'd advised them against poking about in what was over and done with. He'd explained that people wanted to try to forget the explosion of violence that had so suddenly occurred in their midst,

that he himself still prayed for the souls of the Butlers and
Maureen McDowd. The woman had nodded her head, as
though persuaded by what he said. 'I have the camera here,
Father,' the man had remarked as they were leaving. 'Will
I take a snap of you?' Father Sallins had stood by the
hydrangeas, seeing no harm in having his photograph taken.
'I'll send it down to you when it's developed,' the man said,
but the photograph had never arrived. The first he saw of
it was in the Sunday magazine, a poor likeness of himself,
eyelids drooped as though he had drink taken, dark stubble
on his chin.

'This is a terrible thing,' he said in the McDowds'
kitchen, remembering the photograph of that also: the
cream-enamelled electric cooker, the Holy Child on the
green-painted dresser, beside the alarm clock and the stack
of clothes-pegs, the floor carpeted for cosiness, the blue,
formica-topped table, the radio, the television set. In the
photograph the kitchen had acquired an extraneous quality,
just as the photograph of the Butlers' yard had. The harsh,
ordinary colours, the soiled edges of the curtains, the
chipped paintwork, seemed like part of a meticulous composition: the photograph was so much a picture that it
invited questioning as a record.

'We never thought she was going to say that about
Maureen,' Mrs McDowd said. 'It's lies, Father.'

'Of course it is, Mrs McDowd.'

'We all know what happened that night.'

'Of course we do.'

McDowd said nothing. They had taken the money. It
was he who had said that the people should be allowed into
the house. Three thousand, one hundred and fifty pounds
was the sum the woman had written the cheque for, insist-
ing that the extra money was owed.

'You never said she'd been specially chosen, Father?'

'Of course I didn't, Mrs McDowd.'

He'd heard that Superintendent O'Kelly had gone to see

a solicitor to enquire if he'd been libelled, and although he was told he probably had been he was advised that recourse in the courts would be costly and might not be successful. The simple explanation of what had happened at the Butlers' farm had been easy for the people of Drimaghleen and for the police to accept because they had known Mrs Butler and they had known her son. There'd been no mystery, there'd been no doubt.

'Will we say a prayer together?' the priest suggested.

They knelt, and when they rose again Mrs McDowd began to cry. Everyone would know about it, she said, as if the priest had neither prayed nor spoken. The story would get about and people would believe it. '*Disadvantaged people*', she quoted from the newspaper. She frowned, still sobbing, over the words. 'It says the Butlers were disadvantaged people. It says we are disadvantaged ourselves.'

'That's only the way that woman has of writing it down, Mrs McDowd. It doesn't mean much.'

'*These simple farm folk*,' Mrs McDowd read, '*of Europe's most western island form limited rural communities that all too often turn in on themselves.*'

'Don't pay attention,' Father Sallins advised.

'Does disadvantaged mean we're poor?'

'The way that woman would see it, Mrs McDowd.'

There was confusion now in Drimaghleen, in Kilmona and Mountcroe; and confusion, Father Sallins believed, was insidious. People had been separated from their instinct, and other newspaper articles would follow upon this one. More strangers would come. Father Sallins imagined a film being made about Maureen McDowd, and the mystery that had been created becoming a legend. The nature of Maureen McDowd would be argued over, books would be written because all of it was fascinating. For ever until they died her mother and her father would blame themselves for taking the money their poverty had been unable to turn away.

'The family'll see the pictures.'

'Don't upset yourself, Mrs McDowd.'

'No one ever said she was close to being a saint. That was never said, Father.'

'I know, I know.'

Mrs McDowd covered her face with her hands. Her thin shoulders heaved beneath the pain of her distress; sobs wrenched at her body. Too much had happened to her, the priest thought; it was too much for any mother that her murdered daughter should be accused of murder herself in order to give newspaper-readers something to think about. Her husband had turned away from the table she sat at. He stood with his back to her, looking out into the yard. In a low, exhausted voice he said:

'What kind of people are they?'

The priest slowly shook his head, unable to answer that, and in the kitchen that looked different in Jeremiah Tyler's photograph Mrs McDowd screamed. She sat at the blue-topped table with her lips drawn back from her teeth, one short, shrill scream following fast upon another. Father Sallins did not again attempt to comfort her. McDowd remained by the window.

Family Sins

A telegram arrived out of the blue. *Come for the weekend*, Hubert's message read, and I remember the excitement I felt because I valued his friendship more than anyone else's. I had no money for the train journey and had to raise the matter with my father. 'It's hard to come by these days,' my father said, giving me only what he could easily spare. I increased it playing rummy with McCaddy the courthouse clerk, who had a passion for the game.

It was August, 1946. Long warm days cast an unobtrusive spell, one following another in what seemed like orderly obedience. The train I took crept through a landscape that was just beginning to lose its verdancy but was not yet parched. The railway for the last few miles of the journey ran by the sea, which twinkled brilliantly, sunlight dancing on it.

'There's someone called Pamela,' Hubert said, greeting me in no other way. 'Probably I mightn't have mentioned her.'

We walked from Templemairt railway station, away from the sea, into a tangle of small suburban roads. Everywhere there were boarding-houses, cheaper than those by the promenade, Hubert said. Bookies' families stayed there, he said: Sans Souci, Freshlea House, Cois na Farraige. We climbed a hill and passed through iron gates into a garden that was also on a hill, steep rockeries on either side of a path with occasional steps in it. I could see the house above us, through hollyhocks and shrubs, a glass verandah stretching

(29)

the length of its façade.

'Who's Pamela?'

'She spends the summers here. My cousin.'

We entered the house and a voice at once called out. 'Hubert, I should like to meet your friend.'

'Hell,' Hubert muttered. He led me into a small room, its burnt-brown blinds half drawn against the sun. An old woman sat at a piano, turning on the stool as we entered. She was dressed severely, in long, old-fashioned black clothes; her grey hair was swept up and neatly rolled. You could tell she had once been beautiful; and in the wrinkled tiredness of her face her eyes were still young.

'You are very welcome,' she said. 'Hubert does not often invite a friend.'

'It's nice of you to have me, Mrs Plunkett.'

The piano stool swivelled again. The first notes of a Strauss waltz were played. I picked my suitcase up and followed Hubert from the room. In the hall he threw his eyes upwards, but did not speak. Silently we mounted the stairs, and when we reached the first-floor landing a woman's voice called up from some lower part of the house: 'Hubert, don't tell me you forgot the honeycomb?'

'Oh, *God!*' Hubert muttered crossly. 'Leave your case. We'll have to go back for the damn thing.'

I placed my suitcase on the bed of the room we'd entered: a small cell of a place, masculine in character. Just before we left it Hubert said:

'My grandfather had a stroke. You won't be bothered with him. He doesn't come downstairs.'

On a table in the hall there was a dark-framed photograph of the man he spoke of, taken earlier in his lifetime: a stern, hatchet-like face with a tidy grey moustache, hair brushed into smooth wings on either side of a conventional parting, pince-nez, a watch-chain looping across a black waistcoat. At school Hubert had spoken a lot about his grandfather.

'That was Lily who was on about the honeycomb,'

Hubert said as we descended the path between the rockeries. 'A kind of general maid I think you call her. They work the poor old thing to the bone.'

We passed out of the garden and walked back the way we'd come. Hubert talked about boys we'd been at school with, in particular Ossie Richpatrick and Gale and Furney. He'd had news of all three of them: Ossie Richpatrick had become a medical student, Gale had joined the British army, Furney was in a handkerchief business.

'The Dublin Handkerchief Company,' Hubert said. 'He wrote me a letter on their writing-paper.'

'Does he make the handkerchiefs? I can't see Furney making handkerchiefs.'

'He sells them actually.'

Ossie Richpatrick and Gale and Furney had left school the previous summer; Hubert and I more recently, only a matter of weeks ago. It was now August; in October I was, like Ossie Richpatrick, to become a student, though not of medicine. Hubert was uncertain about his future.

'This is the place,' he said. We passed through high wooden doors into what appeared to be a builder's yard. Bricks were stacked, lengths of plumber's piping were tied together with cord. In a shed there was a circular saw. 'This woman sells honey,' Hubert said.

He knocked on a half-open door and a moment later a woman arrived with a honeycomb already in her hand. 'I saw you turning in,' she said. 'How are you, Hubert?'

'I'm all right. Are you well yourself, Mrs Hanrahan?'

'I am of course, Hubert.'

She examined me with curiosity, but Hubert made no attempt to introduce me. He gave the woman some money and received the honeycomb in return. 'I picked that comb out for them. It's good rich honey.'

'You can tell by the look of it.'

'Is your grandmother well? Mr Plunkett no worse, is he?'

'Well, he's still ga-ga, Mrs Hanrahan. No worse than that.'

The woman had placed her shoulder against the door-jamb so that she could lean on it. You could see she wanted to go on talking, and I sensed that had I not been there Hubert would have remained a little longer. As we made our way through the yard he said: 'She lives in ignorance of Hanrahan's evil ways. He died a while back.'

Hubert didn't elaborate on Mr Hanrahan's evil ways, but suggested instead that we go down to the sea. He led the way to a sandy lane that twisted and turned behind small back gardens and came out eventually among sand dunes. He held the honeycomb by one side of its wooden frame. Wind would have blown sand into it, but the day was still, late-afternoon sunshine lightening an empty sky. We walked by the edge of the sea; there was hardly anyone about.

'What's your cousin like?'

'You'll see soon enough.'

Hubert had a lean face, to which a faintly melancholy expression seemed naturally to belong. But when he laughed, or smiled, its bony landscape changed dramatically, delight illuminating every crevice, eyes sparkling like excited sapphires. Hair the colour of wheat was smoothly brushed, never untidy. 'Fancies himself a dandy, does he?' a disagreeable teacher of Greek and Latin had once remarked.

'I'm thinking of going to Africa,' he revealed when we'd turned and begun to make our way back to the house.

Hubert's mother and father had been killed in a car accident in England. 'The last thing that happened before the war,' Hubert used to say, regaling us at school with the story of the tragedy. On Saturday September 2nd, 1939, late at night, they had driven away from a road-house near Virginia Water and unfortunately had had a head-on collision with a lorry belonging to a travelling zoo. There'd been a cage full of apes on the back of the lorry, Hubert subsequently reported, which the impact had caused to become unfastened. He himself had been ten at the time, at a preparatory school in the suburbs of Oxford, and he told how the headmaster had broken the news to him, introducing it with references to courage and manliness. These had failed to prepare him for the death of his parents, because he'd imagined that what was coming next was the news that he would have to be sent home on the grounds that, yet again, the fees hadn't been paid. Already there had been the wireless announcement about the declaration of war, the whole school assembled to hear it. 'You will know no blacker day, Hubert,' the headmaster had asserted before releasing the more personal tidings. 'Take strength at least from that.'

We delivered the honeycomb to the kitchen. 'Lily,' Hubert said, by way of introducing the wiry little woman who was kneading bread on a baking board at the table. 'Mrs Hanrahan says it's good rich honey.'

She nodded in acknowledgement, and nodded a greeting at me. She asked me what kind of a journey I'd had and when I said it had been unremarkable she vouchsafed the information that she didn't like trains. 'I always said it to Hubert,' she recalled, 'when he was going back to school. I suffer on a train.'

'Have you a fag, Lily?' Hubert asked, and she indicated with a gesture of her head a packet of Player's on the dresser. 'I'll pay you back,' he promised. 'I'm taking two.'

'That's seven you owe the kitchen, mind, and I don't want money. You go and buy a packet after supper.'

'I was going to say, Lily, could you lend me a pound?' As he spoke he opened a green purse beside the Player's packet. 'Till Tuesday that would be.'

'It's always till Tuesday with you. You'd think the kitchen was made of Her Ladyships.'

'If Lily was a few years younger,' Hubert said, addressing me, 'I'd marry her tomorrow.'

(33)

He removed a pound note from the purse and smoothed it out on the surface of the dresser, examined the romantic countenance of Lady Lavery, raised it to his lips, and then carefully secreted the note in an inside pocket. 'We're going dancing tonight,' he said. 'Did you ever dance in the Four Provinces Ballroom, Lily?'

'Oh, don't be annoying me.'

We smoked in Hubert's room, a tidily kept place with Leonardo da Vinci's 'Annunciation' on the wall between the windows. Hubert wound up a gramophone and then lay on his bed. I sat on the only chair. Frank Sinatra sang.

'They're trying to grow groundnuts in Africa,' Hubert said. 'I think I'd be interested in that.'

'What are groundnuts?'

'The groundnut is a nut they have an idea about. I think they'll pay my fare.'

He was vague about which African country he referred to, replying when I asked him that it didn't matter. There was another scheme he'd heard about, to do with supplying telephone-boxes, and a third one that involved teaching selected Africans the rudiments of hydraulic engineering. 'You have to go on a course yourself, naturally enough,' Hubert explained. 'Personally I favour the nuts.'

He turned the record over. Sinatra sang 'Begin the Beguine'. Hubert said:

'We can go in on the half-seven train. We'll have to try for a lift back. Don't dawdle in the dining-room.'

At school Hubert had been thought of as 'wild', a reputation he had to some extent inherited from his father's renown at the same school twenty-five years before. For his own part, it was not that he was constantly in breach of the rules, but rather that he tended to go his own way. Short of funds, which regularly he was, he had been known to sell his clothes. The suit of 'sober colouring' which we were permitted to wear on weekend exeats, and for Chapel on Sunday evenings, with either a school, House or Colours tie, he sold in a Dublin secondhand-clothes shop and, never known to go out on exeats himself, managed for Sunday Chapel with the black serge jacket and trousers that was our normal everyday wear. He sold his bicycle to Ossie Richpatrick for eleven shillings, and a suitcase for eightpence. 'I don't understand why that should be,' Hubert had a way of saying in class, voicing what the rest of us felt but didn't always have the courage to say. He didn't mind not understanding; he didn't mind arguing with the Chaplain about the existence of the Deity; he didn't mind leaving an entire meal untouched and afterwards being harangued by the duty prefect for what was considered to be a form of insolence. But, most of all, what marked Hubert with the characteristics of a personality that was unusual were the stories he repeated about his relationship with his grandfather, which was not a happy one. Mr Plunkett's strictures and appearance were endlessly laid before us, a figure emerging of a tetchy elder statesman, wing-collared and humourless, steeped in the Christian morality of the previous century. Mr Plunkett said grace at mealtimes, much as it was said at school, only continuing for longer; he talked importantly of the managerial position he had reached, after a lifetime of devotion and toil, in Guinness's brewery. 'Never himself touches a drop of the stuff, you understand. Having been an abstainer since the age of seven or something. A clerky figure even as a child.' Since Hubert's reports allowed Mrs Plunkett so slight a place in the household, and Lily none at all, his home life sounded spiky and rather cold. At the beginning of each term he was always the first to arrive back at school, and had once returned a week early, claiming to have misread the commencing date on the previous term's report.

'O.K., let's go,' he said when a gong sounded, and we swiftly descended the stairs, Hubert setting the pace. I caught a brief glimpse of a door opening and of a girl. In the hall Hubert struck the gong again as he passed.

(35)

'No need for that,' his grandmother gently reprimanded in the dining-room. 'We are all present and correct.'

The girl smiled at me, so shyly that I was made to feel shy myself. In the absence of her husband Mrs Plunkett said grace while we stood with our hands resting on the backs of our chairs. 'We are quite a houseful now,' she chattily remarked as she sat down. 'Pamela, please pass that salad along to our visitor.'

'Yes, of course.'

Pamela blushed as she spoke, her eyes flittering for a moment in my direction. Hubert, silent beside me, was relishing her discomfiture: I knew that, I could feel it. He and I and his cousin were aware that we had not met; the old woman imagined we had.

'I hope you are a salad-eater.' Mrs Plunkett smiled at me. 'Hubert does not much go in for salad. I'm not sure why.'

'Because Hubert doesn't like the taste,' Hubert replied. 'Lettuce does not seem to him to taste at all. The skin of tomatoes catches in his throat. Chives hang about on his breath. Radishes are nasty little things. And so on.'

His cousin laughed. She was a pretty girl, with dark bobbed hair and blue eyes: I didn't, that evening, notice much else about her except that she was wearing a pale pink dress with white buttons all the way down the front. She became even prettier when she smiled, a dimple appearing in one of her cheeks, her nose wrinkling in a way that became her.

'Well, that's most interesting,' Mrs Plunkett said, a little stiffly, when Hubert ceased to talk about his dislikes.

There was corned beef with the salad. Hubert buttered two slices of brown bread to make a sandwich of his, and all the time he was preparing this his grandmother watched him. She did so uncomfortably, in an odd, dutiful kind of way, and I received the impression that she would have preferred not to. It was what her husband would have done, I

(36)

suddenly realised: as if guided by his silent presence in an upstairs room she was honourably obeying him, keeping faith with his wishes. Mustard was spread on the corned beef, pepper was sprinkled. Mrs Plunkett made no comment. The slow movements of Hubert's knife, a faint whispering under his breath of one of the songs Frank Sinatra had sung, contributed to the considerable unease of both Hubert's cousin and myself. Pamela reddened when she accidentally knocked the little silver spoon out of the salt cellar.

'You're not in a public house, Hubert,' Mrs Plunkett said when he lifted the sandwich to his mouth. 'Pamela, please pour the tea.'

Hubert ignored the reference to a public house. 'Don't dawdle,' he reminded me. 'If we miss the seven-thirty we'll have to cadge a lift and that takes ages.'

Pamela poured the tea. Mrs Plunkett cut her lettuce into fine shreds. She added salad cream, meticulously mixing everything up. She said eventually:

'Are you going in to Dublin?'

'We're going dancing,' Hubert said. 'The Four Provinces Ballroom in Harcourt Street. Music tonight by Ken Mackintosh.'

'I don't think I've heard of Mr Mackintosh.'

'Celebrity spot, the Inkspots.'

'Inkspots?'

'They sing songs.'

On a large round breadboard beside Mrs Plunkett there were several kinds of bread, which she cut very slowly with a battered breadsaw. On the table there was plum jam and raspberry jam, and the honeycomb we had bought from Mrs Hanrahan. There was a fruitcake and a coffee cake, biscuits and shortbread, and when we'd finished our corned beef Lily came in and added to this array a plate of éclairs. She lifted away the plates and dishes we'd finished with. Mrs Plunkett thanked her.

'Mrs Hanrahan said she picked that honeycomb out for you,' Hubert said.

'Well, that was most kind of her.'

'She's lonely since Hanrahan died. She'd talk the legs off you.'

'It's hard for the poor woman. A builder's widow.' Mrs Plunkett explained to me what I already knew. 'He fell off a roof six weeks ago.'

'As a matter of fact,' Hubert said, 'she's better off without him.'

'What on earth d'you mean, Hubert?'

'Hanrahan went after shopgirls. Famous for it.'

'Don't speak so coarsely, Hubert.'

'Is Pam shocked? Are you shocked, Pam?'

'No, no, not at all.' Pamela swiftly replied before her grandmother could answer for her. She had reddened again in her confusion, but being flustered made her more vivacious and was not unattractive.

'Mr Hanrahan was a perfectly decent man,' Mrs Plunkett insisted. 'You're repeating tittle-tattle, Hubert.'

'There's a girl serves in Binchy's, another in Edwards' the cake shop. Hanrahan took both of them to the dunes. D'you remember Hanrahan, Pam?'

She shook her head.

'He painted the drain-pipes one time.'

'You'll need to hurry if you wish to catch the train,' Mrs Plunkett said. As she spoke she drew back the cuff of her sleeve to consult a wristwatch that had not been visible before. She nodded in agreement with the statement she'd just made. Addressing her granddaughter, she said:

'It doesn't matter if you don't finish.'

Doubtfully, Pamela half smiled at Mrs Plunkett. She began to say something, then changed her mind. Vaguely, she shook her head.

'Is Pamela going in to Dublin too?' Hubert said. 'Going to the flicks, Pamela?'

'Isn't she accompanying you? Don't you want to go dancing with the boys, Pamela?'

'No, no.' She shook her head, more vehemently than before. She was going to wash her hair, she said.

'But surely you'd like to go dancing, Pamela?'

Hubert stood up, half a piece of shortbread in one hand. He jerked his head at me, indicating that I should hurry. Pamela said again that she wanted to wash her hair.

'Jesus Christ!' Hubert murmured in the hall. He stifled laughter. 'I'm bloody certain,' he said as we hurried through the garden, 'she remembers Hanrahan. The man made a pass at her.'

In the train he told me when I asked that she was the child of his father's sister. 'She comes over every summer from some back-of-beyond rectory in Roscommon.' He was vague when I asked further questions, or else impatiently brushed them aside. 'Pam's dreary,' was all he said.

'She doesn't seem dreary to me.'

'The old man worships her. Like he did her mother by all accounts.'

In the Four Provinces Ballroom we met girls who were quite different from Hubert's cousin. Hubert said they came from the slums, though this could not have been true since they were fashionably dressed and had money for soft drinks and cigarettes. Their legs were painted—the liquid stockings of that time—and their features were emphasised with lipstick and mascara. But each one I danced with was either stunted or lumpy, and I kept thinking of Pamela's slim figure and her pretty face. Her lips, in particular, I remembered.

We danced to 'As Time Goes By' and 'Autumn Leaves' and 'Falling in Love with Love'. The Inkspots sang. One of the partners I danced with said: 'Your friend's very handsome, isn't he?'

In the end Hubert picked up two girls who were agreeable to being seen home when the evening came to an end.

(39)

Ken Mackintosh and his band began to pack away their instruments. We walked a little way along Harcourt Street and caught a number eleven bus. The girls were nurses. The one allocated to me, being bouncy and talkative, wanted to know what it was like living in a provincial town, as I did, and what my plans were for getting out of it. When I told her she said: 'Maybe I'll run into you when you're a student,' but her voice wasn't exactly loaded with pleasurable anticipation. She was wearing a thick, green woollen coat even though it was August. Her face was flat and pale, her lips garish beneath a fresh coating of lipstick. She had to get up at five o'clock every morning, she said, in order to get to the ward on time. The Sister was a tartar.

When we arrived at the girls' flat Hubert suggested that we might be offered a cup of tea, but the girls would permit us no further than the doorstep of the house. 'I thought we were away,' he murmured disconsolately. His father would have got in, he said. They'd have cooked a meal for his father, anything he wanted. We walked to where we hoped to get a lift to Templemairt. Two hours later a lorry driver picked us up.

*

The next day being a Saturday, Hubert and I went to Phoenix Park races. We missed breakfast and due to pressure of time we missed lunch also—and, in fact, the first race. 'The old man'll have been livid,' Hubert said. 'You understand he takes in what's going on?' Mrs Plunkett and Pamela would have sat waiting for us in the dining-room, he said, then Pamela would have been sent up to see if we were still asleep, and after that Mrs Plunkett would have gone up herself. 'They'll have asked Lily and she'll have told them we've hooked it to the races.' He neither laughed nor smiled, even though he seemed amused. Another two pounds had been borrowed from Lily before we left.

'He'll be livid because he'll think we should have taken Pam with us.'

'Why don't you like Pamela?'

Hubert didn't reply. He said instead: 'I'd love to have heard Hanrahan putting a proposition to her.'

At school all of it would have sounded different. We'd have laughed—I more than anyone—at the report of the lively builder attempting to seduce Hubert's cousin. And somehow it would have been funnier because this had occurred in his grandfather's house, his grandfather being the sort he was. We would have imagined the embarrassment of Hubert's cousin, and Hanrahan saying what harm was a little kiss. We would have imagined the old man oblivious of it all, and would have laughed because Hubert's cousin couldn't bring herself to say anything about it afterwards. Hubert told his stories well.

'He may not,' I said, 'have had a go at her.'

'He couldn't leave them alone, that man. I'm going for this Summer Rain thing.'

We stood in the crowd, examining the list of runners. Announcements were made over loudspeakers; all around us people were talking furiously. Men were in shirtsleeves, women and girls in summer dresses. It was another sunny day.

'Paddy's Pride no good?' I said.

'Could be.' But we both put our bets on Summer Rain and to my surprise the horse won at nine to one. 'Let's have a drink,' Hubert said. Without asking me what I wanted he ordered stout at the bar.

We won again with Sarah's Cottage, lost with Monaghan Lad and King of Them All. We drank further bottles of stout. 'Take Gay Girl for a place,' a man who had dropped into conversation with us in the bar advised. We did so and were again successful. Between us we were now almost seventeen pounds richer than when we started. We watched the last race in high spirits, grasping glasses of stout and urging on a horse called Marino. We hadn't backed it; we hadn't backed anything because Hubert said he could tell our luck had come to an end. Marino didn't win.

'We'll have something to eat and then go to the pictures,' Hubert said.

The grass beneath our feet was littered with discarded race tickets and programmes. The bookmakers were dismantling their stands. Pale evening sunlight slanted over the drifting crowds; voices were more subdued than they had been. I kept thinking of Pamela in the house in Templemairt, of Mrs Plunkett saying grace again in the diningroom, the old man sensing that we weren't present for yet another meal.

'What about *The Moon and Sixpence?*' Hubert suggested, having bought an *Evening Herald* as we left the racecourse. 'George Sanders?'

We ordered two mixed grills at the cinema restaurant, and tea and cakes. We both bought packets of cigarettes. When *The Moon and Sixpence* came to an end we went to an ice-cream parlour and then we caught a Saturday-night bus that brought us almost as far as Templemairt. We walked the last bit, Hubert talking about Africa. Before we reached the town he said:

'He disowned my father, you know. When my father got involved with my mother that was the end of that. My mother was a barmaid, you understand.'

I nodded, having been informed of that before. Hubert said:

'I didn't know that old man existed until I was told after the funeral. He didn't even come to it.'

I didn't say it must have been awful, having both your parents killed at once. We'd often thought so at school and had said it when Hubert wasn't there. We'd often considered it must have affected him, perhaps made him the way he was—careless, it seemed, of what people thought of him.

'You should have heard him when he could talk, laying into me because he thinks I'm like my father. A chip off the old block is what he thinks. My father lived on his wits. A con man, you understand.'

Hubert had often told us this also. His father had briefly been a racing correspondent, had managed a night club, had apparently worked in a bank. But none of these forays into the realm of employment had lasted long; each had been swiftly terminated, either on the grounds of erratic service or for liberties taken with funds. Hubert, at school, had made no bones about his father's reprehensible tendencies, nor about his mother's background. On the contrary, he had taken a certain pride in the fact that his father, in later life, had lived up to the reputation he had established when a schoolboy himself. The apes that had escaped from the circus cage at the time of the tragedy had chattered with delight, scampering over the wreckage. His father would have appreciated that, he said.

A weak crescent moon lightened the darkness as we walked towards Templemairt. The stars were out in force. No car passed us, but even if we'd been aware of headlights behind us I doubt that we'd have bothered to try for a lift. We smoked one cigarette after another, still exhilarated by our triumphant afternoon, and in the circumstances it seemed natural that Hubert should talk about his parents, who had spent a lot of time on racecourses.

'They were drunk, of course, when they crashed that car.'

It was not difficult to believe they were, but nonetheless I did not feel that hearty agreement was in order. I nodded briefly. I said:

'Were you born in England?'

'I believe in the back row of a cinema.'

I had never heard that before, but there was something about Hubert's honesty in other matters that prevented me from suspecting invention. The photograph of his grandfather in the hall was precisely as Mr Plunkett had so often been described, down to his eyebrows being almost a single horizontal line, and the celluloid collar of his shirt.

(43)

'When the lights went up she couldn't move. They had to send for a doctor, but before the ambulance arrived she popped me.'

We entered the house quietly and went to our rooms without further conversation. I had hoped that Pamela might still be up since it wasn't as late as last night. I had even prepared a scene that I felt could easily take place: Pamela in the hall as we closed the front door behind us, Pamela offering us tea in the kitchen and Hubert declining while I politely accepted.

*

'Pam, do you want to play tennis?'

She was as astonished as I was to hear this. A startled look came into her face. She stammered slightly when she replied.

'Three of us?' she said.

'We'll show you how three can play.'

Sunday lunch had already taken place, a somewhat silent occasion because Hubert and I were more than ever out of favour. Mrs Plunkett said quietly, but in the firm tones of one conveying a message as a matter of trust, that her husband had been disappointed because we hadn't accompanied Pamela and herself to church. I did my best to apologise; Hubert ignored the revelation. 'We won a fortune at the races,' he said, which helped matters as little as it would have had the old man been present.

'Tennis would be lovely,' Pamela said.

She added that she'd change. Hubert said he'd lend me a pair of tennis shoes.

A remarkable transformation appeared to have overtaken him, and for a moment I thought that the frosty lunchtime and his grandfather's reported distress had actually stirred his conscience. It then occurred to me that since there was nothing else to do on a Sunday afternoon, tennis with Pamela was better than being bored. I knew what he meant when he said we'd show her how three could play: on the tennis court Hubert belonged in a class far more exalted than my own, and often at school Ossie Richpatrick and I had together played against him and still not managed to win. It delighted me that Pamela and I were to be partners.

Hubert's tennis shoes didn't fit me perfectly, but I succeeded in getting them on to my feet. There was no suggestion that he and I should change our clothes, as Pamela had said she intended to. Hubert offered me a choice of several racquets and when I'd selected one we made our way to the tennis court at the back of the house. We raised the net, measured its height, and knocked up while we waited.

'I'm afraid we can't,' Pamela said.

She was wearing a white dress and tennis shoes and socks of the same pristine freshness. There was a white band in her hair and she was wearing sun-glasses. She wasn't carrying her tennis racquet.

'Can't what?' Hubert said, stroking a ball over the net. 'Can't what, Pam?'

'We're not allowed to play tennis.'

'Who says we're not allowed to? What d'you mean, allowed?'

'Grandmother says we mustn't play tennis.'

'Why on earth not?'

'Because it's Sunday, because you haven't been to church.'

'Oh, don't be so bloody silly.'

'He asked her what we were doing. She had to tell him.'

'The idiotic old brute.'

'I don't want to play, Hubert.'

Hubert stalked away. I wound the net down. I was glad he hadn't insisted that he and I should play on our own.

'Don't be upset by it.' I spoke apologetically. I didn't know what else to say.

'There won't be a quarrel,' she reassured me, and in fact

there wasn't. The raised voices of Hubert and his grand-mother, which I thought we'd hear coming from the house, didn't materialise. Pamela went to change her dress. I took off Hubert's tennis shoes. In the drawing-room at teatime Mrs Plunkett said:

'Hubert's turned his face to the wall, has he?'

'Shall I call him?' Pamela offered.

'Hubert knows the hour of Sunday tea, my dear.'

Lily brought more hot water. She, too, seemed affected by what had occurred, her mouth tightly clamped. But I received the impression that the atmosphere in the drawing-room was one she was familiar with.

'A pity to turn one's face to the wall on such a lovely day,' Mrs Plunkett remarked.

Silence took over then and was not broken until Mrs Plunkett rose and left the room. Strauss began on the piano, tinkling faintly through the wall. Lily came in to collect the tea things.

'Perhaps we should go for a walk,' Pamela said.

We descended the stepped path between the rockeries and strolled past Hanrahan's yard. We turned into the sandy lane that led to the dunes and made our way on to the strand. We didn't refer to what had occurred.

'Are you still at school?' I asked.

'I left in July.'

'What are you going to do now?'

'I'm hoping to study botany.'

She was shyer than I'd thought. Her voice was reticent when she said she hoped to study botany, as if the vaunt-ing of this ambition constituted a presumption.

'What are you going to do?'

I told her. I envied Hubert going to Africa, I said, be-coming garrulous in case she was bored by silence. I men-tioned the cultivation of groundnuts.

'Africa?' she said. When she stopped she took me un-awares and I had to walk back a pace or two. Too late, I realised I had inadvertently disclosed a confidence.

'It's just an idea he has.'

I tried to change the subject, but she didn't seem to hear, or wasn't interested. I watched while she drew a pattern on the sand with the toe of her shoe. More slowly than before, she walked on again.

'I don't know why,' I said, 'we don't have a bathe.'

She didn't reply. Children were running into and out of the sea. Two men were paddling, with their trousers rolled up to their knees. A girl was sunbathing on a li-lo, both hands in the water, resisting the tide that would have carried her away from the shore.

'My bathing-dress is in the house,' Pamela said at last. 'I could get it if you like.'

'Would *you* like?'

She shrugged. Perhaps not, she said, and I wondered if she was thinking that bathing, as much as tennis, might be frowned upon as a breach of the Sabbath.

'I don't think, actually,' she said, 'that Hubert will ever go to Africa.'

*

Lily stood beside my deckchair, a bunch of mint she'd picked in one hand. I hadn't known what else to do, since Hubert had not come out of his room, so I'd wandered about the garden and had eventually found the deckchair on a triangle of grass in a corner. 'I'm going to read for a while,' Pamela had said when we returned from our walk.

'It's understandable they never had to be so severe with Pamela,' Lily said. 'On account of her mother being sensible in her life. Different from Hubert's father.'

I guessed she was talking to me like this because she'd noticed I was bewildered. The pettiness I had witnessed in my friend was a shock more than a surprise. Affected by it, I'd even wondered as I'd walked with Pamela back from the strand if I'd been invited to the house in order to become an

instrument in her isolation. I'd dismissed the thought as a
ridiculous flight of fancy: now I was not so sure.

'It's understandable, Hubert being bad to her. When you
think about it, it's understandable.'

Lily passed on, taking with her the slight scent of mint
that had begun to waft towards me because she'd crushed a
leaf or two. 'He tried to beat me with a walking-stick,'
Hubert had reported at school, and I imagined the appre-
hension Lily hinted at—the father of the son who'd gone to
the bad determined that history should not be repeated, the
mother anxious and agreeing.

'I was looking for you,' Hubert said, sitting down on the
grass beside me. 'Why don't we go down to the hotel?'

I looked at him, his lean face in profile. I remembered
Pamela drawing the pattern on the sand, her silence the
only intimation of her love. When had an intonation or a
glance first betrayed it to him? I wondered.

Hubert pushed himself to his feet and we sauntered off
to the lounge-bar of the hotel beside the railway station.
Without asking me what I would like, Hubert ordered gin
and orange. The tennis we hadn't played wasn't mentioned,
nor did I say that Pamela and I had walked on the strand.

'No need to go tomorrow,' Hubert said. 'Stay on a bit.'

'I said I'd be back.'

'Send them a wire.'

'I don't want to overstay, Hubert. It's good of your
grandmother to have me.'

'That girl stays for three months.'

I'd never drunk gin before. The orange made it pleasantly
sweet, with only a slight after-taste. I liked it better than
stout.

'My father's drink,' Hubert said. 'My mother preferred
gimlets. A gimlet,' he added, 'is gin with lime in it. They
drank an awful lot, you understand.'

He confided to me that he intended to slip away to England himself. He was softening Lily up, he said, with the

intention of borrowing a hundred pounds from her. He knew she had it because she never spent a penny; a hundred pounds would last him for ages, while he found out more about the prospects in Africa.

'I'll pay her back. I'd never not.'

'Yes, of course.'

'Anything would be better than the Dublin Handkerchief Company. Imagine being in the Dublin Handkerchief Company when you were fifty years of age! A lifetime of people blowing their noses!'

We sat there, talking about school, remembering the time Fitzherbert had dressed himself up in the kind of woman's clothes he considered suitable for a streetwalker and demanded an interview with Farquie, the senior languages master; and the time the Kingsmill brothers had introduced a laxative into the High Table soup; and when Prunty and Matchett had appropriated a visiting rugby team's clothes while they were in the showers. We recalled the days of our first term: how Hubert and I had occupied beds next to one another in the junior dormitory, how Miss Fanning, the common-room secretary, had been kind to us, thinking we were homesick.

'One *pour la rue*,' Hubert said.

He held the man who served us in conversation, describing the same mixture of gin and orangeade as he'd had it once in some other bar. There had been iced sugar clinging to the rim of the glass; delicious, he said. The man just stared at him.

'I'll fix it up with Lily tonight,' Hubert said on the way back to the house. 'If she can't manage the hundred I'd settle for fifty.'

We were still talking loudly as we mounted the stepped path between the rockeries, and as we passed through the hall. In the dining-room Mrs Plunkett and Pamela had clearly been seated at the table for some time. When we entered the old woman rose without commenting on our

(49)

lateness and repeated the grace she had already said. A weary expression froze Hubert's features while he waited for her voice to cease.

'We were down in the hotel,' he said when it did, 'drinking gin and orange. Have you ever wandered into the hotel, Pam?'

She shook her head, her attention appearing to be occupied with the chicken leg on her plate. Hubert said the hotel had a pleasant little lounge-bar, which wasn't the description I'd have chosen myself. A rendezvous for the discriminating, he said, even if one encountered difficulty there when it came to a correctly concocted gin and orange. He was pretending to be drunker than he was.

'A rather dirty place, Dowd's Hotel,' Mrs Plunkett interposed, echoing what I knew would have been her husband's view.

'Hanrahan used to drink there,' Hubert continued. 'Many's the time I saw him with a woman in the corner. I've forgotten if you said you remembered the late Hanrahan, Pam?'

She said she didn't. Mrs Plunkett held out her cup and saucer for more tea. Pamela poured it.

'Hanrahan painted the drain-pipes,' Hubert said. 'D'you remember that time, Pam?'

She shook her head. I wanted to tell him to stop. I wanted to remind him that he had already asked his cousin if she remembered Hanrahan painting the drain-pipes, to point out that it wasn't she who had caused the difficulty that afternoon, that it wasn't she who had made us stand there while grace was said again.

'I'm surprised you don't,' Hubert said. 'I'm really very surprised, Pam.'

Mrs Plunkett didn't understand the conversation. She smiled kindly at me, and briefly indicated dishes I might like to help myself to. She lifted a forkful of cold chicken to her mouth.

'It's only that he mentioned you once in Dowd's,' Hubert said. He laughed, his eyes sparkling, as if with delight. 'He asked how you were getting on one time. A very friendly man.'

Pamela turned away from the table, but she couldn't hide what she wished to hide and she couldn't control her emotions. Her cheeks were blazing now. She sobbed, and then she pushed her chair back and hurried from the room.

'What have you said to her?' Mrs Plunkett asked in astonishment.

*

I could not sleep that night. I kept thinking about Pamela, unhappy in her bedroom, and Hubert in his. I imagined Hubert's father and Pamela's mother, children in the house also, the bad son, the good daughter. I imagined the distress suffered in the house when Hubert's father was accused of some small theft at school, which Hubert said he had been. I imagined the misdemeanour forgotten, a new leaf turned, and some time later the miscreant dunned by a debt collector for a sum he could not pay. Letters came to the house from England, pleading for assistance, retailing details of hardship due to misfortune. When I closed my eyes, half dreaming though I was not yet asleep, Mrs Plunkett wept, as Pamela had. She dreaded the letters, she sobbed; for a day or two she was able to forget and then another letter came. 'I will write a cheque': the man I had not seen spoke blankly, taking a cheque-book from his pocket and, at the breakfast table, writing it immediately.

I opened my eyes; I murmured Pamela's name. 'Pamela,' I whispered because repeating it made her face more vivid in my mind. I might have told her that Hubert, at school, had been sought out and admired more than any other boy because he was not ordinary, that he'd been attractive and different in all sorts of ways. I might have begged her not to hate the memory of him when she ceased to love him.

I fell asleep. We played tennis and Hubert easily beat us. A car lay on its side, headlights beaming on the apes that scampered from the broken cage. On the bloody grass of the roadside verge the two dead faces still smiled. 'You will know no blacker day,' the voice of a schoolmaster promised.

In the morning, after breakfast, I packed my suitcase while Hubert sat smoking a cigarette in silence. I said good-bye to Lily in the kitchen, and to Mrs Plunkett. Pamela was in the hall when we passed through it.

'Goodbye,' she said. At breakfast she had seemed to have recovered her composure. She smiled at me now, saying she was sorry I was going.

'Goodbye, Pamela.'

Hubert stood by the open hall-door, not looking at her, gazing out into the sunlit garden. On the way to the railway station we talked again about incidents at school. He mentioned the two nurses we'd accompanied to their doorstep and the luck we'd had at the races. 'A pity we wouldn't have time for a gin and orange,' he said as we passed the hotel.

On the slow train, close at first to the sea and then moving into the landscape that was just beginning to seem parched because of the heatwave, I knew that I would never see Hubert again. A friendship had come to an end because when a little more time went by he would be ashamed, knowing I would not easily forget how he had made his cousin a casualty of the war with his grandfather. There would always be an awkwardness now, and the memory of Hubert at home.

The Third Party

The two men met by arrangement in Buswell's Hotel. The
time and place had been suggested by the man who was
slightly the older of the two; his companion had agreed
without seeking an adjustment. Half-past eleven in the bar:
'I think we'll probably spot one another all right,' the older
man had said. 'Well, she'll have told you what I look
like.'

He was tall, acquiring bulkiness, a pinkish-brown sun-
burn darkening his face, fair curly hair that was turning
grey. The man he met was thinner, with spectacles and a
smooth black overcoat, a smaller man considerably. Lairdman this smaller man was called; the other's name was
Boland. Both were in their early forties.

'Well, we're neither of us late,' Boland said in greeting,
the more nervous of the two. 'Fergus Boland. How are
you?'

They shook hands. Boland pulled out his wallet. 'I'll have
a Jameson myself. What'll I get you?'

'Oh, only a mineral. This time of day, Fergus. A lemonade.'

'A Jameson and a lemonade,' Boland ordered.

'Sure,' the barman said.

They stood by the bar. Boland held out a packet of cigarettes. 'D'you smoke?'

Lairdman shook his head. He cocked an elbow on to the
bar, arranging himself tidily. 'Sorry about this,' he said.

They were alone except for the barman, who set their

two glasses in front of them. They weren't going to sit down; there was no move to do so. 'A pound and tenpence,' the barman said, and Boland paid him. Boland's clothes—tweed jacket and corduroy trousers—were wrinkled: he'd driven more than a hundred miles that morning.

'I mean I'm really sorry,' Lairdman went on, 'doing this to anyone.'

'Good luck.' Boland raised his glass. He had softened the colour of the whiskey by adding twice as much water. 'You never drink this early in the day, I suppose?' he said, constrainedly polite. 'Well, very wise. That's very sensible: I always say it.'

'I thought it mightn't be a drinking occasion.'

'I couldn't face you without a drink in, Lairdman.'

'I'm sorry about that.'

'You've lifted my wife off me. That isn't an everyday occurrence, you know.'

'I'm sorry—'

'It would be better if you didn't keep saying that.'

Lairdman, who was in the timber business, acknowledged the rebuke with a sideways wag of his head. The whole thing was awkward, he confessed, he hadn't slept a wink the night before.

'You're a Dubliner, she tells me,' Boland said, the same politeness to the fore. 'You make blockboard: there's money in that, no doubt about it.'

Lairdman was offended. She'd described her husband as clumsy but had added that he wouldn't hurt a fly. Already, five minutes into the difficult encounter, Lairdman wasn't so sure about that.

'I don't like Dublin,' Boland continued. 'I'll be frank about it. I never have. I'm a small-town man, but of course you'll know.'

He imagined his wife feeding her lover with information about his provincialism. She liked to tell people things; she talked a great deal. Boland had inherited a bakery in the

(54)

town he had referred to, one that was quite unconnected
with the more renowned Dublin bakery of the same name.
A few years ago it had been suggested to him that he should
consider retitling his, calling it Ideal Bread and Cakes, or
Ovenfresh, in order to avoid confusion, but he saw no need
for that, believing, indeed, that if a change should come
about it should be made by the Dublin firm.

'I want to thank you,' Lairdman said, 'for taking all this
so well. Annabella has told me.'

'I doubt I have an option.'

Lairdman's lips were notably thin, his mouth a narrow
streak that smiled without apparent effort. He smiled a little
now, but shook his head to dispel any misconception: he
was not gloating, he was not agreeing that his mistress's
husband had no option. Boland was surprised that he didn't
have a little chopped-off moustache, as so many Dublin
men had.

'I thought when we met you might hit me,' Lairdman
said. 'I remarked that to Annabella, but she said that wasn't
you at all.'

'No, it isn't me.'

'That's what I mean by taking it well.'

'All I want to know is what you have in mind. She doesn't
seem to know herself.'

'In mind?'

'I'm not protesting at your intentions where my wife is
concerned, only asking if you're thinking of marrying her,
only asking if you have some kind of programme. I mean,
have you a place up here that's suitable for her? You're not
a married man, I understand? I'll have another J.J.,' Boland
called out to the barman.

'No, I'm not a married man. What we were hoping was
that—if you're agreeable—Annabella could move herself
into my place more or less at once. It's suitable accommodation all right, a seven-room flat in Wellington Road.
But in time we'll get a house.'

'Thanks,' Boland said to the barman, paying him more money.

'That was my turn,' Lairdman protested, just a little late.

She wouldn't care for meanness, Boland thought. She'd notice when it began to impinge on her, which in time it would: these things never mattered at first.

'But marriage?' he said. 'It isn't easy, you know, to marry another man's wife in Ireland.'

'Annabella and I would naturally like to be married one day.'

'That's what I wanted to put to you. How are you suggesting that a divorce is fixed? You're not a Catholic, I'm to understand?'

'No.'

'No more am I. No more is Annabella. But that hardly matters, one way or another. She's very vague on divorce. We talked about it for a long time.'

'I appreciate that. And I appreciated your suggestion that we should meet.'

'I have grounds for divorce, Lairdman, but a damn bit of use they are to me. A divorce'll take an age.'

'It could be hurried up if you had an address in England. If the whole thing could be filed over there we'd be home and dry in no time.'

'But I haven't an address in England.'

'It's only a thought, Fergus.'

'So she wasn't exaggerating when she said you wanted to marry her?'

'I don't think I've ever known Annabella to exaggerate,' Lairdman replied stiffly.

Then you don't know the most important thing about her, Boland confidently reflected—that being that she can't help telling lies, which you and I would politely refer to as exaggerations. He believed that his wife actually disliked the truth, a rare enough attribute, he imagined, in any human being.

(56)

'I'm surprised you never got married,' he said, genuinely surprised because in his experience cocky little men like this very often had a glamorous woman in tow. He wondered if his wife's lover could possibly be a widower: naturally Annabella would not have been reliable about that.

'I've known your wife a long time,' Lairdman retorted softly, and Boland saw him trying not to let his smile show. 'As soon as I laid eyes on Annabella I knew she was the only woman who would make sense for me in marriage.'

Boland gazed into his whiskey. He had to be careful about what he said. If he became angry for a moment he was quite likely to ruin everything. The last thing he wanted was that the man should change his mind. He lit a cigarette, again offering the packet to Lairdman, who again shook his head. Conversationally, friendlily, Boland said:

'Lairdman's an interesting name—I thought that when she told me.'

'It's not Irish. Huguenot maybe, or part of it anyway.'

'I thought Jewish when she told me.'

'Oh, undoubtedly a hint of that.'

'You know the way you're interested when you're told about a relationship like that? "What's his name?" It's not important, it doesn't matter in the least. But still you ask it.'

'I'm sure. I appreciate that.'

When she'd said his name was Lairdman, Boland had remembered the name from his schooldays. Vaguely, he'd guessed that the man she was telling him about was a boy he couldn't quite place. But knowing the name, he'd recognised in Buswell's bar the adult features immediately.

' "Where did you meet him?" That doesn't matter either. And yet you ask it.'

'Annabella and I—'

'I know, I know.'

At school Lairdman had been notorious for an unexpected reason: his head had been held down a lavatory while his hair was scrubbed with a lavatory brush. Roche and Dead Smith had done it, the kind of thing they tended to do if they suspected uppitiness. Roche and Dead Smith were the bullies of their time, doling out admonitions to new boys who arrived at the school in the summer or winter terms rather than the autumn one, or to boys whose faces they found irritating. Lairdman's head had been scrubbed with the lavatory brush because he kept his hair tidy with perfumed oil that was offensive to Dead Smith.

'I think we were at school together,' Boland said.

Lairdman almost gave a jump, and it was Boland, this time, who disguised his smile. His wife would not have remembered the name of the school in question, not being in the least interested: the coincidence had clearly not been established.

'I don't recollect a Boland,' Lairdman said.

'I'd have been a little senior to yourself.' Deliberately, Boland sounded apologetic. 'But when she said your name I wondered. I was one of the boarders. Up from the country, you know. Terrible bloody place.'

Thirteen boarders there'd been, among nearly a hundred day boys. The day boys used to come noisily up the short, suburban avenue on their bicycles, and later ride noisily away. They were envied because they were returning to warmth and comfort and decent food, because after the weekends they'd talk about how they'd been to the Savoy or the Adelphi or even to the Crystal Ballroom. The boarders in winter would crouch around a radiator in one of the classrooms; in summer they'd walk in twos and threes around the playing-fields. The school matron, a Mrs Porter, was also the cook, but regularly burnt both the breakfast porridge and the barley soup she was given to producing as the main source of sustenance in the evening. An old boy of the school, occupying an attic at the top of a flight of uncarpeted stairs that led out of one of the dormitories, was the junior master, but he appeared to have acquired neither privilege nor distinction through that role: he, too, sat by the radiator in the classroom and dreaded the cooking of Mrs Porter. The bachelor headmaster, a boxer in his time —reputed to have been known in ringside circles as the Belted Earl, an obscurely acquired sobriquet that had remained with him—was a Savonarola-like figure in a green suit, sadistically inclined.

'Oh, I quite liked the place,' Lairdman said.

'You were a day boy.'

'I suppose it made a difference.'

'Of course it did.'

For the first time Boland felt annoyed. Not only was the man she'd become involved with mean, he was stupid as well. All this stuff about an address in England, all this stuff about giving up a seven-room flat, when if he had an iota of commonsense he'd realise you didn't go buying houses for the likes of Annabella because in no way whatsoever could you rely on her doing what she said she was going to do.

'I've always thought, actually, it supplied a sound education,' Lairdman was saying.

The awful little Frenchman who couldn't make himself understood. O'Reilly-Flood, whose method of teaching history was to give the class the textbook to read while he wrote letters. The mathematics man who couldn't solve the problems he set. The Belted Earl in his foul laboratory, prodding at your ears with the sharp end of a tweezers until you cried out in pain.

'Oh, a great place,' Boland agreed. 'A fine academy.'

'We'd probably send our children there. If we have boys.'

'Your children?'

'You'd have no objection? Lord no, why should you? I'm sorry, that's a silly thing to say.'

'I'll have another,' Boland requested of the barman. 'How about your mineral?'

'No, I'm O.K., thanks.'

This time he did not mention, even too late, that he should pay. Instead he looked away, as if wishing to dissociate himself from an over-indulgence in whiskey on an occasion such as this, before it was yet midday. Boland lit another cigarette. So she hadn't told him? She'd let this poor devil imagine that in no time at all the seven-room flat in Wellington Road wouldn't be spacious enough to contain the family that would naturally come trotting along once she'd rid herself of her provincial husband. Of course there'd have to be a divorce, and of course it would have to be hurried up: no one wanted a litter of little bastards in a seven-room flat or anywhere else.

'Good man, yourself,' he said to the barman when his whiskey came. If he ended up having too much to drink, as indeed might happen, he'd spend the night in the hotel rather than drive back. But it was early yet, and it was surprising what a heavy lunch could do.

'I'm sorry about that,' Lairdman repeated, referring again to his slip of the tongue. 'I wasn't thinking.'

'Ah, for heaven's sake, man!'

Boland briefly touched him, a reassuring tap on the shoulder. He could hear her telling him that the reason for their childless marriage had long ago been established. 'Poor old fellow,' she'd probably said, that being her kind of expression. She'd known before their marriage that she couldn't have children; in a quarrel long after it she'd confessed that she'd known and hadn't said.

'Naturally,' Lairdman blandly continued, 'we'd like to have a family.'

'You would of course.'

'I'm sorry that side of things didn't go right for you.'

'I was sorry myself.'

'The thing is, Fergus, is it O.K. about the divorce?'

'Are you saying I should agree to be the guilty party?'

'It's the done thing, as a matter of fact.'

'The done thing?'

'If you find it distasteful—'

'Not at all, of course not. I'll agree to be the guilty party

(60)

and we'll work it out from there.'

'You're being great, Fergus.'

The way he was talking, Boland thought, he might have been drinking. There were people who became easygoing, who adopted that same kind of tone, even if they'd only been with someone else who was drinking: he'd often heard that but he'd never believed it. A sniff of someone else's glass, he'd heard, a vapour in the air.

'D'you remember the cokeman they used to have there? McArdle?'

'Where was that, Fergus?'

'At school.'

Lairdman shook his head. He didn't remember McArdle, he said. He doubted that he'd ever known anyone of that name. 'A cokeman?' he repeated. 'What kind of a cokeman? I don't think I know the word.'

'He looked after the furnace. We called him the cokeman.'

'I never knew that person at all.'

Other people came into the bar. A tall man in a gabardine overcoat who opened an *Irish Times* and was poured a glass of stout without having to order it. An elderly woman and two men who appeared to be her sons. A priest who looked around the bar and went away again.

'You wouldn't have noticed McArdle because you weren't a boarder,' Boland said. 'When you're weekends in a place you notice more.'

'I'm sorry I don't remember you.'

'I wouldn't expect you to.'

She'd be imagining this conversation, Boland suddenly realised. It was she who had suggested this bar for their meeting, speaking as if she knew it and considered it suitable. 'I think I'll go up and see Phyllis,' she used to say, saying it more often as time went by. Phyllis was a friend she had in Terenure, whose own marriage had ended on the rocks and who was suffering from an internal complaint

(61)

besides. But of course Phyllis had just been a name she'd
used, a stalwart friend who would cover up for her if she
needed it. For all he knew, Phyllis might never have been
married, her internal system might be like iron. 'Phone me,'
he used to say, and obediently and agreeably his wife would.
She'd tell him how Dublin looked and how Phyllis was
bearing up. No doubt she'd been sitting on the edge of a
bed in the seven-room flat in Wellington Road.

'It's really good of you to come all this way,' Lairdman
said with a hint of finality in his voice, an indication that
quite soon now the encounter should be brought to an end.
'I really appreciate it. I'll ring Annabella this afternoon and
tell her we know where we stand. You won't mind that,
Fergus?'

'Not at all.'

Boland had often interrupted such a telephone conversation. He would walk into the hall and there she'd be, knees
drawn up, on the second step of the stairs, the receiver
strung through the banisters. She'd be talking quite normally in her slightly high-pitched voice, but when he stepped
through the hall-door she'd wave a greeting and begin to
whisper, the hand that had waved to him now cupped
around the mouthpiece. He'd often wondered what she
imagined he thought, or if she achieved some tremor
of satisfaction from the hushed twilight of this semi-
surreptitious carry-on. The trouble with Annabella was
that sooner or later everything in the world bored her.
'Now, I want to hear,' she would soon be saying to Lairdman, 'every single thing since the moment you left the
house.' And the poor man would begin a long history about
catching a bus and passing through the entrance doors of
his blockboard business, how he had said good morning to
the typist and listened to the foreman's complaint concerning a reprehensible employee, how he'd eaten a doughnut
with his eleven o'clock coffee, not as good a doughnut as
he'd eaten the day before. Later, in a quarrel, she'd fling it

all back at him: who on earth wanted to know about his doughnuts? she'd screech at him, her fingers splayed out in the air so that her freshly applied crimson nail varnish would evenly dry. She had a way of quarrelling when she was doing her nails, because she found the task irksome and needed some distraction. Yet she'd have felt half undressed if her fingernails weren't properly painted, or if her make-up wasn't right or her hair just as she wanted it.

'I'll be able to say,' Lairdman was stating with what appeared to be pride, 'that there wasn't an acrimonious word between us. She'll be pleased about that.'

Boland smiled, nodding agreeably. He couldn't imagine his wife being pleased since she so rarely was. He wondered what it was in Lairdman that attracted her. She'd said, when he'd asked her, that her lover was fun; he liked to go abroad, she'd said, he appreciated food and painting; he possessed what she called a 'devastating' sense of humour. She hadn't mentioned his sexual prowess, since it wasn't her habit to talk in that way. 'Will you be taking those cats?' Boland had enquired. 'I don't want them here.' Her lover would willingly supply a home for her Siamese cats, she had replied, both of which she called 'Ciao'. Boland wondered if his successor even knew of their existence.

'I wonder what became,' he said, 'of Roche and Dead Smith?'

He didn't know why he said it, why he couldn't have accepted that the business between them was over. He should have shaken hands with Lairdman and left it at that, perhaps saying there were no hard feelings. He would never have to see the man again; once in a while he would feel sorry for the memory of him.

'Dead Smith?' Lairdman said.

'Big eejit with a funny eye. There's a barrister called Roche now; I often wonder if that's the same fellow.'

'I don't think I remember either of them.'

'Roche used to go round in a pin-striped blue suit. He

looked like one of the masters.'

Lairdman shook his head. 'I'll say cheerio, Fergus. Again, my gratitude.'

'They were the bright sparks who washed your hair in a lavatory bowl.'

Boland had said to himself over and over again that Lairdman was welcome to her. He looked ahead to an easy widower's life, the house she had filled with her perversities and falsehoods for the last twelve years as silent as a peaceful sleep. He would clear out the memories of her because naturally she wouldn't do that herself—the hoarded magazines, the empty medicine bottles, the clothes she had no further use for, the cosmetics she'd pitched into the corners of cupboards, the curtains and chair-covers clawed by her cats. He would get Molloy in to paint out the rooms. He would cook his own meals, and Mrs Coughlan would still come every morning. Mrs Coughlan wouldn't be exactly sorry to see the back of her, either.

'I don't know why,' Lairdman said, 'you keep going on about your schooldays.'

'Let me get you a decent drink before you go. Bring us two big ones,' he called out to the barman, who was listening to an anecdote the man in the gabardine coat was retailing at the far end of the bar.

'No, really,' Lairdman protested. 'Really now.'

'Oh, go on, man. We're both in need of it.'

Lairdman had buttoned his black overcoat and drawn on a pair of black leather gloves. Finger by finger he drew one of the gloves off again. Boland could feel him thinking that, for the sake of the woman who loved him, he must humour the cuckold.

'It takes it out of you,' Boland said. 'An emotional thing like this. Good luck to you.'

They drank, Lairdman seeming awkward now because of what had been said. He looked a bit like a priest, Boland thought, the black attire and the way he wore it. He tried to imagine the pair of them abroad, sitting down together in a French restaurant, Lairdman being pernickety about a plate of food he didn't like the look of. It didn't make sense, all this stuff about a devastating sense of humour.

'I only mentioned the school,' Boland said, 'because it was the other thing we had in common.'

'As a matter of fact, I'm a governor up there now.'

'Ah, go on!'

'That's why I said we'd maybe send the children there.'

'Well, doesn't that beat the band!'

'I'm pleased myself. I'm pleased they asked me.'

'Sure, anyone would be.'

Stupid he might be, Boland thought, but he was cute as well, the way he'd managed not to make a comment on the Roche and Dead Smith business. Cuteness was the one thing you could never get away from in Dublin. Cute as weasels they were.

'You don't remember it?' he prompted.

'What's that?'

'The lavatory thing.'

'Look here, Boland—'

'I've offended you. I didn't mean that at all.'

'Of course you haven't offended me. It's just that I see no point in harping on things like that.'

'We'll talk of something else.'

'Actually, I'm a bit on the late side.'

The second glove was again drawn on, the buttons of the smooth black overcoat checked to see that all was well for the street. The glove was taken off again when Lairdman remembered there'd have to be a handshake.

'Thanks for everything,' he said.

For the second time, Boland surprised himself by being unable to leave well alone. He wondered if it was the whiskey; the long drive and then the whiskey on top of an empty stomach because of course there hadn't been anything in the house for his breakfast when he'd gone to look,

(65)

not even a slice of bread. 'I'll come down and do you scrambled eggs and a few rashers,' she'd said the night before. 'You'll need something inside you before you set off.'

'I'm interested in what you say about sending your children there,' was what he heard himself saying. 'Would these be your and Annabella's children you have in mind?'

Lairdman looked at him as if he'd gone out of his senses. His narrow mouth gaped in bewilderment. Boland didn't know if he was trying to smile or if some kind of rictus had set in.

'What other children are there?' Lairdman shook his head, still perplexed. He held his hand out, but Boland did not take it.

'I thought those might be the children you had in mind,' he said.

'I don't follow what you're saying.'

'She can't have children, Lairdman.'

'Ah now, look here—'

'That's a medical fact. The unfortunate woman is incapable of mothering children.'

'I think you're drunk. One after another you've had. I thought it a moment ago when you got maudlin about your schooldays. Annabella's told me a thing or two, you know.'

'She hasn't told you about the cats she's going to spring on you. She hasn't told you she can't give birth. She hasn't told you she gets so bored her face turns white with fury. It's best not to be around then, Lairdman. Take my tip on that.'

'She's told me you can't stay sober. She's told me you've been warned off every racecourse in Ireland.'

'I don't go racing, Lairdman, and apart from occasions like this I hardly drink at all. A lot less than our mutual friend, I can promise you that.'

'You have been unable to give Annabella children. She's sorry for you, she doesn't blame you.'

(66)

'Annabella was never sorry for anyone in her life.'

'Now look here, Boland—'

'Look nowhere, man. I've had twelve years of the woman. I'm obliging you by stepping aside. But there's no need for this talk of divorce, Lairdman, in England or anywhere else. I'm just telling you that. She'll come and live with you in your seven-room flat; she'll live in any house you care to buy, but if you wait till Kingdom come you'll not find children trotting along. All you'll have is two Siamese cats clawing the skin off you.'

'You're being despicable, Boland.'

'I'm telling you the truth.'

'You seem to have forgotten that Annabella and myself have talked about all this. She knew you'd take it hard. She knew there'd be bitterness. Well, I understand that. I've said I'm sorry.'

'You're a mean little blockboard man, Lairdman. You belong with your head held down in a lavatory bowl. Were you wringing wet when they let go of you? I'd love to have seen it, Lairdman.'

'Will you keep your damn voice down? And will you stop trying to pick a quarrel? I came out this morning in good faith. I'm aware of the delicacy of the thing, and I'm not saying I've been a saint. But I'll not stand here and be insulted. And I'll not hear Annabella insulted.'

'I think Dead Smith became a vet.'

'I don't care what he became.'

Abruptly, Lairdman was gone. Boland didn't turn his head, or otherwise acknowledge his departure. He examined the row of bottles behind the bar, and in a moment he lit a fresh cigarette.

For half an hour he remained on his own where his usurper had left him. All he could think of was Lairdman as he remembered him, a boy who was pointed out because of what two bullies had done to him. The old cokeman, McArdle, used to laugh over the incident. Sometimes, when the classroom radiator wasn't hot enough, the boarders would go down to McArdle's cokehole and sit around his furnace. He'd tell them obscene stories, all of them to do with the matron and cook, or else he told them about Lairdman. The more Boland thought about it all the more clearly he remembered Lairdman: not much different in appearance, the same trap of a mouth, a propelling pencil and a fountain pen clipped into the pocket of his jacket. He had a bicycle Boland could remember, a new one that had perhaps replaced an older one, a Golden Eagle. 'Oh, we met at a party Phyllis gave,' she had said, but there was no way of knowing how much truth there was in that, presumably none.

Boland ate his lunch in the dining-room of the hotel, among people he did not know, who gave the impression of lunching there regularly. He didn't have to say he'd take nothing to drink because the waitress didn't ask him. There was water in a glass jug on the table; he'd be all right for the journey home, he decided.

'The cod,' he ordered. 'Yes, I'll have the cod. And the cream of celery.'

He remembered a time when the thirteen boarders had smashed a window in an outhouse that no longer had a purpose. Most of the window-panes were broken already, the roof had long ago tumbled in, and one of the walls was so badly split that it had begun to disintegrate. It was forbidden for any boy to enter this small, crumbling building, and the boarders had not done so. They had stood twenty or so yards away throwing stones at the remaining window-panes, as they might have thrown stones at a cockshot. They had meant no harm, and did not realise that an outhouse which was so badly damaged already might be worthy of preservation. Ceremoniously the following morning the Belted Earl had taken his cane to them in the presence of the assembled day boys. Lairdman would have been watching, Boland reflected as he ate his soup: Lairdman might have brought it up just as he himself had brought up the other matter, but of course that wasn't Lairdman's way. Lairdman considered himself a sophisticate; even in the days of his Golden Eagle he would have considered himself that.

Boland crumbled the bread on his side plate, picking up bits of it between mouthfuls of soup. He saw himself, one day in the future, entering the silence of his house. He saw himself on a summer evening pushing open the French windows of the drawing-room and going out into the garden, strolling among its fuchsia bushes and apple trees. He'd known the house all his life; he'd actually been born in it. Opposite O'Connor Motors, it was the last one in the town, yellow-washed and ordinary, but a house he loved.

'Did you say the fish, sir?' the waitress enquired.

'Yes, I did.'

He'd been married in Dublin, she being the daughter of a Dublin wine merchant. The old man was still alive and so was her mother. 'You've taken on a handful,' the old man once had said, but he'd said it playfully because in those days Annabella had been a handful to delight in. What they thought of her now Boland had no idea.

'The plate's hot, sir,' the waitress warned.

'Thanks very much.'

People who'd known him in his childhood had been delighted when he brought her to live among them. They'd stopped him on the street and said he was lucky. They were happy for him: he'd come back from Dublin with a crown of jewels, which was how they saw it. And yet those same people would be delighted when she left. The terrible frustration that possessed her—the denial of children through some mischance within her—turned beauty into wanton eccentricity. It was that that had happened, nothing else.

Slowly he ate his cod, with parsley sauce and cabbage and potatoes. Nobody would mention it much; they'd know what had happened and they'd say to one another that one day, probably, he'd marry again. He wondered if he would. He'd spoken airily of divorce to Lairdman, but in truth he knew nothing of divorce in Ireland these days. A marriage should wither away, he somehow felt, it should rot and die; it didn't seem quite like a cancer, to be swiftly cut out.

He ordered apple tart and cream, and later coffee came. He was glad it was all over: the purpose of his visit to Dublin had been to set a seal on everything that had happened, and in the encounter that had taken place the seal had at some point been set. The air had been cleared, he had accepted the truth it had been necessary to hear from someone else besides his wife. When first she'd told him he'd wondered if she could possibly be making it all up, and he'd wondered it since. Even while he'd waited in Buswell's bar he'd said to himself he wouldn't be surprised if no one turned up.

On the way to the car park two tinker children begged from him. He knew it wasn't coppers they were after, but his wallet or whatever else they could get their fingers on. One held out a cardboard box, the other pressed close to him, with a rug folded over her hands. He'd seen the trick before; Dublin was like that now. 'Go on, along with you,' he ordered them as harshly as he could.

It was because there hadn't been enough for her to do: he thought that as he eased the car through the heavy city traffic. And from the very start she hadn't taken to provincial life. A childless woman in a provincial town had all the time in the world to study its limitations. She had changed the furniture around, and had chosen the wallpapers that her Siamese cats had later damaged. But she'd resisted bridge and tennis, and had deplored the absence of even a cinema café. He'd thought he'd understood; so well used to the limitations himself, he was nevertheless aware that the society he had plunged her into was hardly scintillating. He'd driven her as often as he could to Dublin, before she'd taken to going on her own to visit Phyllis. For years he'd known she wasn't happy, but until she told him he'd never suspected she'd become involved with a man.

He stopped in Mullingar and had a cup of tea. The Dublin evening papers had arrived before him. He read in the *Herald* that the Italian government had been successfully re-formed after the Achille Lauro incident; the dollar was slipping again; a meat-processing plant was to close in Cork. He dawdled over the paper, not wanting to go home. Lairdman would have telephoned her by now. 'Why don't you drive up this afternoon?' he might have said. Maybe she had been packing all day, knowing the encounter was only a formality. 'He won't stand in the way,' Lairdman would have said. 'He'll even supply grounds.' There'd be nothing to keep her, now that all three of them knew where they stood, and it was the kind of thing she'd do, pack up and go when she'd got him out of the way.

A coal fire was burning in the café. A rare welcome these days, he remarked to the woman who'd served him, and pulled a chair up close to it. 'I'd take another cup of tea,' he said.

The little white Volkswagen he'd bought her might be on the road to Dublin already. She wouldn't leave a note because she wouldn't consider it necessary. If the Volkswagen passed by now she would be puzzled at not meeting him on the road; she'd never notice his own car parked outside the café.

'Ah well, you'd need a fire,' the woman said, returning with his tea. 'A shocking foggy old month we're having.'

'I've known better certainly.'

He drove on after he'd had a third cup of tea, keeping an eye out for the Volkswagen. Would she greet him with a touch on the horn? Or would he greet her? He didn't know if he would. Better to wait for the moment.

But over the next fifty or so miles there was no sign of his wife's car. And of course, he told himself, there was no reason why there should be: it was pure conjecture that she'd depart that afternoon, and the amount she had to pack made it unlikely that she could manage to do so in a day. For the next few miles he speculated on how, otherwise, her departure would be. Would Lairdman drive down to assist her? That had not been agreed upon or even touched upon as a possibility: he would instantly put his foot down if it was suggested. Would Phyllis arrive to help her? He would naturally have no objection to that. Certainly, the more he thought about it, the less likely was it that she could be capable of completing the move on her own. She had a way of calling in other people when something difficult had to be undertaken. He imagined her sitting on the second step of the stairs, chattering on the telephone. 'Would you ever . . . ?' she had a way of beginning her demands and her requests.

His headlights caught the familiar sign, in English and Irish, indicating that the town which was his home was the next one. He turned the radio on. 'Dancing in the dark', a sensual female voice lilted, reminding him of the world he supposed his wife and Lairdman belonged to; the thrill of illicit love, tête-à-tête dancing, as the song implied. 'Poor Annabella,' he said aloud, while the music still played. Poor girl, ever to have got herself married to the inheritor of a country-town bakery. Lucky, in all fairness, that cocky little Lairdman had turned up. The music continued, and he imagined them running towards one another along an empty street, like lovers in a film. He imagined their embrace, and then their shared smile before they embraced again. As the dull third party, not even a villain, he had no further part to play.

But as Boland reached the first few houses on this side of the town he knew that none of that was right. Not only had the white Volkswagen not conveyed her to Lairdman in his absence, it would not do so tomorrow or the next day, or next week. It would not do so next month, or after Christmas, or in February, or in the spring: it would not ever do so. It hadn't mattered reminding Lairdman of the ignominy he had suffered as a boy; it hadn't mattered reminding him that she was a liar, or insulting him by calling him mean. All that abuse was conventional in the circumstances, an expected element in the man-to-man confrontation, the courage for it engendered by an intake of John Jameson. Yet something had impelled him to go further: little men like Lairdman always wanted children. 'That's a total lie,' she'd have said already on the telephone, and Lairdman would have soothed her. But soothing wasn't going to be enough for either of them.

Boland turned the radio off. He drew the car up outside Donovan's public house and sat for a moment, swinging the keys between his thumb and forefinger before going in and ordering a bottle of Smithwick's with lime. At the bar he greeted men he knew and stood with them drinking, listening to talk of racehorses and politics. They drifted away when a few more drinks had been taken but Boland remained there for a long time, wondering why he hadn't been able to let Lairdman take her from him.

In Love with Ariadne

Images cluster, fragments make up the whole. The first of Barney's memories is an upturned butter-box—that particular shape, narrower at the bottom. It's in a corner of the garden where the grass grows high, where there are poppies, and pinks among the stones that edge a flowerbed. A dog pants, its paws stretched out on the grass, its tongue trailing from its mouth. Barney picks the pinks and decorates the dog with them, sticking them into its brindle fur. 'Oh, you are bold!' The hem of the skirt is blue, the shoes black. The hat Barney has thrown off is placed again on his head. He has a stick shaped like a finger, bent in the middle. It is hard and shiny and he likes it because of that. The sunshine is hot on his skin. There is a baby's perspiration.

Barney's mother died three years after his birth, but even so his childhood was not unhappy. In the garden at Lisscrea there was Charlie Redmond to talk to, and Nuala was in the kitchen. *Dr G. T. Prenderville* the brass plate on the wall by the hall-door said, and all over the neighbourhood Barney's father was known for his patience and his kindness—a bulky man in a tweed suit, his greying hair brushed straight back, his forehead tanned, a watch-chain looped across his waistcoat. Charlie Redmond made up doggerel, and twice a day came to the kitchen for cups of tea, leaving behind him a basket of peas, or beetroot, or whatever was in season. Because of the slanderous nature of his doggerel, Nuala called him a holy terror.

Lisscrea House, standing by the roadside, was covered

with Virginia creeper. There were fields on one side and on the other the Mulpatricks' cottage. Beyond that was the Edderys' cottage, and an iron gate which separated it from Walsh's public house—single-storeyed and whitewashed like the cottages. Opposite, across the road, were the ruins of a square tower, with brambles growing through them. A mile to the west was the Catholic church, behind white railings, with a shrine glorifying the Virgin just inside the gates. All the rooms at Lisscrea were long and narrow, each with a different, flowered wallpaper. In the hall the patients sat on a row of chairs that stretched between the front door and the stairs, waiting silently until Dr Prenderville was ready. Sometimes a man would draw up a cart or a trap outside, or dismount from a bicycle, and the doorbell would jangle urgently. 'Always listen carefully to what's said at the door,' Dr Prenderville instructed Nuala. 'If I'm out, write a message down.'

When Barney was seven he went to school in Ballinadra, waiting every morning on the road for Kilroy's cart on its way to Ballinadra creamery with churns of milk. The bread van brought him back in the afternoon, and none of that changed until he was allowed to cycle—on Dr Prenderville's old Rudge with its saddle and handle-bars lowered. '*Up the airy mountain*,' Miss Bone's thin voice enunciated in the school-room. Her features were pale, and slight; her fingers stained red with ink. *There goes Miss Bone*, Charlie Redmond's cruel doggerel recorded. *She's always alone.* Miss Bone was tender-hearted and said to be in love with Mr Gargan, the school's headmaster, a married man. '*Quod erat demonstrandum*,' Mr Gargan regularly repeated in gravelly tones.

On the Sunday before he made the journey to school on the Rudge for the first time Barney found his father listening to the wireless in the drawing-room, a thing he never did on a Sunday morning. Nuala was standing in the doorway with a dishcloth in her hand, listening also. They'd have to buy in tea, she said, because she'd heard it would be short, and Dr Prenderville said they'd have to keep the curtains drawn at night as a protection against being bombed from an aeroplane. Charlie Redmond had told Barney a few days before that the Germans ate black bread. The Germans were in league with the Italians, who ate stuff that looked like string. De Valera, Charlie Redmond said, would keep the country out of things.

The war that began then continued for the duration of Barney's time at school. Lisscrea was affected by the shortages that Nuala had anticipated; and De Valera did not surrender the will to remain at peace. It was during those years that Barney decided to follow in his father's and his grandfather's footsteps and become the doctor at Lisscrea.

*

'How're the digs?' Rouge Medlicott asked, and the Pole, Slovinski, again beckoned the waitress—not because he required more coffee but because he liked the look of her.

'Awful,' Barney said. 'I'm moving out.'

When he'd arrived in Dublin at the beginning of the term he found he had not been allocated a set of College rooms and had been obliged to settle for unsatisfactory lodgings in Dún Laoghaire. Greyhounds cluttered the stairs of this house, and broke into a general barking on imagined provocation. Two occupied a territory they had made their own beneath the dining-room table, their cold noses forever investigating whatever flesh they could find between the top of Barney's socks and the turn-ups of his trousers. Rouge Medlicott and Slovinski shared College rooms and at night pursued amorous adventures in O'Connell Street, picking up girls who'd been left in the lurch outside cinemas or ice-cream parlours.

'Why doesn't she come to me?' Slovinski demanded crossly, still waving at the waitress.

'Because you're bloody ugly,' Medlicott replied.

Students filled the café. They shouted to one another across plates of iced buns, their books on the floor beside their chairs, their gowns thrown anywhere. Long, trailing scarves in black and white indicated the extroverts of the Boat Club. Scholars were recognised by their earnest eyes, sizars by their poverty. Nigerians didn't mix. There were tablefuls of engineers and medical practitioners of the future, botanists and historians and linguists, geographers and eager divinity students. Rouge Medlicott and Slovinski were of an older generation, two of the many ex-servicemen of that time. Among these were G.I.s and Canadians and Czechs, a couple of Scots, a solitary Egyptian, and balding Englishmen who talked about Cecil Sharp or played bridge.

'You meet me tonight,' Slovinski suggested in a peremptory manner, having at last succeeded in summoning the waitress. 'What about tonight?'

'Tonight, sir?'

'We'll have oysters in Flynn's.'

'Oh God, you're shocking, sir!' cried the waitress, hurrying away.

Barney had got to know Slovinski and Rouge Medlicott through sitting next to them in biology lectures. He didn't think of them as friends exactly, but he enjoyed their company.

Medlicott had acquired his sobriquet because of the colour of his hair, a quiff of which trailed languorously over his forehead. There was a hint of flamboyance in his attire —usually a green velvet suit and waistcoat, a green shirt and a bulky green tie. His shoes were of soft, pale suede. He was English, and notably good-looking. Slovinski was small and bald, and still wore military uniform—a shade of blue— which Medlicott claimed he had bought in a Lost Property office. Slovinski could play part of Beethoven's Fifth Symphony on his teeth, with his thumbnails.

'I heard of digs,' Medlicott said. 'Out near the Zoo. That

Dutch fellow was after them only he decided to go back to Holland instead.'

It was in this casual way that Barney first came to hear about Gogarty Street, and that evening he went out to inspect the lodgings. A woman with a carefully powdered face and waved black hair opened the door to him. A discreet smear of lipstick outlined her lips, and there was a hint of eye-shadow beneath her myopic-seeming eyes. She was wearing a flowered overall, which she removed in the hall. Beneath was a navy-blue skirt and a cream-coloured blouse that had a fox-terrier brooch pinned to it. She folded the overall and placed it on the hallstand. Normally she would not take in boarders, she explained, but the house was too large, really, for herself and her mother and her daughter, just the three of them. A pity to have rooms and not use them, a pity to have them empty. The trouble was that smaller houses were usually not in districts she cared for. She led the way upstairs while still speaking about the house and household. 'It's a residence that's been in the Lenehan family for three generations,' she said. 'That's another consideration.'

The door of a room on the second floor was opened. 'Fusty,' Mrs Lenehan said, and crossed to the window. The bed was narrow, the bedstead of ornamental iron. There was a wash-stand with an enamel basin on it and a shaving mirror above it on the wall. There was a wardrobe, a chest of drawers, two holy pictures, and a chair. Patterned, worn linoleum partially covered the floor, leaving a darkly varnished surround. There were net curtains and a blind.

'The bathroom and W.C. are off the landing below,' Mrs Lenehan said. In Mr Lenehan's childhood there were two maids and a cook in this house, she went on, and in her own day there'd always been a single maid at least, and a scrubbing woman once a fortnight. Now you couldn't get a servant for love nor money. She noticed Barney glancing at the fireplace, which contained an arrangement of red tissue paper. She said that in the old days there'd have been a fire laid in the grate every morning and coal blazing cheerfully every evening. Now, of course, that was out of the question. 'Thirty shillings would be fair, would it? Breakfast and six p.m. tea, the extra meal on a Sunday.'

Barney said he thought thirty shillings was a reasonable rent for what was offered.

'Of a Friday evening, Mr Prenderville. In advance would be fair, I think.'

'Yes, it would.'

'Best to have a clear arrangement, I always say. No chance for misunderstandings.'

Two days later Barney moved in. When he'd unpacked his suitcases and was waiting for the gong which Mrs Lenehan had told him would sound at six o'clock there was a knock on his door. 'I'm Ariadne,' Mrs Lenehan's daughter said, standing in the doorway with a bar of yellow soap in her hand. 'My mother said give you this.' She was dark-haired, about the same age as Barney. The rather long mauve dress she wore was trimmed with black, and snowy-white beads were looped several times around her neck. Her lips were painted, her hands and wrists delicately slender. Large brown eyes surveyed Barney frankly and with curiosity.

'Thanks very much,' he said, taking the bar of soap from her.

She nodded vaguely, seeming to be no longer interested in him. Quietly she closed the door, and he listened to her footfall on the stairs. As light as gossamer, he said to himself. He was aware of a pleasurable sensation, a tingling on the skin of his head. The girl had brought to the room a whiff of perfume, and it remained after she'd gone. Barney wanted to close the window to keep it with him, but he also wanted just to stand there.

The sounding of the gong roused him from this pleasant reverie. He had never much cared for the appearance of the girls—women sometimes—whom Medlicott and Slovinski admired in cafés or on the streets. Ariadne was different. There was an old-fashioned air about her, and an unusualness. As well, Barney considered her beautiful.

'Fennerty's the name,' a small, jaunty old woman said in the dining-room. Wiry white hair grew tidily on a flat-looking head; eyes like beads peered at Barney. 'Fennerty's the name,' she repeated. 'Mrs Lenehan's mother.'

Barney told her who he was. The last occupant of his room had been employed in Clery's bed-linen department, she replied, a youth called Con Malley from Carlow. Now that someone had replaced him, the house would again be full. There had been difficulty in regularly extracting the rent from Con Malley. 'Mrs Lenehan won't tolerate anything less than promptness,' the old woman warned.

A man of about fifty, wearing a navy-blue belted overcoat and tan gloves, entered the dining-room. 'How're you, Mr Sheehy?' Mrs Fennerty enquired.

Divesting himself of his coat and gloves and placing them on the seat of a chair by the door, the man replied that he wasn't so good. He had a sharply receding chin, with features that had a receding look about them also, and closely clipped hair, nondescript as to colour. The removal of his coat revealed a brown pin-striped suit, with the corner of a handerkerchief peeping from the top pocket, and a tiny badge, hardly noticeable, in the left lapel. This proclaimed Mr Sheehy's teetotalism, the emblem of the Pioneer movement.

'I had a bad debt,' Mr Sheehy said, sitting down at the table. Mrs Fennerty vacated a rexine-covered armchair by the fire and took her place also. Ariadne entered with a laden tray, and placed plates of fried food in front of the three diners. Mrs Fennerty said the thick Yorkshire Relish had been finished the evening before, and when Ariadne returned to the dining-room a minute or so later with a metal tea-pot she brought a bottle of Yorkshire Relish as well.

Neither she nor her mother joined the others at the dining-table.

'Did you know Mattie Higgins?' Mr Sheehy enquired of Mrs Fennerty. When he spoke he kept his teeth trapped behind his lips, as though nervous of their exposure. 'I sold him a wireless set. Three pounds fifteen. I had the price agreed with him, only when I brought it round all he had was a five-pound note. "I'll have that broken into to-night," he said. "Come back in the morning." Only didn't he die that night in his bed?'

Swiftly, the old woman crossed herself. 'You got caught with that one,' she said.

'I was round there at eight o'clock this morning, only the place was in the hands of five big daughters. When I mentioned the wireless they ate the face off of me. A good Pye wireless gone west.'

Mrs Fennerty, still consuming her food, glanced across the room at the radio on the dumbwaiter in a corner. 'Is it a Pye Mrs Lenehan has?'

'It is.'

'I heard the Pye's the best.'

'I told that to the daughters. The one I sold him had only a few fag burns on the cabinet. The five of them laughed at me.'

'I know the type.'

'Five fat vultures, and your man still warming the bed.'

'Strumpets.'

The rest of the meal was taken in a silence that wasn't broken until Ariadne came to clear the table. 'I meant to have told you,' she remarked to Barney. 'Your window gets stuck at the top.'

He said it didn't matter. He had noticed her mother opening the bottom sash in preference to the top one, he added conversationally. It didn't matter in the least, he said.

'The top's stuck with paint,' Ariadne said.

Mrs Fennerty returned to her place by the fire. Mr

Sheehy put on his navy-blue overcoat and his gloves and sat on the chair by the door. Skilfully, with the glass held at an angle, Mrs Fennerty poured out a bottle of stout that had been placed in the fender to warm. On her invitation, accompanied by a warning concerning hasty digestion, Barney occupied the second rexine-covered armchair, feeling too shy to disobey. Mrs Fennerty lit a cigarette. She was a boarder the same as Mr Sheehy, she said. She paid her way, Mrs Lenehan's mother or not. That was why she sat down in the dining-room with Mr Sheehy and whoever the third boarder happened to be.

'Are you at Dowding's?' She referred to a commercial college that offered courses in accountancy and book-keeping, preparing its students for the bank and brewery examinations.

'No. Not Dowding's.' He explained that he was a medical student.

'A doctor buries his mistakes. Did you ever hear that one?' Mrs Fennerty laughed shrilly, and in a sociable way Barney laughed himself. Mr Sheehy remained impassive by the door. Barney wondered why he had taken up a position there, with his coat and gloves on.

'Six feet under, no questions asked,' Mrs Fennerty remarked, again laughing noisily.

Dressed to go out, Mrs Lenehan entered the dining-room, and Mr Sheehy's behaviour was explained. He rose to his feet, and when the pair had gone Mrs Fennerty said:

'Those two are doing a line. Up to the McKee Barracks every evening. Sheehy wouldn't part with the price of anything else. Turn round at the barracks, back by the Guards' Depot. Then he's down in the kitchen with her. That's Ned Sheehy for you.'

Barney nodded, not much interested in Mr Sheehy's courtship of Mrs Lenehan. Nevertheless the subject was pursued. 'Ned Sheehy has a post with the Hibernian Insurance. That's how he'd be selling wireless sets to people. He calls in at houses a lot.'

'I see.'

'He's keen on houses all right. It's the house we're sitting in he has designs on, not Mrs Lenehan at all.'

'Oh, I'm sure—'

'If there's a man in Dublin that knows his bricks and mortar better than Ned Sheehy give me a gander at him.'

Barney said he didn't think he could supply the old woman with such a person, and she said that of course he couldn't. No flies on Ned Sheehy, she said, in spite of what you might think to look at him.

'She made a mistake the first time and she'll make another before she's finished. You could turn that one's head like the wind would turn a weather-cock.'

Ariadne came in with the *Evening Herald* and handed it to her grandmother. Barney smiled at her, but she didn't notice. Mrs Fennerty became engrossed in the newspaper. Barney went upstairs.

In time, he heard footsteps in the room above his, and knew they were Ariadne's. They crossed the room to the window. The blind was drawn down. Ariadne crossed the room again, back and forth, back and forth. He knew when she took her shoes off.

*

Handwritten notes clamoured for attention on the green baize of the board beside the porters' lodge: love letters, brief lines of rejection, relationships terminated, charges of treachery, a stranger's admiration confessed. The same envelope remained on the baize-covered board for months: *R. R. Woodley*, it said, but R. R. Woodley either did not exist or had long since ceased to be an undergraduate. *It is hard to find myself the way I am, and to be alone with not a soul to turn to*: a heart was laid bare within the dust-soiled envelope, its ache revealed to the general curiosity. But other notes, on torn half-sheets of exercise-paper, remained on the green board for only a few hours, disappearing for ever while they were still fresh.

Within their fire-warmed lodge the porters were a suspicious breed of men, well used to attempted circumvention of the law that began where their own rule did. They wore black velvet jockey caps; one carried a mace on ceremonial occasions. They saw to it that bicycles were wheeled through the vast archway they guarded, and that female undergraduates passed in and out during the permitted hours only, that their book was signed when this was necessary. In the archway itself, posters advertised dances and theatrical productions. Eminent visitors were announced. Societies' account sheets were published. There were reports of missionary work in Africa.

Beyond this entrance, dark façades loomed around a cobbled square. Loops of chain protected tidily shorn lawns. The Chapel stared stolidly at the pillars of the Examination Hall. Gold numerals lightened the blue face of the Dining Hall clock. A campanile rose fussily.

Barney attended the lectures of Bore McGusty and Professor Makepeace-Green and the elderly Dr Posse, who had been in the medical school in his father's time. Bore McGusty was a long-winded young man, Professor Makepeace-Green a tetchily severe woman, who particularly objected to Slovinski reading the *Daily Sketch* during her lectures. The students of Barney's age keenly took notes and paid attention, but the recent shedding of years of discipline by the ex-servicemen left them careless of their academic obligations. 'Listen,' Slovinski regularly invited, interrupting Bore McGusty's dissertation on the functioning of the bile-ducts by playing Beethoven on his teeth.

The medical students favoured certain public houses: the International Bar, Ryan's in Duke Street, McFadden's. After an evening's drinking they danced in the Crystal Ballroom, or sat around pots of tea in the café attached to

(84)

the Green Cinema, where the private lives of their mentors were breezily speculated upon, and for the most part scorned. On such occasions Slovinski spoke of his wartime liaisons, and Medlicott retailed the appetites of a baker's widow, a Mrs Claudia Rigg of Bournemouth. For Barney—years later—this time in his life was as minutely preserved as his childhood at Lisscrea. And always, at the heart of the memory, was Mrs Lenehan's household in Gogarty Street.

*

'You've maybe not come across the name Ariadne before,' Mrs Lenehan said one morning in the hall, adding that she'd found it in a story in *Model Housekeeping*. Had a son been born instead of a daughter he'd have been christened Paul, that being a family name on her own side. As soon as she'd seen *Ariadne* written down she'd settled for it.

Barney liked the name also. He thought it suited Mrs Lenehan's daughter, whom increasingly he found himself thinking about, particularly during the lectures of Bore McGusty and Professor Makepeace-Green. Ariadne, he soon discovered, didn't go out to work; her work was in her mother's house and it was there, during the lectures, that he imagined her. She assisted with the cleaning and the preparation of meals, and the washing-up afterwards. She was often on the stairs with a dust-pan and brush; she polished the brass on the front door. Every morning she set the dining-room fire, and lit it every evening. Once in a while she and her mother cleaned the windows.

Mrs Lenehan occasionally sang while she performed her household tasks. Ariadne didn't. There was no trace of reluctance in her expression, only a kind of vagueness: she had the look of a saint, Barney found himself thinking once, and the thought remained with him. In the dining-room he was usually the last to finish breakfast, deliberately dawdling. Ariadne came in with a tray and, seeing him still at the table, absorbed the time by damping the fire down with wet slack and picking up the mantelpiece ornaments and dusting them. Her elegant hands were as delicate as the porcelain she attended to, and her clothes never varied: the same shade of mauve combined repeatedly with mourner's black. 'Good evening, Mr Prenderville,' she sometimes whispered in the dusk of the hall, a fleeting figure passing from one closed door to another.

After he'd been in the lodgings a month Barney was familiar with every movement in the room above his. When Ariadne left it and did not return within a few minutes he said to himself that she was washing her hair, which he imagined wrapped in a towel, the way Nuala wrapped hers before she sat down to dry it at the range. He imagined the glow of an electric fire on Ariadne's long, damp tresses. Staring at a discoloured ceiling, he invaded her privacy, investing every sound she made with his speculations. Would she be sewing or embroidering, as Nuala did in the evening? Nuala pressed flowers betwen the pages of the medical encyclopaedia in the dining-room at Lisscrea, pansies and primulas she asked Charlie Redmond to bring from the garden. Barney wondered if Ariadne did that also. He guessed the moment when she lay down to sleep, and lay in the darkness himself, accompanying her to oblivion.

He didn't tell Rouge Medlicott and Slovinski, or anyone else, about Ariadne. In his letters to his father he mentioned Mrs Lenehan and Mrs Fennerty and Mr Sheehy: Ariadne mightn't have existed. Yet in the noisy cafés and the lecture-halls he continued to feel haunted by her, and wished she was there also. He left the house in Gogarty Street reluctantly each morning, and hurried back to it in the evenings.

*

'Ariadne.'

He addressed her on the first-floor landing one Sunday afternoon. His voice was little more than a whisper; they were shadows in the dim afternoon light. 'Ariadne,' he said again, delighting, while they were alone, in this repetition of her name.

'Yes, Mr Prenderville?'

Mrs Lenehan and Mr Sheehy spent Sunday afternoons with Mrs Fennerty in the dining-room, listening to a radio commentary on a hurling or Gaelic football match, the only time the dining-room wireless was ever turned on. When it was over Mr Sheehy and Mrs Lenehan went to the kitchen.

'Would you like to come for a walk, Ariadne?'

She did not reply at once. He gazed through the gloom, hoping for the gleam of her smile. From the dining-room came the faint sound of the commentator's rapid, excited voice. Ariadne didn't smile. She said:

'This minute, Mr Prenderville?'

'If you are doing nothing better.'

'I will put on my coat.'

He thought of her mother and Mr Sheehy as he waited. He didn't know which direction the McKee Barracks and the Civic Guards' Depot lay in, but wherever these places were he didn't want even to see them in the distance. 'I'm ready,' Ariadne said, having delayed for no longer than a minute. Barney opened the front door softly, and softly closed it behind them. Damp autumn leaves lay thickly on the pavements, blown into mounds and heaps. When the wind gusted, more slipped from the branches above them and gently descended. Ariadne's coat was another shade of mauve, matching her headscarf. There'd been no need to leave the house in that secret way, but they had done so nonetheless, without exchanging a look.

'I love Sunday,' Ariadne said.

He said he liked the day also. He told her about Sundays at Lisscrea because he didn't know how else to interest her. His father and he would sit reading in the drawing-room on a winter's afternoon, or in the garden in the summer. Nuala would bring them tea, and a cake made the day before. His father read books that were sent to him by post from a lending library in Dublin, novels by A. E. W. Mason and E. Phillips Oppenheim and Sapper. Once, laying one down when he had finished it, he changed his mind and handed it to Barney. 'Try this,' he said, and after that they shared the books that came by post. Barney was fourteen or fifteen then.

'Your mother is not there, Mr Prenderville?'

'My mother died.'

He described Lisscrea to her: the long, narrow rooms of the house, the garden where Charlie Redmond had worked for as long as Barney could remember, the patients in the hall. He mentioned the cottages next to Lisscrea House, and Walsh's public house, and the ruined tower he could see from his bedroom window. He repeated a piece of Charlie Redmond's doggerel, and described his prematurely wizened features and Nuala's countrywoman's looks. He told Ariadne about school at Ballinadra, the journey on the milk cart when he was small, the return by the bread van in the afternoon, and then the inheriting of his father's old Rudge bicycle. She'd never known a town like Ballinadra, Ariadne said; she only knew Dublin.

'It isn't much,' he said, but she wanted to know, and he tried to make a picture of the place for her: the single street and the square, O'Kevin's hardware, the grocers' shops that were bars as well, the statue to the men of '98.

'A quiet place,' Ariadne said.

'Oh, a grave.'

She nodded solemnly. She could see the house, she said. She knew what he meant by Virginia creeper. She could see his father clearly.

'What would you have done if I hadn't suggested a walk?'

'Stayed in my room.'

'Doing nothing, Ariadne?' He spoke lightly, almost teasing her. But she was still solemn and did not smile. Maybe tidying her drawers, she said. She called him Mr Prenderville again, and he asked her not to. 'My name's Barney.'

'Just Barney?'

'Barney Gregory.'

Again she nodded. They walked in silence. He said:

'Will you always help your mother in the house?'

'What else would I do?'

He didn't know. He wanted to suggest some work that was worthy of her, something better than carrying trays of food to the dining-room and sweeping the stair-carpet. Even work in a shop was more dignified than what she did, but he did not mention a shop. 'Perhaps a nurse.'

'I would be frightened to be a nurse. I'd be no good at it.'

'I'm sure you would, Ariadne.'

She would care tenderly. Her gentleness would be a blessing. Her beauty would cheer the melancholy of the ill.

'Nuns are better at all that,' she said.

'Did you go to a convent, Ariadne?'

She nodded, and for a moment seemed lost in the memory the question inspired. When she spoke again her voice, for the first time, was eager. 'Will we walk to the convent, Barney? It isn't far away.'

'If you would like to.'

'We have to turn right when we come to Prussia Street.'

No one was about. The front doors of the houses they walked by were tightly closed against the world. Their footsteps were deadened by the sodden leaves.

'I like that colour you wear,' he said.

'An aunt left me her clothes.'

'An aunt?'

'A great-aunt, Aunt Loretta. Half of them she never wore. She loved that colour.'

'It suits you.'

'She used to say that.'

That was why her dresses, and the coat she wore now, were rather long for her. It was her clothes that gave her her old-fashioned air. Had she no clothes of her own? he wondered, but did not ask.

(89)

The convent was a cement building with silver-coloured railings in front of it. The blinds were drawn down in several of its windows; lace curtains ensured privacy in the others. A brass letterbox and knocker gleamed on a green side-door.

'Did you walk here every morning?' he asked.

'When I was small my father used to take me. It wasn't out of his way.'

She went on talking about that, and he formed a picture of her childhood, just as, a few moments ago, she had of his. He saw her, hand in hand with her father, hurrying through the early-morning streets. Her father had worked in Maguire's coal office in Easter Street. Sometimes they'd call in at a shop for his tobacco, half an ounce of Digger.

When they crossed the street he wanted to take her arm, but he didn't have the courage. They could walk to a bus stop, he suggested, and wait for a bus to O'Connell Street. They could have tea somewhere, one of the cinema cafés that were open on a Sunday. But she shook her head. She'd have to be getting back, she said.

They turned and walked the way they'd come, past the silent houses. A drizzle began. They didn't say much else.

*

'God, there's talent for you!' Medlicott exclaimed in the Crystal Ballroom, surveying the girls who stood against the walls. Slovinski conveyed a willowy woman of uncertain age on to the dance-floor, from which, a few minutes later, they disappeared and did not return. Some of the girls who were standing about glanced back at Medlicott, clearly considering him handsome. He approached a lean-featured one with hair the colour of newly polished brass, not at all pretty, Barney considered.

Because he had no knowledge of dance-steps, the partners Barney chose usually excused themselves after a minute or two. 'What line are you in?' a plump one, more tolerant than the others, enquired. He said he worked in a dry-cleaner's, Slovinski having warned him not to mention being a student in case the girls took fright. 'You can't dance,' the plump girl observed, and commenced to teach him.

When the end of the evening came she was still doing so. Medlicott had remained attached to the lean-featured girl, whom he confidently reported he had 'got going'. Outside the dance-hall Barney heard him complimenting her on her eyes, and felt embarrassed because he didn't want to have to tell the plump girl that she, too, had lovely eyes, which wouldn't have been true. Instead, he asked her her name. 'Mavis,' she said.

Medlicott suggested that they should go out to Goatstown in a taxi, since the city bars were closed by now. There were fields in Goatstown, he reminded his companions: after they'd had a couple of nightcaps they could go for a walk through the fields in the moonlight. But Mavis said her father would skin her if she got in late. She took Barney's arm. Her father was fierce-tempered, she confided.

The lean-faced girl didn't want to make the journey to Goatstown either, so Medlicott led her into an alleyway. They kissed one another in a doorway while Mavis and Barney stood some distance away. When her father went wild, Mavis said, nothing could hold him. 'All right,' Barney heard the lean-faced girl say.

A battered Ford car was parked at the far end of the alleyway next to a skip full of builder's rubble. Medlicott and his companion approached it, she teetering on gold-coloured high heels. Medlicott opened one of the back doors. 'Come on in here, darling,' he invited.

It was difficult to know what to say to Mavis, so Barney didn't say anything. She talked about her brothers and sisters; half listening, he imagined Ariadne at Lisscrea. He imagined being engaged to her, and introducing her to Nuala in the kitchen and Charlie Redmond in the garden. He saw himself walking along the road with her, and waiting while she attended mass in the nearby church. He showed her Ballinadra—the rudimentary shops, the statue to the men of '98 in the square.

He glanced at the car and caught a glimpse of brassy hair through the back window. He would introduce her to the tender-hearted Miss Bone. He imagined Miss Bone dismounting from her bicycle outside O'Kevin's hardware. 'Welcome to Ballinadra, Ariadne,' she murmured in her gentle voice.

Three men had turned into the alleyway, and a moment later shouting began. A door of the car was wrenched open; clothing was seized and flung out. One of the lean girl's gold-coloured shoes bounced over the surface of the alleyway, coming to rest near the skip. 'Get that hooer out of my car,' a voice furiously commanded.

In spite of what was happening, Barney couldn't properly detach himself from his thoughts. He walked with Ariadne, from the town to Lisscrea House. On the way he showed her the Lackens' farm and the hay-shed where the Black and Tans had murdered a father and a son, and the ramshackle house at the end of a long avenue, where the bread van used to call every day when he got a lift in it back from school, where mad Mrs Joyce lived. Weeds flowered on the verges; it must have been summer.

'Get out of that bloody car!'

The garments that lay on the ground were pitched into the skip, with the shoe. Medlicott called out incomprehensibly, a humorous observation by the sound of it. 'D'you want your neck broken?' the same man shouted back at him. 'Get out of my property.'

'I'm off,' Mavis said, and Barney walked with her to her bus stop, not properly listening while she told him that a girl who would enter a motor-car as easily as that would come to an unsavoury end. 'I'll look out for you in the Crystal,' she promised before they parted.

On the journey back to Gogarty Street Barney was accompanied by an impression, as from a fantasy, of Mavis's plump body, breasts pressed against his chest, a knee touching one of his, the warm perspiration of her palm. Such physical intimacy was not the kind he had ever associated with Ariadne, but as he approached his lodgings he knew he could not let the night pass without the greater reality of seeing her face, without—even for an instant— being again in her company.

When he arrived at Mrs Lenehan's house he continued to ascend the stairs after he'd reached the landing off which his room lay. Any moment a light might come on, he thought; any moment he would stand exposed and have to pretend he had made a mistake. But the darkness continued, and he switched on no lights himself. Softly, he turned the handle of the door above his, and closed it, standing with his back to the panels. He could see nothing, but so close did the unspoken relationship feel that he half expected to hear his name whispered. That did not happen; he could not hear even the sound of breathing. He remained where he stood, prepared to do so for however many hours might pass before streaks of light showed on either side of the window blinds. He gazed at where he knew the bed must be, confirmed in this conjecture by the creeping twilight. He waited, with all the passion he possessed pressed into a longing to glimpse the features he had come to love. He would go at once then. One day, in some happy future, he would tell Ariadne of this night of adoration.

But as the room took form—the wardrobe, the bed, the wash-stand, the chest of drawers—he sensed, even before he could discern more than these outlines, that he was alone. No sleeping face rewarded his patience, no dark hair lay on the pillow. The window blinds were not drawn down. The bed was orderly, and covered. The room was tidy, as though abandoned.

*

Before the arrival of Professor Makepeace-Green the following morning, the episode in the alleyway and Slovinski's swift spiriting away of the willowy woman from the dance-hall floor were retailed. Barney was commiserated with because he had failed to take his chances. Rouge Medlicott and Slovinski, and several other ex-servicemen, gave him advice as to amorous advancement in the future. His preoccupied mood went unnoticed.

That evening, it was the old woman who told him. When he remarked upon Ariadne's absence in the dining-room she said their future needs in this respect would be attended to by a maid called Biddy whom Mrs Lenehan was in the process of employing. When he asked her where Ariadne had gone she said that Ariadne had always been religious.

'Religious?'

'Ariadne's working in the kitchen of the convent.'

Mr Sheehy came into the dining-room and removed his navy-blue overcoat and his tan gloves. A few minutes later Mrs Lenehan placed the plates of fried food in front of her lodgers, and then returned with the metal tea-pot. Mr Sheehy spoke of the houses he had visited during the day, in his capacity as agent for the Hibernian Insurance Company. Mrs Lenehan put her mother's bottle of stout to warm in the fender.

'Is Ariadne not going to live here any more?' Barney asked Mrs Fennerty when Mr Sheehy and Mrs Lenehan had gone out for their walk to the McKee Barracks.

'I'd say she'll stop in the convent now. Ariadne always liked that convent.'

'I know.'

Mrs Fennerty lit her evening cigarette. It was to be expected, she said. It was not a surprise.

'That she should go there?'

'After you took Ariadne out, Barney. You follow what I mean?'

He said he didn't. She nodded, fresh thoughts agreeing

(94)

with what she had already stated. She poured her stout.
She had never called him Barney before.

'It's called going out, Barney. Even if it's nothing very
much.'

'Yes, but what's that to do with her working in the convent?'

'She didn't tell you about Lenehan? She didn't mention
her father, Barney?'

'Yes, she did.'

'She didn't tell you he took his life?' The old woman
crossed herself, her gesture as swift as it always was when
she made it. She continued to pour her stout, expertly
draining it down the side of the glass.

'No, she didn't tell me that.'

'When Ariadne was ten years old her father took his life
in an upstairs room.'

'Why did he do that, Mrs Fennerty?'

'He was not a man I ever liked.' Again she paused, as
though to dwell privately upon her aversion to her late
son-in-law. 'Shame is the state Ariadne lives in.'

'Shame?'

'Can you remember when you were ten, Barney?'

He nodded. It was something they had in common, he'd
said to Ariadne, that for both of them a parent had died.
Any child had affection for a father, Mrs Fennerty was
saying.

'Why did Mr Lenehan take his life?'

Mrs Fennerty did not reply. She sipped her stout. She
stared into the glow of the fire, then threw her cigarette end
into it. She said Mr Lenehan had feared arrest.

'Arrest?' he repeated, stupidly.

'There was an incident on a tram.' Again the old woman
blessed herself. Her jauntiness had left her. She repeated
what she'd told him the first evening he sat with her: that
her daughter was a fool where men were concerned. 'At that
time people looked at Ariadne on the street. When the girls

(95)

at the convent shunned her the nuns were nice to her. She's never forgotten that.'

'What kind of an incident, Mrs Fennerty?'

'A child on a tram. They have expressions for that kind of thing. I don't even like to know them.'

He felt cold, even though he was close to the fire. It was as though he had been told, not of the death of Ariadne's father but of her own. He wished he had taken her arm when they went for their walk. He wished she'd said yes when he'd suggested they should have tea in a cinema café. Not so long ago he hadn't even known she existed, yet now he couldn't imagine not loving her.

'It would have been no good, Barney.'

He asked her what she meant, but she didn't answer. He knew anyway. It would have been no good because what seemed like a marvel of strangeness in Ariadne was damage wrought by shame. She had sensed his love, and fear had come, possibly revulsion. She would have hated it if he'd taken her arm, even if he'd danced with her, as he had with Mavis.

'Ariadne'll stay there always now,' the old woman said, sipping more of her stout. Delicately, she wiped a smear of foam from her lips. It was a silver lining that there'd been the convent kitchen to go to, that the same nuns were there to be good to her.

'She'd still be here if I hadn't taken the room.'

'You were the first young man, Barney. You couldn't be held to blame.'

*

When Barney returned to Dublin from Lisscrea at the beginning of his second term he found, unexpectedly, that he had been allocated College rooms. He explained that in Gogarty Street, and Mrs Lenehan said it couldn't be helped. 'Mr Sheehy and myself are getting married,' she added in the hall.

Barney said he was glad, which was not untrue. Mr Sheehy had been drawn towards a woman's property; for her part, Mrs Lenehan needed more than a man could offer her on walks to the McKee Barracks. Mrs Lenehan had survived the past; she had not been damaged; second time round, she had settled for Mr Sheehy.

In the dining-room he said goodbye to Mrs Fennerty. There was a new young clerk in Ned Sheehy's office who was looking for digs, she said. He would take the vacant room, it wouldn't be empty for long. A student called Browder had moved into Ariadne's a week or so after her going. It hadn't been empty for long either.

It was snowing that evening. Huge flakes clung to Barney's overcoat as he walked to the convent, alone in the silence of the streets. Since Ariadne's going he had endlessly loitered by the convent, but its windows were always blank, as they were on that Sunday afternoon. Tonight, a dim light burned above the green side-door, but no curtain twitched as he scanned the grey façade, no footsteps disturbed the white expanse beyond the railings. In the depths of the ugly building were the strangeness and the beauty as he had known them, and for a moment he experienced what was left of his passion: a useless longing to change the circumstances there had been.

While he was still in Mrs Lenehan's house he had thought that somehow he might rescue Ariadne. It was a romantic urge, potent before love began to turn into regret. He had imagined himself ringing the convent bell, and again seeing Ariadne's face. He had imagined himself smiling at her with all the gentleness he possessed, and walking again with her; and persuading her, when time had passed, that love was possible. 'You'll get over her,' his father had said in the holidays, guessing only that there had been some girl.

*

A bus creeps through the snow: years later, for Barney, there is that image, a fragment in the cluster that makes the whole. It belongs with the upturned butter-box in the grass and the pinks in the brindle hair of the dog, with Rouge Medlicott and Slovinski, and the jockey-capped porters, and the blue-faced Dining Hall clock. A lone figure stares out into the blurred night, hating the good sense that draws him away from loitering gloomily outside a convent.

A Trinity

Their first holiday since their honeymoon was paid for by the elderly man they both called Uncle. In fact, he was related to neither of them: for eleven years he had been Dawne's employer, but the relationship was more truly that of benefactor and dependants. They lived with him and looked after him, but in another sense it was he who looked after them, demonstrating regularly that they required such care. 'What you need is a touch of the autumn sun,' he had said, ordering Keith to acquire as many holiday brochures as he could lay his hands on. 'The pair of you're as white as bedsheets.'

The old man lived vicariously through aspects of their lives, and listened carefully to all they said. Sharing their anticipation, he browsed delightedly through the pages of the colourful brochures and opened out on the kitchen table one glossy folder after another. He marvelled over the blue of the Aegean Sea and the flower markets of San Remo, over the Nile and the pyramids, the Costa del Sol, the treasures of Bavaria. But it was Venice that most vividly caught his imagination, and again and again he returned to the wonder of its bridges and canals, and the majesty of the Piazza San Marco.

'I am too old for Venice,' he remarked a little sadly. 'I am too old for anywhere now.'

They protested. They pressed him to accompany them. But as well as being old he had his paper-shop to think about. He could not leave Mrs Withers to cope on her own;

it would not be fair.

'Send me one or two postcards,' he said. 'That will be sufficient.'

He chose for them a package holiday at a very reasonable price: an air flight from Gatwick Airport, twelve nights in the fairyland city, in the Pensione Concordia. When Keith and Dawne went together to the travel agency to make the booking the counter clerk explained that the other members of that particular package were an Italian class from Windsor, all of them learning the language under the tutelage of a Signor Bancini. 'It is up to you if you wish to take the guided tours of Signor Bancini,' the counter clerk explained. 'And naturally you have your own table for breakfast and for dinner.'

The old man, on being told about the party from Windsor, was well pleased. Mixing with such people and, for just a little extra, being able to avail themselves of the expertise of an Italian language teacher amounted to a bonus, he pointed out. 'Travel widens the mind,' he said. 'I deplore I never had the opportunity.'

But something went wrong. Either in the travel agency or at Gatwick Airport, or in some anonymous computer, a small calamity was conceived. Dawne and Keith ended up in a hotel called the Edelweiss, in room two hundred and twelve, in Switzerland. At Gatwick they had handed their tickets to a girl in the yellow-and-red Your-Kind-of-Holiday uniform. She'd addressed them by name, had checked the details on their tickets and said that that was lovely. An hour later it had surprised them to hear elderly people on the plane talking in North of England accents when the counter clerk at the travel agency had so specifically stated that Signor Bancini's Italian class came from Windsor. Dawne had even remarked on it, but Keith said there must have been a cancellation, or possibly the Italian class was on a second plane. 'That'll be the name of the airport,' he confidently explained when the pilot referred

over the communications system to a destination that didn't
sound like Venice. 'Same as he'd say Gatwick. Or Heath-
row.' They ordered two Drambuies, Dawne's favourite
drink, and then two more. 'The coach'll take us on,' a stout
woman with spectacles announced when the plane landed.
'Keep all together now.' There'd been no mention of an
overnight stop in the brochure, but when the coach drew in
at the Edelweiss Hotel Keith explained that that was clearly
what this was. By air and then by coach was how these
package firms kept the prices down, a colleague at work had
told him. As they stepped out of the coach it was close on
midnight: fatigued and travel-stained, they did not feel like
questioning their right to the beds they were offered. But
the next morning, when it became apparent that they were
being offered them for the duration of their holiday, they
became alarmed.

'We have the lake, and the water-birds,' the receptionist
smilingly explained. 'And we may take the steamer to
Interlaken.'

'An error has been made,' Keith informed the man, keeping the register of his voice even, for it was essential to be
calm. He was aware of his wife's agitated breathing close
beside him. She'd had to sit down when they realised that
something was wrong, but now she was standing up again.

'We cannot change the room, sir,' the clerk swiftly
countered. 'Each has been given a room. You accompany
the group, sir?'

Keith shook his head. Not this group, he said, a different
group; a group that was travelling on to another destination.
Keith was not a tall man, and often suffered from what he
considered to be arrogance in other people, from officials of
one kind or another, and shop assistants with a tendency to
assume that his lack of stature reflected a diminutive personality. In a way Keith didn't care for, the receptionist
repeated:

'This is the Edelweiss Hotel, sir.'

(101)

'We were meant to be in Venice. In the Pensione Concordia.'

'I do not know the name, sir. Here we have Switzerland.'

'A coach is to take us on. An official said so on the plane. She was here last night, that woman.'

'Tomorrow we have the fondue party,' the receptionist went on, having listened politely to this information about an official. 'On Tuesday there is the visit to a chocolate factory. On other days we may take the steamer to Interlaken, where we have teashops. In Interlaken mementoes may be bought at fair prices.'

Dawne had still not spoken. She, too, was a slight figure, her features pale beneath orange-ish powder. 'Mingy,' the old man had a way of saying in his joky voice, and sometimes told her to lie down.

'Eeh, idn't it luvely?' a voice behind Keith enthused. 'Been out to feed them ducks, 'ave you?'

Keith did not turn round. Speaking slowly, giving each word space, he said to the receptionist: 'We have been booked on to the wrong holiday.'

'Your group is booked twelve nights in the Edelweiss Hotel. To make an alteration now, sir, if you have changed your minds—'

'We haven't changed our minds. There's been a mistake.'

The receptionist shook his head. He did not know about a mistake. He had not been told that. He would help if he could, but he did not see how help might best be offered.

'The man who made the booking,' Dawne interrupted, 'was bald, with glasses and a moustache.' She gave the name of the travel agency in London.

In reply, the receptionist smiled with professional sympathy. He fingered the edge of his register. 'Moustache?' he said.

Three aged women who had been on the plane passed through the reception area. Had anyone noticed, one of them remarked, that there were rubber linings under the sheets? Well, you couldn't be too careful, another agreeably responded, if you were running a hotel.

'Some problem, have we?' another woman said, beaming at Keith. She was the stout woman he had referred to as an official, flamboyantly attired this morning in a two-tone trouser-suit, green and blue. Her flesh-coloured spectacles were decorated with swirls of metal made to seem like gold; her grey hair was carefully waved. They'd seen her talking to the yellow-and-red girl at Gatwick. On the plane she'd walked up and down the aisle, smiling at people.

'My name is Franks,' she was saying now. 'I'm married to the man with the bad leg.'

'Are you in charge, Mrs Franks?' Dawne enquired. 'Only we're in the wrong hotel.' Again she gave the name of the travel agency and described the bald-headed counter clerk, mentioning his spectacles and his moustache. Keith interrupted her.

'It seems we got into the wrong group. We reported to the Your-Kind-of-Holiday girl and left it all to her.'

'We should have known when they weren't from Windsor,' Dawne contributed. 'We heard them talking about Darlington.'

Keith made an impatient sound. He wished she'd leave the talking to him. It was no good whatsoever going on about Darlington and the counter clerk's moustache, confusing everything even more.

'We noticed you at Gatwick,' he said to the stout woman. 'We knew you were in charge of things.'

'I noticed *you*. Well, of course I did, naturally I did. I counted you, although I dare say you didn't see me doing that. Monica checked the tickets and I did the counting. That's how I know everything's O.K. Now, let me explain to you. There are many places Your-Kind-of-Holiday sends its clients to, many tours, many different holidays at different prices. You follow me? Something to suit every pocket, something for every taste. There are, for instance, villa holidays for the adventurous under-thirty-fives. There are treks to Turkey, and treks for singles to the Himalayas. There is self-catering in Portugal, November reductions in Casablanca, February in Biarritz. There's Culture-in-Tuscany and Sunshine-in-Sorrento. There's the Nile. There's Your-Kind-of-Safari in Kenya. Now, what I am endeavouring to say to you good people is that all tickets and labels are naturally similar, the yellow with the two red bands.' Mrs Franks suddenly laughed. 'So if you simply followed other people with the yellow-and-red label you might imagine you could end up in a wildlife park!' Mrs Franks' speech came hurriedly from her, the words tumbling over one another, gushing through her teeth. 'But of course,' she added soothingly, 'that couldn't happen in a million years.'

'We're not meant to be in Switzerland,' Keith doggedly persisted.

'Well, let's just see, shall we?'

Unexpectedly, Mrs Franks turned and went away, leaving them standing. The receptionist was no longer behind the reception desk. The sound of typing could be heard.

'She seems quite kind,' Dawne whispered, 'that woman.'

To Keith it seemed unnecessary to say that. Any consideration of Mrs Franks was, in the circumstances, as irrelevant as a description of the man in the travel agent's. He tried to go over in his mind every single thing that had occurred: handing the girl the tickets, sitting down to wait, and then the girl leading the way to the plane, and then the pilot's voice welcoming them aboard, and the air hostess with the smooth black hair going round to see that everyone's seat-belt was fastened.

'Snaith his name was,' Dawne was saying. 'It said *Snaith* on a plastic thing in front of him.'

'What are you talking about?'

'The man in the travel place was called Snaith. *G. Snaith* it said.'

'The man was just a clerk.'

'He booked us wrong, though. That man's responsible, Keith.'

'Be that as it may.'

Sooner or later, Dawne had guessed, he'd say 'Be that as it may'. He put her in her place with the phrase; he always had. You'd make an innocent remark, doing your best to be helpful, and out he'd come with 'Be that as it may'. You expected him to go on, to finish the sentence, but he never did. The phrase just hung there, making him sound uneducated.

'Are you going to phone up that man, Keith?'

'Which man is this?'

She didn't reply. He knew perfectly well which man she meant. All he had to do was to get through to Directory Enquiries and find out the number of the travel agency. It was no good complaining to a hotel receptionist who had nothing to do with it, or to a woman in charge of a totally different package tour. No good putting the blame where it didn't belong.

'Nice to have some young people along,' an elderly man said. 'Nottage the name is.'

Dawne smiled, the way she did in the shop when someone was trying to be agreeable, but Keith didn't acknowledge the greeting because he didn't want to become involved.

'Seen the ducks, 'ave you? Right champion them ducks are.'

The old man's wife was with him, both of them looking as if they were in their eighties. She nodded when he said the ducks were right champion. They'd slept like logs, she said, best night's sleep they'd had for years, which of course would be due to the lakeside air.

'That's nice,' Dawne said.

Keith walked out of the reception area and Dawne followed him. On the gravel forecourt of the hotel they didn't say to one another that there was an irony in the catastrophe that had occurred. On their first holiday since their honey-moon they'd landed themselves in a package tour of elderly people when the whole point of the holiday was to escape the needs and demands of the elderly. In his bossy way Uncle had said so himself when they'd tried to persuade him to accompany them.

'You'll have to phone up Snaith,' Dawne repeated, irritating Keith further. What she did not understand was that if the error had occurred with the man she spoke of it would since have become compounded to such a degree that the man would claim to be able to do nothing about their immediate predicament. Keith, who sold insurance over the counter for the General Accident insurance company, knew something of the complications that followed when even the slightest uncertainty in a requirement was passed into the programme of a computer. Somewhere along the line that was what had happened, but to explain it to Dawne would take a very long time. Dawne could work a till as well as anyone; in the shop she knew by heart the price of Mars bars and the different kinds of cigarettes and tobacco, and the prices of all the newspapers and magazines, but otherwise Keith considered her slow on the uptake, often unable to follow simple argument.

'Hi, there!' Mrs Franks called out, and they turned and saw her picking her way across the gravel towards them. She had a piece of pink paper in her hand. 'I've been doing my homework!' she cried when she was a little closer. She waved the pink paper. 'Take a look at this.'

It was a list of names, a computer print-out, each name a series of tiny dots. *K. and H. Beale*, they read, *T. and G. Craven, P. and R. Fineman*. There were many others, including *B. and Y. Nottage*. In the correct alphabetical position they were there themselves, between *J. and A. Hines* and *C. and L. Mace*.

'The thing is,' Dawne began, and Keith looked away. His wife's voice quietly continued, telling Mrs Franks that their holiday had been very kindly paid for by the old man whom they lived with, who had been her employer before they ever moved in to live with him, who still was. They called him Uncle but he wasn't a relation, a friend really— well, more than that. The thing was, he would be angry because they were not in Venice, he having said it should be Venice. He'd be angry because they were in a package for the elderly when he wanted them to have a rest from the elderly, not that she minded looking after Uncle herself, not that she ever would. The person in the travel agency had said the Windsor people were quite young. 'I always remember things like that,' Dawne finished up. 'Snaith he was called. G. Snaith.'

'Well, that's most interesting,' Mrs Franks commented, and added after a pause: 'As a matter of fact, Dawne, Mr Franks and myself are still in our fifties.'

'Be that as it may,' Keith said. 'At no time did we book a holiday in Switzerland.'

'Well, there you are, you see. The ticket you handed to me at Gatwick is as clear as daylight, exactly the same as the Beales' and the Maces', the same as our own, come to that. Not a tither of difference, Keith.'

'We need to be conveyed to our correct destination. An arrangement has to be made.'

'The trouble is, Keith, I don't know if you know it but you're half a continent away from Venice. Another thing is, I'm not employed by Your-Kind, nothing like that. They just reduce our ticket a bit if I agree to keep an eye. On location we call it.' Mrs Franks went on to say that her husband had also scrutinised the piece of pink paper and was in complete agreement with her. She asked Keith if he had met her husband, and said again that he was the man with the bad leg. He'd been an accountant and still did a lot of accountancy work one way or another, in a private capacity. The Edelweiss Hotel was excellent, she said. Your-Kind would never choose an indifferent hotel.

'We are asking you to get in touch with your firm in London,' Keith said. 'We do not belong with your group.'

In silence, though smiling, Mrs Franks held out the pink list. Her expression insisted that it spoke for itself. No one could gainsay the dotted identification among the others.

'Our name is there by mistake.'

A man limped across the gravel towards them. He was a large man of shambling appearance, his navy-blue pin-striped jacket and waistcoat at odds with his brown trousers, his spectacles repaired with Sellotape. The sound of his breath could be heard as he approached. He blew it through half-pursed lips in a vague rendition of a Gilbert and Sullivan melody.

'These are the poor lost lambs,' Mrs Franks said. 'Keith and Dawne.'

'How do?' Mr Franks held a hand out. 'Silly thing to happen, eh?'

It was Mr Franks who eventually suggested that Keith should telephone Your-Kind-of-Holiday himself, and to Keith's surprise he got through to a number in Croydon without any difficulty. 'Excuse me a minute,' a girl said when he finished. He heard her talking to someone else and he heard the other person laughing. There was a trace of laughter in the girl's voice when she spoke again. You couldn't change your mind, she said, in the middle of a package. In no circumstances whatsoever could that be permitted. 'We're not changing our minds,' Keith protested, but while he was explaining all over again he was cut off because he hadn't any more coins. He cashed a traveller's cheque with the receptionist and was supplied with a number of five-franc pieces, but when he re-dialled the number the girl he'd spoken to couldn't be located so he explained everything to another girl. 'I'm sorry, sir,' this girl said, 'but if we allowed people to change their minds on account of they didn't like the look of a place we'd be out of business in no time.' Keith began to shout into the telephone, and

Dawne rapped on the glass of the booth, holding up a piece of paper on which she'd written *G. Snaith the name was.* 'Some sort of loony,' Keith heard the girl say in Croydon, the mouthpiece being inadequately muffled. There was an outburst of giggling before he was cut off.

*

It was not the first time that Keith and Dawne had suffered in this way: they were familiar with defeat. There'd been the time, a couple of years after their marriage, when Keith had got into debt through purchasing materials for making ships in bottles; earlier—before they'd even met—there was the occasion when the Lamb and Flag had had to let Dawne go because she'd taken tips although the rules categorically forbade it. Once Keith had sawn through the wrong water pipe and the landlords had come along with a bill for nearly two hundred pounds when the ceiling of the flat below collapsed. It was Uncle who had given Dawne a job in his shop after the Lamb and Flag episode and who had put them on their feet by paying off the arrears of the handicraft debt. In the end he persuaded them to come and live with him, pointing out that the arrangement would suit all three of them. Since his sister's death he had found it troublesome, managing on his own.

In Interlaken they selected a postcard to send him: of a mountain that had featured in a James Bond film. But they didn't know what to write on it: if they told the truth they would receive the old man's unspoken scorn when they returned—a look that came into his eyes while he silently regarded them. Years ago he had openly said—once only—that they were accident-prone. They were unfortunate in their dealings with the world, he had explained when Dawne asked him; lame ducks, he supposed you could say, if they'd forgive the expression, victims by nature, no fault of their own. Ever since, such judgements had been expressed only through his eyes.

'You choose your piece of gâteau,' Dawne said, 'up at the counter. They put it on a plate for you. Then the waitress comes along and you order the tea. I've been watching how it's done.'

Keith chose a slice of glazed greengage cake and Dawne a portion of strawberry flan. As soon as they sat down a waitress came and stood smiling in front of them. 'Tea with milk in it,' Dawne ordered, because when she'd said they were going abroad someone who'd come into the shop had warned her that you had to ask for milk, otherwise the tea came just as it was, sometimes no more than a tea-bag and a glass of hot water.

'A strike?' Dawne suggested. 'You're always hearing of strikes in airports.'

But Keith continued to gaze at the blank postcard, not persuaded that an attempt at falsehood was wise. It wasn't easy to tell the old man a lie. He had a way of making such attempts feel clumsy, and in the end of winkling out the truth. Yet his scorn would continue for many months, especially since he had paid out what he would call—a couple of hundred times at least—'good money' for their tickets. 'That's typical of Keith, that is,' he'd repeatedly inform his customers in Dawne's hearing, and she'd pass it on that night in bed, the way she always passed his comments on.

Keith ate his greengage slice, Dawne her strawberry flan. They did not share their thoughts, although their thoughts were similar. 'You've neither of you a head for business,' he'd said after the ships-in-bottles calamity, and again when Dawne unsuccessfully attempted to make a go of dress-making alterations. 'You wouldn't last a week in charge of things downstairs.' He always referred to the shop as 'downstairs'. Every day of his life he rose at five o'clock in order to be downstairs for the newspapers when they arrived. He'd done so for fifty-three years.

The plane couldn't land at the Italian airport, Keith wrote, *owing to a strike. So it had to come down here instead. It's good in a way because we're seeing another country as well! Hope your cold's cleared up*, Dawne added. *It's really lovely here!* X X X

They imagined him showing the postcard to Mrs Withers. 'That's typical, that is,' they imagined him saying and Mrs Withers jollying him along, telling him not to be sarky. Mrs Withers was pleased about earning the extra; she'd been as keen as anything when he'd asked her to come in full time for a fortnight.

'Could happen to anyone, a strike,' Dawne said, voicing Mrs Withers' response.

Keith finished his greengage slice. 'Call in to Smith's for a will-form,' he imagined the cross, tetchy voice instructing Mrs Withers, the postcard already tucked away on the Embassy Tipped shelf. And when she arrived with the will-form the next morning he'd let it lie around all day but have it in his hand when she left, before he locked the shop door behind her. 'Silly really,' Mrs Withers would say when eventually she told Dawne about it.

'I'd just as soon be here,' Dawne whispered, leaning forward a bit, daring at last to say that. 'I'd just as soon be in Switzerland, Keithie.'

He didn't reply, but looked around the teashop: at the display of cake in the long glass cabinet that served also as a counter—apricot and plum and apple, carrot cake and Black Forest gâteau, richly glazed fruitcake, marzipan slices, small lemon tarts, orange éclairs, coffee fondants. Irritated because his wife had made that statement and wishing to be unpleasant to her by not responding, he allowed his gaze to slip over the faces of the couples who sat sedately at round, prettily arranged tables. In a leisurely manner he examined the smiling waitresses, their crimson aprons matching the crimson of the frilled tablecloths. He endeavoured to give the impression that the waitresses attracted him.

'It's really nice,' Dawne said, her voice still shyly low.

He didn't disagree; there was nothing wrong with the place. People were speaking in German, but when you spoke in English they understood you. Enoch Melchor, in Claims, had gone to somewhere in Italy last year and had got into all sorts of difficulties with the language, including being given the head of a fish when he thought he'd ordered peas.

'We could say we liked it so much we decided to stay on,' Dawne suggested.

She didn't seem to understand that it wasn't up to them to decide anything. Twelve days in Venice had been chosen for them; twelve days in Venice had been paid for. 'No better'n a sewer,' Enoch Melchor had said, not that he'd ever been there. 'Stinks to high heaven,' he'd said, but that wasn't the point either. Memories of Venice had been ordered, memories that were to be transported back to London, with glass figurines for the mantelpiece because Venice was famous for its glass. The menus at the Pensione Concordia and the tunes played by the café orchestras were to be noted in Dawne's day-to-day diary. Venice was bathed in sunshine, its best autumn for years, according to the newspapers.

They left the teashop and walked about the streets, their eyes stinging at first, until they became used to the bitter breeze that had got up. They examined windows full of watches, and went from one to another of the souvenir shops because notices said that entrance was free. There was a clock that had a girl swinging on a swing every hour, and another that had a man and a woman employing a cross-saw, another that had a cow being milked. All sorts of tunes came out of different-shaped musical boxes: 'Lily Marlene', 'The Blue Danube', 'Lara's Theme' from *Doctor Zhivago*, the 'Destiny Waltz'. There were oven gloves with next year's calendar printed on them in English, and miniature arrangements of dried flowers, framed, on velvet. In the chocolate shops there were all the different brands, Lindt,

Suchard, Nestlé, Cailler, and dozens of others. There was chocolate with nuts, and chocolate with raisins, with nougat and honey, white chocolate, milk or plain, chocolate with fudge filling, with cognac or whiskey or chartreuse, chocolate mice and chocolate windmills.

'It's ever so enjoyable here,' Dawne remarked, with genuine enthusiasm. They went into another teashop, and this time Keith had a chestnut slice and Dawne a blackcurrant one, both with cream.

*

At dinner, in a dining-room tastefully panelled in greypainted wood, they sat among the people from Darlington, at a table for two, as the clerk in the travel agency had promised. The chicken-noodle soup was quite what they were used to, and so was the pork chop that followed, with apple sauce and chipped potatoes. 'They know what we like,' the woman called Mrs Franks said, making a round of all the tables, saying the same thing at each.

'Really lovely,' Dawne agreed. She'd felt sick in her stomach when they'd first realised about the error; she'd wanted to go to the lavatory and just sit there, hoping it was all a nightmare. She'd blamed herself because it was she who'd wondered about so many elderly people on the plane after the man in the travel place had given the impression of young people, from Windsor. It was she who had frowned, just for a moment, when the name of the airport was mentioned. Keith had a habit of pooh-poohing her doubts, like when she'd been doubtful about the men who'd come to the door selling mattresses and he'd been persuaded to make a down payment. The trouble with Keith was, he always sounded confident, as though he knew something she didn't, as though someone had told him. 'We'll just be here for the night,' he'd said, and she'd thought that was something he must have read in the brochure or that the clerk in the travel place had said. He couldn't help himself, of course; it was the way he was made. 'Cottonwool in your brain-box, have you?' Uncle had rudely remarked, the August Bank Holiday poor Keith had got them on to the slow train to Brighton, the one that took an hour longer.

'Silver lining, Keithie.' She put her head on one side, her small features softening into a smile. They'd walked by the lakeside before dinner. Just by stooping down, she'd attracted the birds that were swimming on the water. Afterwards she'd changed into her new fawn dress, bought specially for the holiday.

'I'll try that number again tomorrow,' Keith said.

She could see he was still worried. He was terribly subdued, even though he was able to eat his food. It made him cross when she mentioned the place they'd bought the tickets, so she didn't do so, although she wanted to. Time enough to face the music when they got back, better to make the best of things really: she didn't say that either.

'If you want to, Keithie,' she said instead. 'You try it if you've a call to.'

Naturally he'd feel it more than she would; he'd get more of the blame, being a man. But in the end it mightn't be too bad, in the end the storm would be weathered. There'd be the fondue party to talk about, and the visit to the chocolate factory. There'd be the swimming birds, and the teashops, and the railway journey they'd seen advertised, up to the top of an alp.

'Banana Split?' the waiter offered. 'You prefer Meringue Williams?'

They hesitated. Meringue Williams was meringue with pears and ice-cream, the waiter explained. Very good. He himself would recommend the Meringue Williams.

'Sounds lovely,' Dawne said, and Keith had it too. She thought of pointing out that everyone was being nice to them, that Mrs Franks was ever so sympathetic, that the man who came round to ask them if the dinner was all right had been ever so pleasant, and the waiter too. But she

decided not to because often Keith just didn't want to cheer
up. 'Droopy Drawers', Uncle sometimes called him, or
'Down-in-the-Dumps Donald'.

All around them the old people were chattering. They
were older than Uncle, Dawne could see; some of them
were ten years older, fifteen even. She wondered if Keith
had noticed that, if it had added to his gloom. She could
hear them talking about the mementoes they'd bought and
the teashops they'd been to; hale and hearty they looked,
still as full of vim as Uncle. 'Any day now I'll be dropping
off my twig,' he had a way of saying, which was nonsense of
course. Dawne watched the elderly mouths receiving spoon-
fuls of banana or meringue, the slow chewing, the savouring
of the sweetness. A good twenty years Uncle could go on for,
she suddenly thought.

'It's just bad luck,' she said.

'Be that as it may.'

'Don't say that, Keithie.'

'Say what?'

'Don't say "Be that as it may".'

'Why not?'

'Oh just because, Keithie.'

They had in common an institution background: they had
not known their parents. Dawne could remember Keith
when he was eleven and she was nine, although at that time
they had not been drawn to one another. They'd met again
later, revisiting their children's home for the annual dance,
disco as it was called these days. 'I got work in this shop,'
she'd said, not mentioning Uncle because he was only her
employer then, in the days when his sister was alive. They'd
been married for a while before he became an influence in
their lives. Now they could anticipate, without thinking, his
changes of heart and his whims, and see a mile off another
quarrel with the Reverend Simms, whose church occasionally he attended. Once they'd tried to divert such quarrels,
to brace themselves for changes of heart, to counter the

whims that were troublesome. They no longer did so. Although he listened carefully, he took no notice of what they said because he held the upper hand. The Smith's will-forms and an old billiard room—'the happiest place a man could spend an hour in'—were what he threatened them with. He met his friends in the billiard room; he read the *Daily Express* there, drinking bottles of Double Diamond, which he said was the best bottled beer in the world. It would be a terrible thing if men of all ages could no longer play billiards in that room, terrible if funds weren't available to keep it going for ever.

Mrs Franks made an announcement. She called for silence, and then gave particulars of the next day's pro-gramme. There was to be a visit to the James Bond moun-tain, everyone to assemble on the forecourt at half-past ten. Anyone who didn't want to go should please tell her tonight.

'We don't have to, Keithie,' Dawne whispered when Mrs Franks sat down. 'Not if we don't want to.'

The chatter began again, spoons excitedly waved in the air. False teeth, grey hair, glasses; Uncle might have been among them except that Uncle never would because he claimed to despise the elderly. 'You're telling *me*, are you? You're telling *me* you got yourselves entangled with a bunch of O.A.P.s?' As clearly as if he were beside her Dawne could hear his voice, enriched with the pretence of amaze-ment. 'You landed up in the wrong country and spent your holiday with a crowd of geriatrics! You're never telling me that?'

Sympathetic as she was, Mrs Franks had played it down. She knew that a young couple in their thirties weren't meant to be on a package with the elderly; she knew the error was not theirs. But it wouldn't be any use mentioning Mrs Franks to Uncle. It wouldn't be any use saying that Keith had got cross with the receptionist and with the people in Croydon. He'd listen and then there'd be a silence. After that he'd begin to talk about the billiard room.

'Had a great day, did you?' Mrs Franks said on her way out of the dining-room. 'All's well that ends well, eh?'

Keith continued to eat his Meringue Williams as if he had not been addressed. Mr Franks remarked on the Meringue Williams, laughing about it, saying they'd all have to watch their figures. 'I must say,' Mrs Franks said, 'we're lucky with the weather. At least it isn't raining.' She was dressed in the same flamboyant clothes. She'd been able to buy some Madame Rochas, she said, awfully good value.

'We don't have to say about the old people,' Dawne whispered when the Frankses had passed on. 'We needn't mention that.'

Dawne dug into the deep glass for the ice-cream that lay beneath the slices of pear. She knew he was thinking she would let it slip about the old people. Every Saturday she washed Uncle's hair for him since he found it difficult to do it himself. Because he grumbled so about the tepid rinse that was necessary in case he caught a cold afterwards, she had to jolly him along. She'd always found it difficult to do two things at once, and it was while washing his hair that occasionally she'd forgotten what she was saying. But she was determined not to make that mistake again, just as she had ages ago resolved not to get into a flap if he suddenly asked her a question when she was in the middle of counting the newspapers that hadn't been sold.

'Did you find your friends from Windsor then?' an old woman with a walking frame enquired. 'Eeh, it were bad you lost your friends.'

Dawne explained, since no harm was meant. Other old people stood by to hear, but a few of them were deaf and asked to have what was being said repeated. Keith continued to eat his Meringue Williams.

'Keithie, it isn't their fault,' she tentatively began when the people had passed on. '*They* can't help it, Keithie.'

'Be that as it may. No need to go attracting them.'

'I didn't attract them. They stopped by. Same as Mrs Franks.'

'Who's Mrs Franks?'

'You know who she is. That big woman. She gave us her name this morning, Keithie.'

'When I get back I'll institute proceedings.'

She could tell from his tone that that was what he'd been thinking about. All the time on the steamer they'd taken to Interlaken, all the time in the teashop, and on the cold streets and in the souvenir shops, all the time they'd been looking at the watch displays and the chocolate displays, all the time in the grey-panelled dining-room, he had been planning what he'd say, what he'd probably write on the very next postcard: that he intended to take legal proceedings. When they returned he would stand in the kitchen and state what he intended, very matter-of-fact. First thing on Monday he'd arrange to see a solicitor, he'd state, an appointment for his lunch-hour. And Uncle would remain silent, not even occasionally inclining his head, or shaking it, knowing that solicitors cost money.

'They're liable for the full amount. Every penny of it.'

'Let's try to enjoy ourselves, Keithie. Why don't I tell Mrs Franks we'll go up the mountain?'

'What mountain's that?'

'The one she was on about, the one we sent him a post-card of.'

'I need to phone up Croydon in the morning.'

'You can do it before ten-thirty, Keithie.'

The last of the elderly people slowly made their way from the dining-room, saying goodnight as they went. A day would come, Dawne thought, when they would go to Venice on their own initiative, with people like the Windsor people. She imagined the Windsor people in the Pensione Concordia, not one of them a day older than themselves. She imagined Signor Bancini passing among them, translating a word or two of Italian as he went. There was laughter in the dining-room of the Pensione Concordia, and bottles of red wine on the tables. The young people's names were Désirée and Rob, and Luke and Angélique, and Sean and Aimée. 'Uncle we used to call him,' her own voice said. 'He died a while back.'

Keith stood up. Skilful with the tablecloths, the waiter wished them goodnight. In the reception area a different receptionist, a girl, smiled at them. Some of the old people were standing around, saying it was too cold to go for a walk. You'd miss the television, one of them remarked.

*

The warmth of their bodies was a familiar comfort. They had not had children because the rooms above the shop weren't suitable for children. The crying at night would have driven Uncle mad, and naturally you could see his point of view. There'd been an error when first they'd lived with him; they'd had to spend a bit terminating it.

They refrained from saying that their bodies were a comfort. They had never said so. What they said in their lives had to do with Keith's hoping for promotion, and the clothes Dawne coveted. What they said had to do with their efforts to make a little extra money, or paying their way by washing the woodwork of an old man's house and tacking down his threadbare carpets.

When he heard their news he would mention the savings in the Halifax Building Society and the goodwill of the shop and the valuation that had been carried out four years ago. He would mention again that men of all ages should have somewhere to go of an evening, or in the afternoons or the morning, a place to be at peace. He would remind them that a man who had benefited could not pass on without making provision for the rent and the heating and for the replacing of the billiard tables when the moment came. 'Memorial to a humble man,' he would repeat. 'Shopkeeper of this neighbourhood.'

In the darkness they did not say to one another that if he hadn't insisted they needed a touch of the autumn sun they wouldn't again have been exposed to humiliation. It was as though, through knowing them, he had arranged their failure in order to indulge his scorn. Creatures of a shabby institution, his eyes had so often said, they could not manage on their own: they were not even capable of supplying one another's needs.

In the darkness they did not say that their greed for his money was much the same as his greed for their obedience, that greed nourished the trinity they had become. They did not say that the money, and the freedom it promised, was the galaxy in their lives, as his cruelty was the last pleasure in his. Scarcely aware that they held on to one another beneath the bedclothes, they heard his teasing little laugh while they were still awake, and again when they slept.

Honeymoon in Tramore

They stayed in a boarding-house, St Agnes's, run by a Mrs
Hurley. 'You have it written all over you!' this woman said
when she opened the door to them. She eyed a speck of
confetti on the lapel of his navy-blue suit and then glanced
briefly at the rounding of Kitty's stomach. It was the summer of 1948, a warm afternoon in July.

Mrs Hurley was a middle-aged landlady in a brown
coat, who apologised for the wellington boots she was
wearing: she'd been brushing down the yard. Her fingernails were enamelled a vivid shade of pink, her hair was
contained by a tidy blue hairnet which partially disguised
an arrangement of pins and curling papers. They would be
very happy in St Agnes's, she said; they'd have the place to
themselves because there was no one else stopping in the
house at the moment. When they were carrying their two
suitcases upstairs she said that marriage was a God-given
institution and added that her husband went to mass every
morning of his life, on his way to work with the county
council. 'Your tea'll be on the table at six on the dot,' she
said.

On their own, they embraced. He put his hand under his
wife's skirt and felt for the warm flesh at the top of her
stockings. 'Jesus, you're terrible,' she murmured thickly at
him, as she had on the bus when he'd pressed himself close
against her. She was sweating because of her condition and
the July heat. Her face was sticky with perspiration, and
small patches of it had developed on her dress, beneath each

armpit. 'Jesus,' she whispered again. 'Oh Jesus, go easy now.'

He didn't want to go easy. They were free of the farm, and of her father and her aunt and her Uncle Ned Whelan. He had a right to his desires.

'That woman'll be listening,' she whispered in the same slurred voice, but it didn't matter if the woman was listening. It didn't even matter if the woman opened the door and walked in. The bed made creaking sounds when she wriggled away from him, saying again that he was terrible, giggling as she said it. The bedroom smelt of flies, as if the windows hadn't been opened for a long time. 'God, you're great, Kitty,' he said, his own voice thickening also.

He was thirty-three, Kitty two years older. At fifteen he had been taken from the orphans' home in Cork by Kitty's father and her Uncle Ned Whelan. The two men had let it be known that they could do with a young fellow on the farm, and Father Horan, who was their parish priest at that time, had made enquiries of Father Lyhane at the orphans' home on their behalf. 'Davy Toome's a good lad,' Father Lyhane had said, and a few weeks later, after the recommendation had been passed on to the farmers and after Father Horan had been assured that the candidate would be strong enough for farm-work, a label with that name on it had been attached to the boy and he'd been forwarded by train. 'And did you never do farm-work before?' Kitty's Uncle Ned Whelan had asked, sitting beside him in the cart as they slowly progressed on the road from the railway junction. But Davy had never even seen fields with corn in them before, let alone taken part in farm-work. 'I'm thinking,' said Kitty's uncle, who'd spent an hour in Doolin's public house at the railway junction, 'that it could be we bought a pig in a poke.' He said it again in the kitchen when they arrived, while his wife and his brother-in-law were examining Davy, silently agreeing that he was not as strong as the priest had claimed. 'Will you for God's sake take off that label!' the woman said to him, and then, in a gentler voice, asked him about his name. She'd never heard of Toome before, she said, so he told them that his name had been given to him when the orphans' home had taken him in as an infant, that there'd been a priest connected with it then who'd had an interest in naming the orphans. His first name was in memory of St David. Toome meant a burial mound. 'Is he right in the head?' he afterwards heard Kitty's father asking his brother-in-law and her uncle reply-ing that you wouldn't know, the way he was talking about burial mounds.

'Will you come on now, for heaven's sake!' Kitty rebuked him in the bedroom at St Agnes's. 'And let me take off my hat.'

She pushed him away from her and told him to open the window. It was she who had chosen Tramore for the week-end of their honeymoon, saying she'd heard it was lovely, with a sandy little beach. Kitty knew what she wanted, her aunt used to say, and you couldn't budge her when she made up her mind. 'Would you accompany me to Cork?' she had suggested one day four months ago. 'I'm a stranger to the city, Davy.' He hadn't been back to Cork since he'd come to the farm, and he didn't really know his way around it; but it turned out that Kitty had never been there at all. 'We'll fix it to go on a Saturday,' she said, and on the bus he felt proud to be sitting there with her, a big handsome girl, the daughter of his employer: he hoped that on the streets they'd maybe meet someone from the orphans' home. She'd looked out the window most of the time, not saying very much to him, her round face pink with excitement. She was good-looking in a way he admired, better-looking than any of the other girls at mass, or the tinker girls whom he'd caught once stealing turnips from the field, who'd shouted over a hedge at him that their sister would marry him. Her hair was very fine and very black, like a dark mist encircling her face. He'd heard her aunt calling her sullen, but he'd never noticed that himself, even though sometimes a blankness came into her face and stayed there till she roused herself. Her three brothers had all been born with something wrong with them and had died in childhood, before he had come to the farm. Nobody mentioned them; he hadn't even known about her brothers until one of the men who came to help with the harvest referred to them in passing. Her mother had died giving birth to the last of them.

'Are you O.K., pet?' Kitty said, putting lipstick on at the dressing-table. 'Isn't it great we're on our own?'

He leaned against the window-frame, looking at her, seeing her in the looking-glass as well. She had to go to see a Mr Minogue, she'd said eventually on the bus, a chemist in McHenry Street.

'Great,' he said from the window.

'Can you hear the sea there?'

He shook his head. They'd found the chemist's shop, having had to ask for directions to McHenry Street. If her mother was alive she'd have accompanied her, she said all of a sudden, and then she said she couldn't go into the chemist's shop alone. Her voice became different. Her legs wouldn't have taken her, she said, and then she told him she was in trouble. Her aunt had found out about the chemist, she said, only she'd refused to accompany her. 'Take Toome to show you the way,' her aunt had said.

'Will we go down, pet?'

He moved to where she stood by the dressing-table but when he put his arms around her she said sharply that she didn't want to get messed up again. She'd spilt powder on the glass top of the dressing-table, the same peach shade that was on her cheeks. She'd put on perfume he could smell, a strong sweet smell that made him want to try again to put his arms around her. But already she had crossed the room to the door. She opened it and he followed her downstairs.

'I've done you black puddings,' Mrs Hurley said in the

dining-room, placing before them plates of fried sausages and fried eggs and slices of the delicacy she spoke of.

'God, I love black pudding,' Kitty said, and he passed her his because as a boy in the orphans' home he had developed a revulsion for this dark composition of pig's blood and entrails. The table they sat at was empty of other guests, as Mrs Hurley had promised. He smiled at his bride across it. On the way downstairs she had kept repeating that this would be their first meal as husband and wife. She attached importance to the fact. She'd said it again as they sat down. Through the wooden hatch that opened into the kitchen the voice of Mrs Hurley could be heard raised in abuse, speaking about a greyhound.

'Are you hungry, pet?'

He wasn't; he shook his head.

'D'you know what it is,' Kitty said, cutting into a soda farl, 'I could eat the head off of a horse.'

A low mumble of protest had begun in the kitchen, which he guessed must emanate from Mrs Hurley's husband. 'Errah, have a pick of sense, will you?' the landlady stridently interrupted. 'Would any animal in its sane mind keep getting into a cement mixer?'

Kitty giggled. She'd nearly died, she said, when Mrs Kilfedder gave her a kiss at the wedding. 'One thing about Kilfedder,' she added, 'he keeps his hands to himself.'

At that moment a man in shirtsleeves entered the dining-room. He greeted them and introduced himself as Mr Hurley. He enquired if they'd like another pot of tea, already seizing the metal tea-pot and moving towards the hatch with it. They'd find St Agnes's restful, he said, no children for miles around. The hatch opened and Mrs Hurley's freshly rouged face appeared. She had removed her hairnet, and the hair it had controlled, now seen to be a shade of henna, fluffed elaborately about her head. 'Have they butter enough?' she demanded of her husband, in the same uncompromising tone she had employed when protesting about the activities of the greyhound. 'It's good country butter,' she shouted at her guests. 'Fresh as a daisy.'

'We have plenty,' Kitty replied. 'It's good butter all right, Mrs Hurley.'

The tea-pot was handed back through the hatch and placed on the table. 'There's a big attraction in Tramore tonight,' Mr Hurley said. 'Have you ever heard tell of the Carmodys?'

When they said they hadn't he told them that the Carmodys ran a Wall of Death that was reputed to be great entertainment. She had never seen a Wall of Death yet, Kitty said when he'd gone. 'D'you like the sausages, pet?'

He nodded, holding his cup out for tea. Under the table the calves of their legs were pressed together.

'Coddy Donnegan wanted to take me once, only I said I couldn't watch it.'

'Maybe we wouldn't bother in that case.'

'I'd watch anything with yourself, Davy. Maybe we'd walk down by the sea as well.'

He nodded again and she leaned forward to say she was feeling fine, a reference to the fact that she had recently been subject to bouts of sickness in her stomach. They'd have a few drinks after the Wall of Death and the walk, she suggested, in case it wouldn't look good, coming back to the bedroom too soon. She winked and nudged him with her knee. Under the table he put his hand on her lightly stock-inged leg. 'Oh Jesus, lay off now,' she whispered.

It wasn't Coddy Donnegan, she'd told him in McHenry Street, standing outside the chemist's shop. She'd never been in love with Coddy Donnegan. She'd never been in love until the other thing happened, until there was a man taking her hand in a way Coddy Donnegan wouldn't do in a million years—a cousin of Father Tolan's, who was destined himself for the priesthood. He'd been about in the parish for the summer holidays; she'd have put down her life for him, she said. 'He'd marry me if he knew, Davy. He'd give up the priesthood, only I'd never tell him.'

They finished the meal Mrs Hurley had prepared for them. 'I'll just go upstairs a minute,' she said. 'I won't be a tick, pet.'

Waiting in the hall, Davy examined the pictures on the walls. A light burned beneath the Virgin and Child; there were reproductions of Victorian paintings, one of a match-seller, another of a shawled woman with a basket of lavender. He turned away from them, and the face of the chemist crept into his recollection: the jaw dark, the chin pimpled beneath a raw shave, eyes magnified behind heavily lensed spectacles, cheeks as pale as the white coat he wore. 'Come in,' Mr Minogue had welcomed them that day, knowing what they wanted although nothing had been said yet. It was the afternoon when his shop was closed, and he led them through the stillness of it into a room at the back, where there were no chairs to sit on, only a table with a rubber sheet on it. 'I take a grave risk,' Mr Minogue announced without preamble, his unsmiling countenance reflecting eloquently the gravity he spoke of. 'The assistance I offer you in your distress is offered for humanitarian reasons only. But the risk must be covered, you understand that? It is not of my own volition that I charge a fee.' While he spoke he did not remove his bulbously magnified eyes from their faces, revolving his stare in a circle around each, sliding it from one to the other. 'You may know the fee?' he said, and when Kitty placed the money before him his grey, closely barbered head bowed over the notes he counted. 'Yes, this is correct,' he said, speaking directly to Davy, clearly assuming him to be the father of the unwanted child and the source of the fee. He placed the notes in a wallet he'd taken out of the back pocket of his trousers, and jerked his head at Davy, indicating that he should return to the shop and wait there. But before Davy could do so both he and the abortionist were taken by surprise because without any warning whatsoever Kitty cried out that she couldn't do it. She would burn in hell for it, she shrieked in sudden, shrill, unexpected emotion; she could never confess it, there was no penance she could be given. 'I'd rather die as I stand, sir,' she said to Mr Minogue, and gave way to tears. They flooded on her flushed, round cheeks; the humane abortionist stood arrested, one hand still in the back pocket of his trousers. 'Hail Mary, Mother of God!' Kitty cried, shrill again. 'Sweet Mother, don't abandon me!' The money was handed back, no further word was spoken. Mr Minogue removed his white coat and led the way to the door of his shop, glancing before he opened it around the edge of an advertisement for liver salts pasted to its glass. The street was empty. As there had been no salutation, so there was no farewell.

'Are we right so?' Kitty said, descending the stairs.

He opened the hall-door and they stepped out into the evening. It was warm and quiet on the terraced cul-de-sac, in which St Agnes's was the last house. They still couldn't hear the sea and Kitty said the waves wouldn't be big in that case. 'I'm sorry,' she'd said outside the chemist's shop, still sobbing, and then they'd walked for ages through the streets, before having a cup of tea in a café. She was calm by that time; it had never for a second occurred to her that she couldn't do it, she said, but the sin when she'd handed Mr Minogue the money had been like something alive in the room with them. 'I swear to God, Davy.' He'd said he understood, but in fact he didn't. He was confused because there was so much to take in—her being in trouble, the purpose of their journey being revealed, and then the episode with Mr Minogue. He was the man on the farm, the labourer who worked in the yard and the fields: it had been strange enough being asked to go to Cork with her. In the café, after she'd drunk two cups of tea, she said she was better. She ate a bun with currants in it, but he couldn't eat

anything himself. Then he brought her to the orphans'
home just to look at the outside of. 'God, Davy, what am I
going to do?' she suddenly cried when they were standing
there, as suddenly as she'd said in the back room of the
chemist's that she couldn't go through with it.

'It's down at the strand,' a man told them when they
asked about the Wall of Death. He pointed out the way,
and soon they heard the music that accompanied it and the
roar of the motor-cycle's engine. '. . . to see again the moonlight over Clara,' moaned a tenor voice, robbed of its mel-
lifluous quality by the scratching of a gramophone needle.
'. . . and to see the sun going down on Galway Bay.' They
paid the admission charge and climbed up rickety stairs,
like a ladder, that led to the top of the circular wooden wall.
A platform ran around the circumference, with a balustrade
to prevent the jostling audience from falling into the pit
below. 'God, it's great,' Kitty shouted above the noise, and
Davy gave her arm a squeeze. A small, wizened man in red
gaiters and black leather clothes, with a spotted red neckerchief, mounted the quivering motor-cycle that stood on its
pedestal in the centre of the pit. He pushed it forward and
ran it on to the incline at the bottom of the wall, gradually
easing it on to the wall itself. Each circle he made increased
the angle of his machine until in the end, close to the
balustrade over which the audience leaned, he and his
motor-cycle were horizontal. The timbers of the wall and
of the platform shuddered, the roar of the engine was deaf-
ening. Waving above his head, the performer descended,
the same circular motion in reverse. The audience clapped
and threw coins into the pit. 'Are you O.K.?' Davy shouted,
for in the excitement Kitty had closed her eyes. In the pit
the motor-cycle was returned to its stand. The man bowed
his gratitude for the money that still lay on the ground, and
then threw out an arm in a sudden, dramatic gesture. He
was joined immediately by a woman, dressed in red and
black clothing also, who climbed on to the pillion of his

motor-cycle and when it reached the centre of the wall clambered on to his back. She stood on his shoulders, with his spotted neckerchief streaming from between her teeth. Kitty screamed and closed her eyes again. More coins were thrown.

'Is she his wife, Davy?' Kitty asked as they walked away.

'I'd say she was.'

'Wouldn't it be shocking if she came off?'

'I'd say she wouldn't.'

'God, I love the smell of the sea, Davy.'

If she hadn't been wearing stockings she'd have paddled, she said, and he told her about a time they'd been taken from the orphans' home to the seaside at Courtmacsherry. He continued to tell her about this while they walked back to the town and went in search of a public house. They found one that was as quiet as St Agnes's, a murky place that Kitty said was cosy. Two elderly men sat at the counter, steadily drinking, not conversing. The publican was shifting sacks of meal in the grocery that adjoined the bar. Davy called out to him, ordering bottles of stout.

'Was it terrible in the orphans' home?' Kitty asked when he'd carried them to the table she was sitting at. 'Did you hate it the whole time?'

He said he hadn't. It hadn't been bad; he'd never known anywhere else until he came to the farm. 'Jeez, it looks like a prison,' she'd said that day, looking up at the orphans' home from the street.

'It's terrible, though, no family to turn to,' she said now. 'I have the half of it myself, with no mother.'

'You get used to the way it is.'

A week after their visit to Cork her aunt said to him in the yard that Kitty would marry him if he asked her. Her aunt stood there in the early-morning sunlight, a heavily made woman who was always dressed in black. She more than anyone, more than her husband or her brother or Kitty herself, knew that ever since he'd arrived at the farm with a

label on him he'd had a notion of Kitty. The aunt was the
sharpest of them, her eyes as black as her clothes, always
watchful. She had noticed him looking at Kitty across the
table when they all sat down to their dinner; he'd never
been able to help looking at her, and it embarrassed him
every time her aunt caught him. Did she guess that he lay
in bed at night imagining Kitty's lips on his own, and the
lovely white softness of her? They would have the farm
between them was what she omitted to say in the yard because it was not necessary to say it: Kitty would inherit the
farm since there was no one else, and if he married her he
would no longer be the hired man, with the worst of the
work always reserved for him. 'I'll ask her so,' he said, and
because of the day there had been in Cork it was easier to
pluck up the courage. Before that, Kitty had always ordered
him about in the way her father and her uncle did when
they all worked together at certain seasons, making hay or
lifting the potatoes. He had never disliked her for it, any
more than he'd ever felt he had a right to resent Coddy
Donnegan's rusty old Vauxhall arriving in the yard and
Coddy Donnegan waiting in it, and the way he'd push open
a door of the car when he heard the sound of her heels tip-
tapping across the concrete. Father Tolan's cousin had
never come near the farm; all that was a mystery.

'Would there be anything to eat in here, pet? Would they
have biscuits?'

At the bar he ordered two more bottles of stout and enquired if biscuits could be supplied. The publican said he
had gingersnaps and went to the grocery to weigh out half
a pound.

'Oh, great,' Kitty said. She crumbled one in her mouth.
He poured out the stout. The day before her aunt had made
her suggestion in the yard he had noticed Kitty going up to
Coddy Donnegan after mass, and Coddy Donnegan had
turned away from her as if they'd had a quarrel, which was
understandable in view of her friendship with Father

Tolan's cousin. After that, Coddy Donnegan's Vauxhall never again drove up to the farm.

'We'll never forget our honeymoon,' Kitty said. 'I wish we had a camera. I'd love to take snaps of Tramore.'

He knew what she meant. For the rest of their lives they'd be at the farm, milking every morning and evening, taking the churns down to the creamery, ploughing and sowing and ditching. No matter how you fixed it there was never enough time, except for the couple of hours you took to go to mass. He always rode to mass on his bicycle, and on Sunday afternoons he rode over to Doolin's at the old railway junction, where no trains came any more. A new road passed by Doolin's now and on Sunday afternoons there would always be bicycles propped up against its window, and the same dozen or so faces inside. 'I hear you're marrying in,' one of the men said to him on the Sunday after Kitty agreed. 'More power to your elbow, Davy!' No one was displeased at his good fortune, in Doolin's or anywhere else. Father Tolan came up to the farm specially and walked down to the mangold field to shake his hand and to congratulate him. Even Ned Whelan, who rarely had a good word to say on any subject, wagged his head at him in an approving way.

'I love the taste of gingersnaps and stout,' Kitty said. 'Did you know gingersnaps were my favourite?'

'They're all the man had.'

Suddenly she asked him if he was happy. She repeated the question, putting it differently, asking him if he was contented in himself. He said he was.

'Will you ever forget the day we went to Cork, Davy?'

From her voice, he thought she was maybe getting drunk, that her condition made the stout go to her head. She was looking at him, giggling. She leaned closer to him and said that on the bus that day she'd thought to herself she wouldn't mind being married to him.

'You were good to me that day, Davy, d'you know that?'

'I always had a notion of you, Kitty.'

'I never noticed it till that day, pet. That was the first time I knew it.'

He went to the bar for two further bottles of stout. He had wondered if the men in Doolin's knew the state she was in, and if they imagined he was the man involved. The same applied where her father and her uncle were concerned, and Father Tolan. He didn't know if there'd been talk or not.

'Didn't it work out O.K. in the end?' she said when he returned with the stout. She asked if there were any more biscuits and he went back to buy another quarter pound. When he returned to where they sat she said:

'Were you ever jealous of Coddy, pet?'

He nodded, pouring his stout from the bottle, and she laughed because she'd made him feel awkward. He looked away, wishing she hadn't brought up Coddy Donnegan. Then he turned and clumsily attempted to kiss her on the lips, but found them gritty with biscuit crumbs.

'Oh, Coddy's the right romantic! It was maybe ten or eleven times he said would we get married.'

He frowned, feeling that something wasn't quite right, yet for the moment uncertain as to what it was.

'Did I tell you poor Coddy cried?' she said. 'The day I told him I was marrying yourself?'

After that the conversation became confused. Kitty again mentioned her surprise when Mrs Kilfedder had embraced her at the wedding. She counted up the wedding guests, and said it must have been the biggest wedding for a long time. Her father had had to sell two bullocks to pay for it. 'Did you see the cut of old Feehy, without a collar on tie?' She went through all the guests then, commenting or their dress and wondering why other women hadn't embraced her. 'Will we take back a few bottles?' she suggested, nudging him and winking. 'Hey!' she called out to the publican. 'Put a dozen stout in a bag for us, mister.'

When Davy had paid for them they left the public house, Kitty talking about a girl called Rose she'd been at the Presentation convent with, wondering where she was now. She hung on to his arm; he listened vaguely. Turning into the cul-de-sac, they met Mr Hurley exercising a greyhound, a dejected animal which in the course of conversation Mr Hurley said was worth a fortune. 'Is it the one that gets into the cement mixer?' Kitty asked, and Mr Hurley explained that the greyhound only got into the cement mixer the odd time.

Kitty laughed shrilly. The trouble with a habit like that, she pointed out, was that the creature might get turned into concrete. 'Will you take a stout, Mr Hurley? We brought home a few bottles.'

Mr Hurley instantly fell into step with them and when they arrived at the house he led them round to the back, incarcerating the greyhound in a shed on the way. 'Sit down on a chair,' he said in the kitchen and his wife produced glasses, saying it was unusual to have guests bringing drink back to St Agnes's, but where was the harm in it? 'Good luck!' said Mr Hurley.

Details of the Wall of Death were given, and details of the wedding. The unexpected embrace of Mrs Kilfedder was retailed, and reference made to Kitty's father singing 'Lily of Laguna' and to old Feehy without his collar or tie. 'Poor Coddy Donnegan hadn't the heart to attend,' Kitty said. 'He's a fellow from the slaughterhouse, Mrs Hurley. I went out with poor Coddy for three years.'

'They take it hard,' agreed Mrs Hurley.

'He cried, poor Coddy.'

'I had a similar case myself. A fellow by the name of O'Gorman.'

'A chancer,' said Mr Hurley beneath his breath. 'A real oiler.'

'O'Gorman could have charmed the leaves off the trees. I heard him called the handsomest man in Tramore.'

'The story is told,' Mr Hurley said in the same low voice, 'that he fecked a crucifix off a nun.'

' "Well, I'll never marry now" was what poor Coddy came out with when I told him. "I'll keep myself by for you, Kitty." '

'Where'd the point be in that, though?' Mrs Hurley interposed. 'Is poor Coddy a bit slow?'

'It's only his way of putting the thing, Mrs Hurley.'

The dozen bottles took an hour to drink, during which time Mr Hurley gave Davy a number of racing tips. He talked about famous greyhounds he had known or had even had a hand in the breeding of, but Davy was more interested in what the two women were discussing and was unable to prevent himself from listening. He heard Kitty saying the husband she'd married would do anything for you. He watched her leaning closer to Mrs Hurley and heard her referring to the cousin of Father Tolan. 'Errah, go on, are you serious?' Mrs Hurley exclaimed, glancing across at him, and he guessed at once what she'd been told—that the lapse of the priest's cousin had determined him in his vocation, that God had gained in the end.

'Held back all summer,' Mr Hurley continued. 'Put every penny in your pocket on him.'

Davy promised he would, although he had never in his life backed a horse and hadn't heard what the one Mr Hurley recommended was called. Kitty stood up and was swaying back and forth, her eyes blearily staring. 'I don't know should I have eaten the gingersnaps,' she muttered uneasily, but Mrs Hurley said a gingersnap never did anyone any harm. Mr Hurley was talking about another horse, and Davy kept nodding.

'You're a good man,' the landlady whispered as he went by her. He had one arm around Kitty, holding her up. He shook his head, silently disclaiming the goodness Mrs Hurley imbued him with.

'Are you all right?' he asked Kitty on the stairs, and she

didn't reply until they were in the bedroom, when she said she wasn't. He lifted the china jug out of the basin on the wash-stand and after she had finished being sick he carried the basin across the landing to the lavatory.

'God, I'm sorry, pet,' she managed to say before she fell asleep, lying across the bed.

Even though she couldn't hear him, he said it didn't matter. It had never occurred to him before that a cousin of Father Tolan's who came to the parish for his holidays must have attended mass on Sundays, yet he had never seen him there. Nor had he ever heard anyone else but Kitty mention him. She had painted a picture of a saintly young man who had since become a priest, and in her befuddled state she'd wanted Mrs Hurley to know about him too. She had wanted Mrs Hurley to know that it wasn't anything crude that had occurred, like going with Coddy Donnegan in the back of a bloodstained Vauxhall.

'It's all right, Kitty.' He spoke aloud, sitting beside her on the bed, looking down into her face. In the bedroom there was the rancid smell of her vomit; her breath as he pulled the dress over her head was cloyed with it. Again he looked down into her face, understanding why she had told the lies. When she'd approached Coddy Donnegan after mass that day he'd probably retorted that she'd let herself get into that condition in order to catch him.

Davy stood up and slowly took his clothes off. He was lucky that she had gone with Coddy Donnegan because if she hadn't she wouldn't now be sleeping on their honeymoon bed. Once more he looked down into her face: for eighteen years she had seemed like a queen to him and now, miraculously, he had the right to kiss her. He straightened her slackened body, moving her arms and legs until she was lying comfortably. Slowly he pulled the bedclothes up and turned the light out; then he lay beside her and caressed her in the darkness. He had come to the farm with a label round his neck; he had come out of nowhere, from rooms and corridors that were as bleakly anonymous as the orphan home's foundling inmates. He had been known as her father's hired man, but now he would be known as her husband. That was how people would refer to him, and in the end it wouldn't matter when she talked about Coddy Donnegan, or lowered her voice to mention the priest's cousin. It was natural that she should do so since she had gained less than he had from their marriage.

The Printmaker

In the large room Charlotte hangs her prints to dry, like clothes on clothes-lines. Three cows, framed by the legs and belly of a cow, have rested for an instant beneath its udder: all over the room this stark image is multiplied, in black and white and tones of green.

The reality was years ago, in France: Charlotte senses that confidently, without being able to recall the moment of observation. Familiar to her is the feeling that a glance from the window, or from a motor-car, has been retained for half a lifetime. 'This is still the Langevins' land,' Monsieur Langevin said in English, the first time he drove her in his white Citroën the fifteen kilometres from Massuery to St Cérase. Obediently she inspected the fields to her right, treeless and uninteresting, cattle grazing. Perhaps there were three cows also.

In the room the suspended sheets are scrutinised, and one in every seven or eight rejected. Fragile, tapering fingers loosen the tiny, variously coloured pegs that hold the prints in place; each inferior reproduction floats softly to the bare-wood floor. Intent upon her task, Charlotte moves silently in the room, seeming almost a ghost among the ubiquitous repetition of what she has created. At thirty-nine she is as thin as ever, her bones as apparent as her flesh. Bright azure eyes illuminate a slender face that is still a girl's. Shattered only twice in Charlotte's appearance is the illusion that time has been defeated; grey strands creep through hair that once was as pale as corn, and on the backs of her hands are the telltale signs that sun and weather do not pass gently by.

One by one, she picks up the rejected prints where they have dropped. She tears each in half and bundles it into the wooden box that is the room's repository for wastepaper. Then she examines one of the suspended sheets, holding it obliquely against the light to see if it has wholly dried. Satisfied that this is so, she releases the pegs and trims the paper in her guillotine. She signs it and writes in pencil *1/50*, then places it in a pale green portfolio. She repeats all this with each remaining print, then loosely ties the folder's tattered ribbons.

'To look at, there is *l'église* St Cérase,' Monsieur Langevin said, that first Wednesday afternoon. He stopped the car in the Place de la Paix and pointed out the way. There was nothing much else in the town, he warned. A park beside the Maison de la Presse, tea-rooms and cafés, the Hostellerie de la Poste. But the church was quite impressive. 'Well, anyway, the façade,' Monsieur Langevin added.

Charlotte walked to it, admired the façade and went inside. There was a smell of candlegrease and perhaps of incense: it was difficult precisely to identify the latter. Charlotte was seventeen then, her presence in the Langevin household arranged by her father, who set great store by what he referred to as 'perfect French'. Some acquaintance of his had a connection with a cousin of Madame Langevin; an arrangement had been made. 'I've been good about your drawing,' her father had earlier claimed, in the parental manner of that time. 'I'm only asking in return that you acquire the usefulness of perfect French.' Her father did not believe in her talent for drawing; a businessman himself, he anticipated for his only child a niche in some international commercial firm, where the French she had perfected would float her to desirable heights. Charlotte's father had her interests—as he divined them—at heart. A prosperous marriage would come later. He was a conventional man.

In the church of St Cérase she walked by confessionals and the Stations of the Cross, taking no interest at seventeen, only wishing her father hadn't been insistent on sending her to Massuery. She had every Wednesday afternoon to herself, when Madame Langevin took her children riding. She had Sunday afternoons as well, and every evening when the children had gone to bed. But what on earth could she do on Sunday afternoons except go for a walk in the woods? And in the evenings the family seemed surprised if she did not sit with them. There were in all five children, the youngest still an infant. The twins were naughty and, though only six, knew how to tease. Colette sulked. Guy, a dark-haired boy of ten, was Charlotte's favourite.

This family's details were recorded in an unfinished letter in Charlotte's handbag: the sulking, the teasing, Guy's charm, the baby's podginess. Her mother would read between the lines, winkling out an unhappiness that had not been stated; her father would skip a lot. *Madame Langevin's sister is here on a visit. She is tall and languid, an incessant smoker, very painted up, beautifully dressed. Madame Langevin's quite different, smartly dressed too, and just as good-looking in her way, only nicer in the sense that she wants people to be all right. She smiles a lot and worries. Monsieur Langevin does not say much.*

Outside a café in the square she completed the letter, pausing often to make the task last. It was July and necessary to sit in the shade. *There hasn't been a cloud in the sky since I arrived.* She drank tea with lemon and when she'd sealed the envelope and written the address she watched the people going by. But there were few of them because of the heat of the afternoon—a woman in a blue dress, with sun-glasses and a poodle, a child on a bicycle, a man delivering shoe-boxes from a van. Charlotte bought a stamp in a *tabac* and found the park by the Maison de la Presse. The seats were dusty, and whitened with bird droppings; sunlight didn't penetrate the foliage of the trees, but at least the place was cool and empty. She read the book she'd brought, *The Beautiful and Damned*.

Twenty-two years later Charlotte sees herself sitting there, and can even recall the illustration on the cover of the novel—a girl with a cigarette, a man in evening dress. *Madame Langevin's conscientious about speaking French to me*, a line in her letter reported. *Monsieur practises his English*. Charlotte was timid then, and innocent of almost all emotion. In her childhood she'd been aware of jealousy, and there'd always been the affection she felt for her father and her mother; but she had no greater experience of the vagaries of her heart, or even of its nature, and only loneliness concerned her at first at Massuery.

In the room set aside for her work Charlotte slips a green Loden overcoat from a coat-hanger and searches for her gloves, the park at St Cérase still vividly recurring. She might have wept that afternoon, protected by the human absence around her; she rather thought she had. After an hour she had gone to the museum, only to find it shut. Beneath a flamboyant female figure representing Eternal Peace she had waited in the Place de la Paix for the bus that would take her back to the gates of Massuery.

'Describe to me England,' Madame Langevin's sister requested that evening, practising her English also. 'Describe to me the house of your father. The food of England is not agreeable, *n'est-ce pas?*'

Replying, Charlotte spoke in French, but the tall, beautifully dressed woman stopped her. She wanted to hear the sound of English, it made a change. She yawned. The country was tedious, but so was Paris in July.

So Charlotte described the house where she lived, and her mother and her father. She explained how toast was made because Madame Langevin's sister particularly wanted to know that, and also how English butchers hung their beef. She wasn't sure herself about the beef and she didn't know the names of the various joints, but she did her best.

Madame Langevin's sister lay listening on a sofa, her cigarette in a black holder, her green silk dress clinging to her
legs.

'I have heard of Jackson's tea,' she said.

Charlotte had not. She said her parents did not have servants. She did not know much about the Royal Family, she
confessed.

'Pimm's Number One,' Madame Langevin's sister
prompted. '*Qu'est-ce que c'est que ça?*'

The Massuery estate was extensive. Beyond the gardens
there were fields where sheep grazed, and beyond the fields
there were plantations of young trees, no more than a foot
high. On the slopes beyond them, firs grew in great pro-
fusion, and sometimes the chain-saws whirred all day long,
an ugly sing-song that grated on Charlotte's nerves.

In front of the house, early every morning, gardeners
raked the gravel. An old man and a boy, with rakes wider
than Charlotte had ever seen before, worked for an hour,
destroying every suspicion of a weed, smoothing away the
marks of yesterday's wheels. The same boy brought vegetables to the house an hour or so before lunch, and again in
the evening.

Marble nymphs flanked the front door at Massuery. A
decorated balustrade accompanied the steps that rose to the
left and right before continuing grandly on, as a single
flight. The stone of the house was greyish-brown, the
slatted shutters of its windows green. Everything at Massuery was well kept up, both inside and out. The silver, the
furniture, the chandeliers, the tapestries of hunting scenes,
the chess-board marble of the huge entrance hall, were all
as lovingly attended to as the gravel. The long, slender
stair-rods and the matching brass of the banister were regularly polished, the piano in the larger of the two salons kept
tuned, the enamel of the dining-room peacocks never
allowed to lose its brilliance. Yet in spite of all its grandeur,
Massuery possessed only one telephone. This was in a small

room on the ground floor, specially set aside for it. A striped wallpaper in red and blue covered the walls, matching the colours of an ornate ceiling. A blue-shaded light illuminated the telephone table and the chair in front of it. There were writing materials and paper for noting messages on. Madame Langevin's sister, with the door wide open, sat for hours in the telephone room, speaking to people in Paris or to those who, like herself, had left the city for the summer months.

'*Mon Dieu!*' Monsieur Langevin would sometimes murmur, passing the open door. Monsieur Langevin was grey at the temples. He was clean-shaven, of medium height, with brown eyes that became playful and indulgent in his children's presence. But the children, while agreeable to their father's spoiling of them, were equally fond of their mother, even though it was she who always punished them for their misdemeanours. There was the day the twins put the cat in the chimney, and the day the bough of the apricot tree collapsed beneath their weight, and the morning old Pierre couldn't find his shoes, not a single pair. There were occasions when Colette refused to speak to anyone, especially to Charlotte, when she lay on her bed, her face turned to the wall, and picked at the wallpaper. Monsieur Langevin was as angry about that as he was about the cat in the chimney, but in each case it was Madame Langevin who arranged for whatever deprivation appeared to her to be just.

Madame Langevin's sister was having an affair. Her husband arrived at the house every Thursday night, long after dinner, close on midnight. He came on the Paris train and remained until Sunday evening, when he took a sleeper back again. He was a vivacious man, not as tall as his wife, with a reddish face and a small black moustache. After his first weekend Madame Langevin told Charlotte that her sister had married beneath her, but even so she spoke affectionately of her brother-in-law, her tone suggesting that she was relaying a simple fact. Madame Langevin would not speak ill of anyone, nor would she seek, maliciously, to wound: she was not that kind of woman. When she mentioned her sister's love affair, she did so with a shrug. On her sister's wedding day she had guessed that one day there would be such a development: with some people it was a natural thing. '*Le monde*,' Madame Langevin said, her tone neither condemning her sister nor disparaging her brother-in-law in his cuckold role.

*

Charlotte descends dimly lit stairs from her flat to the street, the green portfolio under her arm. The chill of a December morning has penetrated the house. The collar of her Loden overcoat is turned up, a black muffler several times wound round her neck. Does it happen, she wonders, in other people's lives that a single event influences all subsequent time? When she was five she was gravely ill, and though she easily remembers the drama there was, and how she sensed a closeness to death and was even reconciled to it, the experience did not afterwards pursue her. She left it, snagged in its time and place, belonging there while she herself went lightly on. So, too, she had left behind other circumstances and occurrences, which had seemed as if they must surely cast perpetually haunting shadows: they had not done so. Only that summer at Massuery still insistently accompanies her, established at her very heart as part of her.

'It is the yellow wine of the Jura,' Monsieur Langevin said, in English still. 'Different from the other wines of France.'

From the windows of Massuery you could see the mountains of the Jura. Spring and early summer were sometimes cold because of wind that came from that direction. So they told her: the Jura was often a conversational topic.

'Is there a doctor at hand?' Madame Langevin's sister

enquired, quoting from an English phrase-book she had made her husband bring her from Paris. 'What means "at hand"? *Un medicin sur le main? C'est impossible!*' With the precision of the bored, Madame Langevin's sister selected another cigarette and placed it in her holder.

'The lover is a younger man,' Madame Langevin passed on in slowly articulated French. 'Assistant to a pharmacist. One day of course he will wish to marry and that will be that.'

First thing in the morning, as soon as I open my eyes, the smell of coffee being made wafts through my open window. It is the servants' breakfast, I think. Later, at half-past eight, ours is served in an arbour in the garden, and lunch is taken there too, though never dinner, no matter how warm the evening. On Sundays Monsieur Langevin's mother comes in a tiny motor-car she can scarcely steer. She lives alone except for a house-keeper, in a village thirty kilometres away. She is small and formidable, and does not address me. Sometimes a man comes with her, a Monsieur Ogé with a beard. He speaks to me in detail about his health, and afterwards I look up the words I do not know. Other relations occasionally come on Sundays also, Madame's cousin from Saulieu and her husband, and the widow of a general.

During the war, when there were only women and children at Massuery, a German soldier was discovered in the grounds. He had made himself a shelter and apparently lived on the remains of food thrown out from the house. He would not have been discovered had he not, in desperation, stolen cheese and bread from a larder. For more than a week the women lived with the knowledge of his presence, catching glimpses of him at night, not knowing what to do. They assumed him to be a deserter and yet were not certain, for he might as easily have been lost. In the end, fearing they were themselves being watched for a purpose they could not fathom, they shot him and buried him in the garden. '*Ici,*' Madame Langevin said, pointing at a spot in the middle of a great oval flowerbed where roses grew. '*C'était moi,*' she added, answering Charlotte's unasked question. On a wet night she and her mother-in-law and a maidservant had waited for the soldier to emerge. Her first two shots had missed him and he'd advanced, walking straight towards them. Her third shot made him stagger, and then she emptied both barrels into his body. She'd only been married a few months, not much older than Charlotte was now. *She seems so very gentle*, Charlotte wrote. *You can't imagine it.*

On August 14th, a date that was to become enshrined in Charlotte's consciousness, she was driven again to her Wednesday-afternoon freedom by Monsieur Langevin. But when they came to the Place de la Paix, instead of opening the car door as usual and driving on to his mid-week appointment, he said:

'I have nothing to do this afternoon.'

He spoke, this time, in French. He smiled. Like her, he said, he had hours on his hands. He had driven her to St Cérase specially, she realised then. On all previous Wednesday afternoons it had been convenient to give her a lift and, now, when it was not, he felt some kind of obligation had been established.

'I could have caught the bus at the gates,' she said.

He smiled again. 'That would have been a pity, Charlotte.'

This was the first intimation of his feelings for her. She didn't know how to reply. She felt confused, and knew that she had flushed. *He's such a charming man*, she'd written. *Both Monsieur and Madame are charming people. There's no other word for it.*

'Let me drive you some place, Charlotte. There's nothing to do here.'

She shook her head. She had a few things to buy, she said, after which she would return to Massuery as usual, on the bus. She would be all right.

'What will you do, Charlotte? Look at the front of the church again? The museum isn't much. It doesn't take long to drink a cup of coffee.'

The French her father wished her to perfect was far from perfect yet. Haltingly, she replied that she enjoyed her Wednesday afternoons. But even as she spoke she knew that what she'd come to enjoy most about them was the drive with Monsieur Langevin. Before, she hadn't dared to allow that thought to form. Now, she could not prevent it.

'I'll wait,' Monsieur Langevin said, 'while you do your shopping.'

When she returned to the car he drove to a country hotel, almost fifty kilometres away. It was ivy-covered, by a river, with doves in the garden and a stream near by. They sat at a table beneath a beech tree, but nobody came hurrying out to ask them what they'd like. The garden was deserted; the hotel seemed so too. Everyone was sleeping, Monsieur Langevin said.

'Are you happy at Massuery, Charlotte?'

She was three feet away from him, yet she could feel a fondness that made her faintly dizzy. Her flesh tingled, as though the tips of his fingers had touched her forearm and were sending reverberations through her body. Yet they hadn't. She tried to think of his children, endeavouring to imagine Colette and the twins at their most tiresome. She tried to think of Madame Langevin, to hear her soft, considerate voice. But nothing happened. All there was was the presence of the man she was with, his white car drawn up in the distance, the small round table at which they sat. A deception was taking place. Already they were sharing a deception.

'Yes, I am happy at Massuery now.'

'You were not at first?'

'I was a little lonely.'

*

Charlotte walks swiftly through the grey December streets with her portfolio. There was another print, a long time ago, of that round white table, and two faceless figures sitting at it. There was one of three women blurred by heavy rain, waiting like statues among the dripping shrubs. There was one of Massuery caught in dappled sunlight, another of children playing, another of a white Citroën with nobody in it.

'They like you, Charlotte. Guy most of all perhaps.'

'I like them now too.'

They returned to the car when they had talked a while. Only, perhaps, an hour had passed: afterwards she calculated it was about an hour. No one had served them.

'Everyone is still asleep,' he said.

How had it happened that he put his arms around her? Had they stopped in their walk across the grass? Afterwards she realised they must have. But in her memory of the moment she was only aware that she had murmured protests, that the palms of both her hands had pressed against his chest. He hadn't kissed her, but the passion of the kiss was there. Afterwards she knew that too.

'Dear Charlotte,' he said, and then: 'Forgive me.'

She might have fainted and, as though he sensed it, he took her arm, his fingers lightly supporting her elbow, as a stranger on the street might have. He told her, as he drove, about his childhood at Massuery. The old gardener had been there, and nothing much had changed in the house. A forest of birches that had been sold for timber after the war had been replanted. In the fields where sunflowers were grown for their oil now there had been wheat before. He remembered carts and even oxen.

The white Citroën turned in at the gates and glided between the plane trees on the drive, its tyres disturbing the gravel. There'd been an oak close to the house, but its branches had spread too wide and it had been felled. He pointed at the place. They walked up the steps together, and into the hall.

That evening at dinner Madame Langevin's sister tried out a new phrase. 'My friend and I desire to attend a theatre,' she repeated several times, seeking guidance as to emphasis and pronunciation. No one remarked upon the fact that Charlotte had returned in the car with Monsieur Langevin, when always previously on Wednesdays she had arrived back on the bus. No one had noticed; no one was interested. It had been just a moment, she told herself, just the slightest thing. She hadn't been able to reply when he asked her to forgive him. He hadn't even taken her hand.

When Sunday came, Monsieur Langevin's mother brought the bearded Monsieur Ogé who talked about his health, and the widow of the general was there also. The deceived husband was in particularly good spirits that day. '*Mon chéri*,' Madame Langevin's sister murmured on the telephone after he'd left for the railway station in the evening. '*C'est trop cruel.*'

When Wednesday came Madame Langevin asked Charlotte if she'd mind taking the bus to St Cérase today because her husband was not going in that direction. And the following Wednesday, as though a precedent had been set by that, it seemed to be assumed that she would take the bus also. Had Madame Langevin somehow discovered? Her manner did not suggest it, but Charlotte remembered her philosophical tone when she'd first spoken of her sister's relationship with the pharmacist's assistant, her matter-of-fact acceptance of what clearly she considered to be an absurdity.

Sitting at the café where her solitary presence had become a Wednesday-afternoon feature, Charlotte tried to feel relieved that she'd been saved a decision. But would she really have said no if he'd offered, again, to drive her somewhere pleasant, or would her courage have failed her? Alone at the café, Charlotte shook her head. If he'd asked her, her longing to be with him would have quenched her conventional protests: courage did not come into it.

That day, she went again to the museum and sat in the dusty park. She sketched a hobby-horse that lay abandoned by a seat. The deception was still there, even though he'd changed his mind. Nothing could take it from them.

'*Tu es triste,*' Guy said when she bade him goodnight that evening. '*Pourquoi es-tu triste, Charlotte?*' Only three weeks were left of her time at Massuery: that was why she was sad, she replied, which was the truth in part. '*Mais tu reviendras,*' Guy comforted, and she believed she would. It was impossible to accept that she would not see Massuery again.

*

The man nods appreciatively. He knows what he wants and what his clients like. The décor he supplies is enhanced by a pale-framed pleasantry above a minibar or a television set. In the bedrooms of fashionable hotels—and in boardrooms and directors' dining-rooms and the offices of industrial magnates—Charlotte's summer at Massuery hangs.

While her patron examines what she has brought him today, she sees herself walking in the Massuery woods, a lone, slight figure among the trees. What was it about her that had made a man of the world love her? She'd not been without a kind of beauty, she supposes, but often she'd been awkward in her manner and certainly ill-informed in conversation, naive and credulous, an English schoolgirl whose clothes weren't smart, who hardly knew how to make up her face and sometimes didn't bother. Was it her very artlessness that had attracted his attention? Had he somehow delighted in the alarmed unease that must have been displayed in her face when he said he'd wait for her to finish her shopping? With long hindsight, Charlotte believes she had noticed his attention from the very first day she arrived at Massuery. There was a fondness in the amused glances he cast at her, which she had not understood and had not sought to. Yet as soon as he permitted the *frisson* between them, as soon as his manner and his words created it, she knew that being in his company was in every way different from being in Madame Langevin's, though, before, she had assumed she liked them equally. With that same long hindsight, Charlotte believes she came to love Monsieur Langevin because of his sense of honour and his strength, yet she knows as well that long before she was aware of these qualities in him her own first stirrings of emotion had surfaced and, with unconscious propriety, been buried.

Madame Langevin's sister embraced her warmly the day Charlotte left Massuery. 'Farewell,' she wished her, and enquired if that was what was said on such occasions in England. The children gave her presents. Monsieur Langevin thanked her. He stood with his hands on Colette's shoulders, removing one briefly to shake one of Charlotte's. It was Madame Langevin who drove her to the railway station, and when Charlotte looked back from the car she saw in Monsieur Langevin's eyes what had not been there a moment before: the anguish of the sadness that already claimed their clandestine afternoon. His hands remained on his daughter's shoulders but even so it was as if, again, he'd spoken. At the railway station Madame Langevin embraced her, as her sister had.

Journeying through late September sunshine, Charlotte wept in a corner of her compartment. He respected Madame Langevin too much to betray her in the way her sister betrayed the husband she'd once chosen. Nor was he a man to cause his children pain in order to gratify a selfishness in himself. She knew all that, and in turn respected him. Her resignation was melancholy on that train journey, but with the balm of passing time it became more bearable.

'You're miles away, Charlotte,' young men would later amusedly accuse, and she'd apologise, already back at Massuery. Listening to the young men's chatter, she descended again the wide staircase, and walked in the woods. Such memories made it easier when with embarrassed gaucheness the young men seized her hand, or kissed her. When proposals came, her private reply was to see the white car waiting for her in the Place de la Paix, while aloud she apologised to whoever had got it into his head that she was free to love him.

*

'These'll ring the changes,' the man who has commissioned the new prints says. When a business room or the bedrooms of a hotel are repainted he always likes to have fresh curtains and fresh prints as well; it's something that's expected. In six months' time, he says, he may be ready for another contribution from her. 'That's something to be thinking about, my love.' He always calls her that. He has mahogany-coloured hair with a spring in it; the stubble on his chin and neck grows so slightly and so softly that he hardly has to shave. 'We'll send a cheque,' he says.

Charlotte thanks him. There are other such men, and women too, who remember her when they want something new and unexacting for their décor. They admire her prints more than Charlotte does herself; for her the prints are by the way. What matters more is the certainty of her faith: even without thinking she knows that time, for her lover also, has failed to absorb the passion that was not allowed. For all the years that have passed she has thought of him as that; and dwelling on the nature of love during all that time she has long ago concluded that it's a mystery, appearing to come from nowhere, no rhyme nor reason to it. The truth will not yield: why did so unsuitably, so cruelly almost, two people love?

Daylight hasn't properly penetrated the December drabness. Fog shrouds the streets; the pavements are dampened by it. Busy with their assets and take-overs, the men of the business rooms have probably never noticed the prints that hang there. 'How charming that is!' a woman, half-dressed in a hotel bedroom, may have remarked after the scurry of afternoon love or in some idle moment during a weekend's deceit.

Charlotte sits for a while in the corner of a bar, her green portfolio empty beside her. No one else, except two barmen, are there so early in the day. She sips with pleasure the glass of red wine that has been brought to her; she lights a cigarette and with slow deliberation drops the spent match into the discoloured plastic ashtray in front of her. Then idly, on the cover of her folder, she sketches a funeral procession, sombre between two lines of plane trees. When eventually he sees it the man with the mahogany hair will display no curiosity, for he never does; in the rooms destined for her funeral scene no one will wonder either.

She finishes her wine and catches the eye of the taller barman. He brings her another glass. She remembers her father being angry, and her mother frowning in bewilderment. She never told them what she might have; but her father was angry because she had no ambition, because one young man after another was so summarily rejected. 'You're alone so,' her mother sadly observed. Charlotte did not attempt to explain, for how could happily married people understand that such flimsiness could become the heart of a human existence? Ambitions in this direction or that, and would-be husbands keenly persuading, seemed empty of seriousness, ludicrous almost, compared with what she had.

She has never seen Monsieur Langevin's handwriting, but imagines it is large and sloping, a little like Guy's was. She knows she'll never see it, for the thoughts that occur to her from time to time leave no illusions behind them: no letter will ever inform her that Madame Langevin, a month or so ago, was thrown from her horse—as once, unable to help herself, she dreamed. The funeral is not a hope, only another image from her printmaker's stock. Why should an

honourable deception end in romance? Rewards for decency
are not duly handed out.

Their love affair, for her, is there among the memories of
a summer, with the people of a household, the town she
visited, Guy saying she will return, the sound of the gravel
raked, the early-morning smell of coffee. For Monsieur
Langevin, the deception is lived with every day, pain
blinked away, words bitten back. For both of them, the pattern of their lives has formed around a moment in an afternoon. It is not often so, her lover tells her in yet another
silent conversation. He, too, is grateful.

Coffee with Oliver

That is Deborah, Oliver said to himself: my daughter has come to see me. But at the pavement table of the café where he sat he did not move. He did not even smile. He had, after all, only caught a glimpse of a slight girl in a yellow dress, of fair hair, and sun-glasses and a profile: it might not be she at all.

Yet, Oliver insisted to himself, you know a thing like that. You sense your flesh and blood. And why should Deborah be in Perugia unless she planned to visit him? The girl was alone. She had hurried into the hotel next to the café in a businesslike manner, not as a sightseer would.

Oliver was a handsome man of forty-seven, with greying hair, and open, guileless features. This morning he was dressed as always he was when he made the journey to Perugia: in a pale-cream linen suit, a pale shirt with a green stripe in it, and the tie of an English public school. His tan shoes shone; the socks that matched the cream of his suit were taut over his ankles.

'*Signorina!*'

He summoned the waitress who had just finished serving the people at the table next to his and ordered another cappuccino. This particular girl went off duty at eleven and the waitress who replaced her invariably made out the bill for one cappuccino only. It was fair enough, Oliver argued to himself, since he was a regular customer at the café and spent far more there than a tourist would.

'*Si, signore. Subito.*'

(155)

What he had seen in the girl who'd gone into the hotel was a resemblance to Angelica, who was slight and fair-haired also, and had the same quick little walk and rather small face. If the girl had paused and for some reason taken off her dark glasses he would at once, with warm nostalgia, have recognised her mother's deep, dark eyes, of that he was certain. He wouldn't, of course, have been so sure had it not been for the resemblance. Since she'd grown up he'd only seen photographs of his daughter.

It was best to let whatever Deborah had planned just happen, best not to upset the way she wanted it. He could ask for her at the reception desk of the hotel. He could be waiting for her in the hall, and they could lunch together. He could show her about the town, put her into the picture gallery for an hour while he waited at the café across the street; afterwards they could sit over a drink. But that would be all his doing, not Deborah's, and it wouldn't be fair. Such a programme would also be expensive, for Deborah, in spite of being at a smart hotel, might well not be able to offer a contribution: it would not be unlike Angelica to keep her short. Oliver's own purpose in being in Perugia that morning was to visit the Credito Italiano, to make certain that the monthly amount from Angelica had come. He had cashed a cheque, but of course that had to be made to last.

'*Prego, signore,*' the waitress said, placing a fresh cup of coffee in front of him and changing his ashtray for an un-used one.

He smiled and thanked her, then blew gently at the foam of his cappuccino and sipped a little of the coffee. He lit a cigarette. You could sit all day here, he reflected, while the red-haired Perugians went by, young men in twos and threes, and the foreign students from the language schools, and the tourists who toiled up, perspiring, from the car parks. Idling time away, just ruminating, was lovely.

Eventually Oliver paid for his coffee and left. He should

perhaps buy some meat, in case his daughter arrived at his house at a mealtime. Because it was expensive he rarely did buy meat, once in a blue moon a packet of cooked turkey slices, which lasted for ages. There was a butcher's he often passed in a side street off the via dei Priori, but this morning it was full of women, all of them pressing for attention. Oliver couldn't face the clamour and the long wait he guessed there'd be. The butcher's in Betona might still be open when he arrived off the five-past-twelve bus. Probably best left till then in any case, meat being tricky in the heat.

He descended from the city centre by a steep short cut, eventually arriving at the bus stop he favoured. He saved a little by using this particular fare-stage, and though he did not often make the journey to Perugia all such economies added up. What a marvellous thing to happen, that Deborah had come! Oliver smiled as he waited for his bus in the midday sunshine; the best things were always a surprise.

*

Deborah had a single memory of her father. He'd come to the flat one Sunday afternoon and she'd been at the top of the short flight of stairs that joined the flat's two floors. She hadn't known who he was but had watched and listened, sensing the charged atmosphere. At the door the man was smiling. He said her mother was looking well. He hoped she wouldn't mind, he said. Her mother was cross. Deborah had been five at the time.

'You know I mind,' she'd heard her mother say.

'I was passing. Unfriendly just to pass, I thought. We shouldn't not ever talk to one another again, Angelica.'

Her mother's voice was lowered then. She spoke more than she had already, but Deborah couldn't hear a word.

'Well, no point,' he said. 'No point in keeping you.'

Afterwards, when Deborah asked, her mother told her who the man was. Her mother was truthful and found deception difficult. When two people didn't get on any

(157)

more, she said, it wasn't a good idea to try to keep some surface going.

He'd lit a cigarette while they'd been talking. Softly, he'd tried to interrupt her mother. He'd wanted to come in, but her mother hadn't permitted that.

'I'm here because of a mistake? Is that it?' Deborah pinned her mother down in a quarrel years after that Sunday afternoon. It was her mother's way of putting it when her marriage came up: two people had made a mistake. Mistakes were best forgotten, her mother said.

*

The dwelling Oliver occupied, in the hills above the village of Betona, was a stone building of undistinguished shape and proportions. It had once housed sheep during the frozen winter months, and wooden stair, resembling a heavily constructed ladder, led to a single upstairs room, where shepherds had sought privacy from their animals. Efforts at conversion had been made. Electricity had been brought from the village; a kitchen, and a lavatory with a shower in it, had been fitted into the space below. But the conversion had an arrested air, reflecting a loss of interest on the part of Angelica who, years ago, had bought the place as it stood. At the time of the divorce she had made over to him the ramshackle habitation. She herself had visited it only once; soon after the divorce proceedings began she turned against the enterprise, and work on the conversion ceased. When Oliver returned on his own he found the corrugated roof still letting in rain, no water flowing from either the shower or the lavatory, the kitchen without a sink or a stove, and a cesspit not yet dug. He had come from England with his clothes and four ebony-framed pictures. 'Well, anyway it's somewhere to live,' he said aloud, looking around the downstairs room, which smelt of concrete. He sighed nonetheless, for he was not deft with his hands.

The place was furnished now, though modestly. Two

folding garden chairs did service in the downstairs room.
There was a table with a fawn formica surface, and a pitch-
pine bookcase. Faded rugs covered most of the concrete
floor. The four heavily framed pictures—scenes of Suffolk
landscape—adorned the rough stone walls to some effect.
Across a corner there was a television set.

The cesspit remained undug, but in other directions
Oliver had had a bit of luck. He'd met an Englishman on
one of his visits to the Credito Italiano and had helped with
a language difficulty. The man, in gratitude, insisted on
buying Oliver a cup of coffee and Oliver, sensing a usefulness in this acquaintanceship, suggested that they drive together in the man's car to Betona. In return for a summer's
lodging—a sleeping-bag on the concrete floor—the man
replaced the damaged corrugated iron of the roof, completed the piping that brought water to the shower and the
lavatory, and installed a sink and an antique gas stove that
someone had thrown out, adapting the stove to receive
bottled gas. He liked to work like this, to keep himself occupied, being in some kind of distress. Whenever Oliver
paused in the story of his marriage his companion had a
way of starting up about the business world he'd once belonged to, how failure had led to bankruptcy: finding the
interruption of his own narration discourteous, Oliver did
not listen. Every evening at six o'clock the man walked
down to the village and returned with a litre of red wine
and whatever groceries he thought necessary. Oliver explained that since he himself would not have made these
purchases he did not consider that he should make a contribution to their cost. His visitor was his guest in the matter
of accommodation; in fairness, it seemed to follow, he
should be his visitor's guest where the odd egg or glass of
wine was concerned.

'Angelica was never easy,' Oliver explained, continuing
the story of his marriage from one evening to the next.
'There was always jealousy.' His sojourn in the Betona hills

was temporary, he stated with confidence. But he did not add that, with his sights fixed on something better, he often dropped into conversation with lone English or American women in the rooms of the picture gallery or at the café next to the hotel. He didn't bore his companion with this information because it didn't appear to have much relevance. He did his best only to be interesting about Angelica, and considered he succeeded. It was a dispute in quite a different area that ended the relationship, as abruptly as it had begun. As well as hospitality, the visitor claimed a sum of money had been agreed upon, but while conceding that a cash payment had indeed been mooted, Oliver was adamant that he had not promised it. He did not greatly care for the man in the end, and was glad to see him go.

*

When Angelica died two years ago Deborah was twenty. The death was not a shock because her mother had been ill, and increasingly in pain, for many months: death was a mercy. Nonetheless, Deborah felt the loss acutely. Although earlier, in her adolescence, there had been arguments and occasionally rows, she'd known no companion as constant as her mother; and as soon as the death occurred she realised how patient with her and how fond of her Angelica had been. She'd been larky too, amused by unexpected things, given to laughter that Deborah found infectious. In her distress at the time of her mother's death it never occurred to her that the man who'd come to the flat that Sunday afternoon might turn up at the funeral. In fact, he hadn't.

'You'll be all right,' Angelica had said before she died, meaning that there was provision for Deborah to undertake the post-graduate work she planned after she took her degree. 'Don't worry, darling.'

Deborah held her hand, ashamed when she remembered how years ago she'd been so touchy because Angelica once too often repeated that her marriage was a mistake. Her mother had never used the expression again.

'I was a horrid child,' Deborah cried forlornly before her mother died. 'A horrid little bully.'

'Darling, of course you weren't.'

At the funeral people said how much they'd always liked her mother, how nice she'd been. They invited Deborah to visit them at any time, just to turn up when she was feeling low.

*

When Oliver stepped off the bus in the village the butcher's shop was still open but he decided, after all, not to buy a pork chop, which was the choice he had contemplated when further considering the matter on the bus. A chop was suitable because, although it might cost as much as twenty thousand lire, it could be divided quite easily into two. But supposing it wasn't necessary to offer a meal at all? Supposing Deborah arrived in the early afternoon, which was not unlikely? He bought the bread he needed instead, and a packet of soup, and cigarettes.

He wondered if Deborah had come with a message. He did not know that Angelica had died and wondered if she was hoping he might be persuaded to return to the flat in the square. It was not unlikely. As he ascended the track that led to his property, these thoughts drifted pleasurably through Oliver's mind. 'Deborah, I'll have to think about that.' He saw himself sitting with his daughter in what the man who'd set the place to rights had called the patio—a yard really, with two car seats the man had rescued from a dump somewhere, and an old table-top laid across concrete blocks. 'We'll see,' he heard himself saying, not wishing to dismiss the idea out of hand.

He had taken his jacket off, and carried it over his arm. '*E caldo!*' the woman he'd bought the bread from had exclaimed, which indicated that the heat was excessive, for in Betona references to the weather were only made when extremes were reached. Sweat gathered on Oliver's forehead and at the back of his neck. He could feel it becoming clammy beneath his shirt. Whatever the reason for Deborah's advent he was glad she had come because company was always cheerful.

In the upstairs room Oliver took his suit off and carefully placed it on a wire coat-hanger on the wall. He hung his tie over one linen shoulder, and changed his shirt. The trousers he put on were old corduroys, too heavy in the heat, but the best he could manage. In the kitchen he made tea and took it out to the patio, with the bread he'd bought and his cigarettes. He waited for his daughter.

*

After Angelica's death Deborah felt herself to be an orphan. Angelica's brother and his wife, a well-meaning couple she hardly knew, fussed about her a bit; and so did Angelica's friends. But Deborah had her own friends, and she didn't need looking after. She inherited the flat in London and went there in the university holidays. She spent a weekend in Norfolk with her uncle and his wife, but did not do so again. Angelica's brother was quite unlike her, a lumpish man who wore grey, uninteresting suits and had a pipe, and spectacles on a chain. His wife was wan and scatterbrained. They invited Deborah as a duty and were clearly thankful to find her independent.

Going through her mother's possessions, Deborah discovered neither photographs of, nor letters from, her father. She did not know that photographs of herself, unaccompanied by any other form of communication, had been sent to her father every so often, as a record of her growing up. She did not know of the financial agreement that years ago had been entered into. It did not occur to her that no one might have informed the man who'd come that Sunday afternoon of Angelica's death. It didn't occur to her to find some way of doing so herself. None of this entered Deborah's head because the shadowy figure who had smiled and lit a cigarette belonged as deeply in the grave as her mother did.

She had no curiosity about him, and her uncle did not mention him. Nor did any of Angelica's friends on the occasions when they invited Deborah to lunch or drinks, since she had not just turned up as they'd suggested at the funeral. In reply to some casual query by a stranger, she once replied that her father was probably dead. The happiness of her relationship with Angelica was what she thought about and moodily dwelt upon, regretting that she had taken it for granted.

*

The heat was at its most intense at three o'clock, but afterwards did not lose its fervour. The concrete blocks of Oliver's patio, the metal ribs of the car chairs, the scorching upholstery, the stone of the house itself, all cancelled the lessening of the sun's attack by exuding the heat that had been stored. By half-past five a kind of coolness was beginning. By seven it had properly arrived. By half-past eight there was pleasure in its relief.

Perhaps he had been wrong, Oliver thought later, not to approach the girl: thoughtfulness sometimes was misplaced. If she had waited for the day to cool she would have found herself too late for the last bus to Betona, and a taxi would have been outrageously expensive. Angelica would have taken a taxi, of course, though in other ways, as he well knew, she could be penny-pinching.

But Deborah didn't come that evening, nor the next day, nor the day after that. So Oliver made the journey into Perugia again, long before it was time for his next visit to the Credito Italiano. The only explanation was that the girl had not been Deborah at all. But he still felt she was, and was bewildered. He even wondered if his daughter was lying low because she'd been sent to spy on him.

'*Si, signore?*' The clerk in the reception of the hotel smiled at him, and in slow Italian Oliver made his query. He wrote down Deborah's name on a piece of paper so that there could be no confusion. He remembered the date of the day he'd last sat at the café. From the photograph he had of her he described his daughter.

'*Momento, signore. Scusi.*' The clerk entered a small office to one side of the reception desk and returned some minutes later with a registration form. On it were Deborah's name and signature, and the address of the flat in London. She had stayed one night only in the hotel.

'Student,' a girl who had accompanied the clerk from the office said. 'She search a room in Perugia.'

'A room?'

'She ask.' The girl shrugged. 'I no have room.'

'Thank you.' Oliver smiled at both of them in turn. The clerk called after him in Italian. The girl had given Deborah the name of an agency, not twenty metres away, where rooms were rented to students. 'Thank you,' Oliver said again, but did not take the details of the agency. At the café he ordered a cappuccino.

Deborah had enrolled on a course—language or culture, or perhaps a combination. Perugia was famous for its courses; students came from all over the place. Sometimes they spent a year, or even longer, depending on the course they'd chosen. He knew that because now and again he dropped into conversation with one, and in return for a grappa or a cappuccino supplied some local information. Once he'd had lunch with a well-to-do young Iranian who'd clearly been grateful for his company.

'*Ecco, signore!*' The waitress who went off duty at eleven placed his coffee in front of him.

'*Grazie.*'

'*Prego, signore.*'

He lit a cigarette. Once he'd had a lighter and a silver cigarette case, given to him by a Mrs Dogsmith, whom he'd met in the Giardini Carducci. For a moment he saw again the slim, faintly embossed case, and the initials curling around one another at the bottom left-hand corner of the lighter. He'd sold both of them years ago.

A woman came out of the hotel and paused idly, glancing at the café tables. She was taller than Mrs Dogsmith and a great deal thinner. A widow or divorcee, Oliver guessed, but then a man came out of the hotel and took her arm.

'Your mother gave you so much.' Angelica's irrational chatter lurched at him suddenly. 'But still you had to steal from her.'

He felt himself broken into, set upon and violated, as he remembered feeling at the time. The unpleasant memory had come because of Deborah, because Deborah's presence put him in mind of Angelica, naturally enough. More agreeably, he recalled that it was he who'd chosen that name for their daughter. 'Deborah,' he'd suggested, and Angelica had not resisted it.

Not wishing to think about Angelica, he watched the waddling movement of a pigeon on the pavement, and then listened to a conversation in Italian between a darkly suited man and his companion, a woman in a striped red dress. They were talking about swimwear; the man appeared to be the proprietor of a fashion shop. Young people in a group went by, and Oliver glanced swiftly from face to face, but his daughter was not among them. He ordered another cappuccino because in ten minutes or so the early-morning waitress would be going off duty.

It was a silliness of Angelica's to say he'd stolen from his mother. He more than anyone had regretted the sad delusions that had beset his mother. It was he who had watched her becoming vague, he who had suffered when she left all she possessed to a Barnardo's home. Angelica belonged to a later time; she'd hardly known his mother.

Slowly Oliver lit and smoked another cigarette, filling in time while he waited for the new waitress to arrive. As soon as he saw her he crumpled up the little slip that had accompanied his first cup of coffee, and placed on the table the money for the second. But this morning, when he'd gone only a few yards along the street, the waitress came hurrying after him, jabbering in Italian. He smiled and shook his head. She held out the money he'd left.

'Oh! *Mi dispiace!*' he apologised, paying her extra.

*

'Deborah.'

She heard her name and turned. A middle-aged man was smiling at her. She smiled back, thinking he was one of the tutors whom she couldn't place.

'Don't you recognise me, Deborah?'

They were in the square. He had risen from the edge of a wooden stage that had been erected for some public meeting. The two girls Deborah was with had walked on a yard or so.

'My dear,' the man said, but seventeen years had passed since Deborah had caught her one glimpse of her father that Sunday afternoon. Neither features nor voice were familiar. 'It's really you!' the man said.

Bewildered, Deborah shook her head.

'I'm Oliver,' Oliver said. 'Your father.'

*

They sat outside, at the nearest café. She didn't take off her sun-glasses. She'd spoken to the girls she'd been with and they'd walked on. She had a class at two, she'd said.

'Time at least for a coffee,' Oliver said.

She had a look of him, even though she was more like Angelica. It had been a disappointment, the deduction that she hadn't come here to seek him out. A disappointment that it was no more than a coincidence, her presence in Perugia.

'You knew of course?' he said. 'You did have my address?'

She shook her head. She'd had no idea. She hadn't even been aware that he was not in England.

'But, Deborah, surely Angelica—'

'No, she never did.'

Their coffee came. The waiter was young and unshaven, not neatly in a uniform like the girls at the café by the hotel. He glanced at Deborah with interest. Oliver thought he heard him making a sound with his lips, but he could not be sure.

'I often think of you and your mother in that flat.'

*

Deborah realised he didn't know Angelica had died, and found it difficult to break the news. She did so clumsily, or so she thought.

'My God!' he said.

Deborah dipped a finger into the foam of her coffee. She didn't like the encounter; she wished it hadn't taken place. She didn't like sitting here with a man she didn't know and didn't want to know. 'Apparently he's my father,' she'd said to her companions, momentarily enjoying the sophistication; but later, of course, all that would have to be explained.

'Poor Angelica!' he said.

Deborah wondered why nobody had warned her. Why hadn't her grey-suited uncle or one of Angelica's friends advised against this particular Italian city? Why hadn't her mother mentioned it?

Presumably they hadn't warned her because they didn't know. Her mother hadn't ever wanted to mention him; it wasn't Angelica's way to warn people against people.

'She used to send me a photograph of you every summer,' he said. 'I wondered why none came these last two years. I never guessed.'

She nodded meaninglessly.

'Why are you learning Italian, Deborah?'

'I took my degree in the history of art. It's necessary to improve my Italian now.'

'You're taking it up? The history of art?'

'Yes, I am.'

'It's lovely you're here.'

'Yes.'

She had chosen Perugia rather than Florence or Rome because the course was better. But if she'd known she wouldn't have.

'Not really a coincidence,' he was saying, very softly. 'These things never are.'

Just for a moment Deborah felt irritated. What had been the use of Angelica's being generous, unwilling to malign, bending over backwards to be decent, when this could happen as a result? What was the good of calling a marriage a mistake, and leaving it at that? But the moment passed; irritation with the dead was shameful.

'Is it far from here, where you live?' she asked, hoping that it was.

*

Oliver tore a cheque-stub from his cheque-book and wrote his address on it, then tore out another and drew a map. He wrote down the number of the Betona bus.

'It's lovely you're here,' he said again, giving his daughter the cheque-stubs. An excitement had begun in him. If he hadn't been outside the hotel that morning he'd never even have known she was in Perugia. She might have come and gone and he'd have been none the wiser. Angelica had died, the two of them were left; he wouldn't have known that, either.

'If you don't mind,' he heard his daughter saying and felt she was repeating something he hadn't heard the first time, 'I don't think I'll visit you.'

'You've been told unpleasant things, Deborah.'

'No, not at all.'

'We can be frank, you know.'

Angelica had been like that, he knew it to his cost. In his own case, she had laid down harsh conditions, believing that to be his due. The half-converted house and the monthly transfer of money carried the proviso that he should not come to the flat ever again, that he should not live in England. That wasn't pleasant, but since it was what she wanted he'd agreed. At least the money hadn't ceased when the woman died. Oliver smiled, feeling that to be a triumph.

'Angelica was always jealous. It was jealousy that spoilt things.'

'I never noticed that in her.'

He smiled again, knowing better. Heaven alone knew what this girl had been told about him, but today, now that she was here and Angelica was not, it didn't matter.

'A pity you feel you can't come out to Betona. The bus fare's quite a bit, else I'd come in oftener while you're here.'

'Actually, to tell the truth, I'd rather we didn't have to meet.' Deborah's tone was matter-of-fact and sharp. A note of impatience had entered it, reminding Oliver not of his wife, but strangely of his mother.

'I only come in once a month or so.' He slid a cigarette from his packet of MS. 'Angelica tried to keep us apart,' he said, 'all these years. She made the most elaborate arrangements.'

Deborah rooted in her handbag and found her own cigarettes and matches. Oliver said he'd have offered her one of his if he'd known she smoked. She said it didn't matter.

'I don't want any of this hassle,' she said.

(169)

'Hassle, Deborah? A cup of coffee now and again—'
'Look, honestly, not even that.'

Oliver smiled. It was always better not to argue. He'd never argued with Angelica. It was she who'd done the arguing, working herself up, making it sound as though she were angrily talking to herself. Deborah could easily sleep in the downstairs room; there were early-morning buses to Perugia. They could share the expenses of the household: the arrangement there'd been with the bankrupt man had been perfectly satisfactory.

'Sorry,' Deborah said, and to Oliver her voice sounded careless. She blew out smoke, looking over her shoulder, no doubt to see if her friends were still hanging around. He felt a little angry. He might have been just anyone, sitting there. He wanted to remind her that he had given her life.

'It's simple at Betona,' he said instead. 'I'm not well off. But I don't think you'd find it dreadful.'

'I'm sure I wouldn't. All the same—'

'Angelica was well off, you know. She never wanted me to be.'

*

Deborah missed her two o'clock lesson because it was harder than she'd anticipated to get away. She was told about all sorts of things, none of which she'd known about before. The Sunday afternoon she remembered was mentioned. 'I wasn't very well then,' Oliver said. It was after that occasion that a legal agreement had been drawn up: in return for financial assistance Oliver undertook not to come to the flat again, not ever to attempt to see his child. He was given the house near Betona, no more than a shack really. 'None of it was easy,' he said. He looked away, as if to hide emotion from her. The photographs he annually received were a legality also, the only one he had insisted on himself. Suddenly he stood up and said he had a bus to catch.

'It's understandable,' he said. 'Your not wanting to come to Betona. Of course you have your own life.'

He nodded and went away. Deborah watched him disappearing into the crowd that was again collecting, after the afternoon siesta.

*

Who on earth would have believed that he'd outlive Angelica? Extraordinary how things happen; though, perhaps, in a sense, there was a fairness in it. Angelica had said he always had to win. In her unpleasant moods she'd said he had to cheat people, that he could not help himself. As a gambler was in thrall to luck, or a dipsomaniac to drink, his flaw was having to show a gain in everything he did.

On the bus journey back to Betona Oliver did not feel angry when he recalled that side of Angelica and supposed it was because she was dead. Naturally it was a relief to have the weight of anger lifted after all these years, no point in denying it. The trouble had been it wasn't easy to understand what she was getting at. When she'd found the three or four pieces among his things, she'd forgotten that they were his as much as his mother's, and didn't even try to understand that you couldn't have told his mother that, she being like she was. Instead Angelica chose to repeat that he hadn't been able to resist 'getting the better of' his mother. Angelica's favourite theme was that: what she called his pettiness and his meanness left him cruel. He had often thought she didn't care what she said; it never mattered how she hurt.

On the bus Angelica's face lolled about in Oliver's memory, with his mother's and—to Oliver's surprise—his daughter's. Angelica pleaded about something, tears dripped from the old woman's cheeks, Deborah simply shook her head. 'Like cancer in a person,' Angelica said. Yet it was Angelica who had died, he thought again.

Deborah would come. She would come because she was

(171)

his flesh and blood. One day he'd look down and see her on the path, bringing something with her because he wasn't well off. Solicitors had drawn up the stipulations that had kept them apart all these years; in ugly legal jargon all of it was written coldly down. When Deborah considered that, she would begin to understand. He'd sensed, before they parted, a shadow of unease: guilt on Angelica's behalf, which wasn't surprising in the circumstances.

The thought cheered Oliver considerably. In his house, as he changed his clothes, he reflected that it didn't really matter, the waitress running after him for the money. In all, over the months that had passed since this waitress had begun to work at the café, he'd probably had twenty, even thirty, second cups of coffee. He knew it didn't matter because after a little time it hadn't mattered that the bankrupt man had made a scene, since by then the roof was repaired and the plumbing completed. It hadn't mattered when Mrs Dogsmith turned nasty, since already she'd given him the lighter and the cigarette case. That was the kind of thing Angelica simply couldn't understand, any more than she'd understood the confusions of his mother, any more than, probably, she'd understood their daughter. You couldn't keep flesh and blood apart; you actually weren't meant to.

In the kitchen Oliver put the kettle on for tea. When it boiled he poured the water on to a tea-bag he'd already used before setting out for Perugia. He carried the glass out to the patio and lit a cigarette. The car seats were too hot to sit on, so he stood, waiting for them to cool. There'd been no reason why she shouldn't have paid for their coffee since she, after all, had been the cause of their having it. Eighteen thousand lire a cappuccino cost at that particular café, he'd noticed it on the bill.

A Husband's Return

As dawn lightened Maura Brigid's bedroom the eyes of the
Virgin Mary surveyed her waking face dispassionately. Two
fingers of the Holy Child blessed her from a tiny pedestal
above the room's single window. Sleepily recollected, the
routine of the day before passed unobtrusively through her
thoughts, prefacing the daytime shadow of her desertion by
the man she'd loved. This pall of shame reclaimed its
potency in the first moments of every day, establishing itself
afresh, as the sacred statues did. Then, this morning,
Maura Brigid remembered that her sister Bernadette had
died.

In his bedroom across the landing Maura Brigid's
brother, Hiney, awoke with the occasion already alive in his
consciousness. In the town the family had travelled to a
banner had been suspended high up across a street, offering
a welcome on behalf of a carnival in the future. Halfway between white iron railings and the church, on a hill, there
was a shrine, a pietà, in white also. The yellow grain of the
coffin was vivid in the sunshine, the face of the priest wan
and distressed. Hiney pushed back the bedclothes, the
action assisting him to dispel these recollections of a time
spent unhappily in an unfamiliar place. Bernadette had run
away from the farmhouse with her sister's husband: that sin
had still been ugly at the funeral.

Affected also by the recent death, Mrs Colleary, the
mother of Maura Brigid and Hiney, rose an hour later. She
released the two blinds in her bedroom and dressed herself

in the nondescript wear of a farmer's widow. He would
have gone after Bernadette, she reflected, thinking of her
husband; he would have brought her back, and the danger
was that he might even have killed Lawless, for his anger
had always been difficult to control. It was as well he'd been
spared all of it, because nothing he might have done could
have lessened the disgrace into which the family had been
dragged. Mrs Colleary told her rosary, and prayed for the
soul of her husband, and for her daughter's soul. It was the
morning of a Tuesday in May, a month after the funeral.

In another bedroom an old man, distantly related to the
family, remained in his bed. Of everyone in the farmhouse,
only he no longer dwelt on the scandal that had occurred.
He had been upset by it at the time, but with the passing
years it had settled in his mind, as had so much else in a
long life. He was a small, wizened man who had spent most
of that life on this farm. His relationship to the remaining
Collearys was vague.

The house where the family lived was large and square
and white, facing a grassy hill, its back to the distant sea.
The hall-door had been nailed in place a long time ago, to
keep out draughts; a slated roof, obtusely pitched, was
scarcely visible. The gravel sweep that lay between the
house and the hill was weedless; the windows that looked
out on it were curtained heavily with net and velveteen.
The front of the house was where appearances were kept
up. At the back a cobbled yard, with a hay-barn and out-
houses, and a feed shed where potatoes and swill were
boiled, was less tidy. A porch in need of repair led to
sculleries and kitchen.

Weeding a field of mangolds that ran to the edge of the
cliffs, Hiney heard in the distance the engine of the post
van, and knew by the direction it came from that the van
was on its way to the farmhouse. Would an abrupt, buff-
enveloped notice announce the withdrawal of the tillage
grant? Or was there at last a communication from the

Appeal Commissioners? Sunshine warmed Hiney's thin shoulders and his head as he bent over the mangolds, the impassive solemnity of his countenance unaffected by speculation. His waistcoat hung loosely; his collarless shirt was held at the neck by a stud. More likely it was the bill for the diesel that brought the post van down the avenue, he guessed.

The old man was visited in his bedroom by Mrs Colleary. She spoke to him about the weather, reporting that it was a brightly sunny morning. But it was always uncertain whether or not he comprehended what was related to him, and this morning he gave no sign that he did. The old man's age was as mysterious as his relationship to the family; he was perhaps ninety-four or -five. Mrs Colleary visited him first thing every morning to make sure he was all right.

Maura Brigid fried bacon in the kitchen. She had set the table the night before, the last to leave the kitchen, as she always was. She pushed the bacon to one side of the pan and dropped slices of griddle bread into the fat. She heard her brother's footsteps in the yard, and for an instant imagined his slow walk and his wide, well-shaved face, his dark hair brushed flat on either side of its parting, his lips set dourly, his blue eyes expressionless. Work was what Hiney thought about, work that had been completed, work that had yet to be done. His life was the fields, and his tractor, and the weather.

The letter that had arrived lay on the stone floor of the scullery passage, just inside the door from the yard. When there was a letter the postman opened the back door and placed it on the passage floor, propped against the wall, since there was no letterbox and nowhere else to put it. Entering the house, Hiney picked up the communication that had just been delivered. It was not the bill for the diesel, nor was it about the tillage grant, nor the appeal that had been lodged with the tax commissioners. It was a white envelope, addressed in a sloping hand to Maura Brigid.

Hiney was curious about it. He turned the envelope over, but nothing was written on the back.

In the kitchen Mrs Colleary said she thought the old man would get up today. She always knew if he intended to get up when she visited him first thing. The anticipation of his intentions might have shown as a glimpse in his eyes or in some variation of the sound he emitted when she spoke to him: she had no idea how the impression was conveyed, only that she received it.

'I have an egg ready to fry for him,' Maura Brigid said, that being what the old man had for breakfast. Bacon he couldn't manage.

Hiney placed the letter on the table beside his sister's knife and fork. He sat where he always sat, on the chair that had been his father's in his lifetime. 'Move into his place, Hiney,' Mrs Colleary had said a few weeks after her husband's death in 1969, when Hiney was still a boy.

'Did Paídín bring a letter?' Mrs Colleary did not question the delivery of a letter since the letter was clearly there and could have arrived by no other means than with the postman: her query was her way of expressing surprise. She could see that the letter was a personal one, and from where she stood she could see it was addressed to her daughter.

Maura Brigid, having placed three plates of food on the table, sat down herself. Mrs Colleary poured the tea. Maura Brigid examined the envelope much as her brother had done. She did not recognise the handwriting.

Dear Mrs Lawless, I am writing to you from my conscience. There is repentance in Michael, that's all I'm writing to say to you. There is sorrow in him also, left behind after the death. Poor Michael is tormented in his heart over the way he was tempted and the sin there was. He told me more times than once that he would endeavour to make recompense to you for the pain he inflicted on you. I am writing to advise you to pray to Our Lady for guidance at this time in your life. I am asking you to recollect the forgiveness She displayed in Her Own Life.

(176)

'It's from Father Mehegan,' Maura Brigid said, 'the priest that did the funeral.'

She handed the letter to her mother because all letters that came to the farm were read in that general way. Mrs Colleary noted without comment what Father Mehegan had written. Hiney read the letter in silence also.

'I hear him on the stairs,' Mrs Colleary said. A few moments later the old man entered the kitchen, his shirt not yet buttoned, his trousers hitched up with ragged braces. A vest that had been drained of its whiteness through washing was exposed, its two buttons not fastened either. He sat down in his usual place to await his breakfast. Maura Brigid rose to fry his egg.

'Is he off the hunger strike yet?' the old man enquired, lost in a confusion that evoked for him a distant past. 'Will MacSwiney go to the end, Hiney?'

'He will.' Hiney nodded in his solemn way. Indulging such dislocation of time was not unusual in the farmhouse.

'I was saying he would myself.'

Michael does not know I'm writing to you, the priest's letter ended. *That's in confidence between us.* It was three years since Michael Lawless and Bernadette had run off in the middle of a July night. Maura Brigid had been married for six months at the time and no particular lack of accord between husband and wife had warned of what was to occur. No hint as to the direction of her affections had ever slipped from Bernadette. No note had been left behind.

'Isn't it a terrible thing, Hiney, that they'd let poor Mac-Swiney go to the end?'

'It is all right.'

'I'd say they'd pay the price of it.'

'I'd say they would.'

Hiney folded the letter and returned it to its envelope. Bernadette had died of an internal infection; she'd been two days in hospital. A message had come to them through their own priest, Father Brennan, from a parish more than sixty miles away. They had not known that Bernadette and Michael Lawless had been living there. After their flight the two had not been spoken of.

'I put my faith in Collins to this day,' the old man said. 'Won't Collins have a word to say when Terry MacSwiney goes?'

Hiney nodded, and so did Mrs Colleary. It was she who had led the silence in the house, her anger and her pain eventually becoming creased into her features. She had offered Maura Brigid no comfort. That Lawless had shattered the lives of both her daughters was how she registered what had occurred. Nor was it any consolation that she had never liked Michael Lawless, believing at the time of his marriage to Maura Brigid that he was after what he could extract to his advantage from the farm, while comfortably living as a member of the household. His running away might have seemed to disprove such an intention, but not for Mrs Colleary. In the humiliation of the scandal there was little room for reason, and no desire to pursue it. The Collearys, and the family Mrs Colleary had come from herself, were well known and well respected in the neighbourhood. They farmed their land, they did not miss mass, there had never been talk of debts to shopkeepers or supply merchants. 'I would see Lawless hung,' Mrs Colleary had said, the last time she mentioned her son-in-law's name.

Maura Brigid tilted the frying-pan and spooned fat on to the yolk of the egg. She wondered if Bernadette had been pregnant. Was that the cause of it, something going wrong inside her? At the funeral no details had been given because none had been asked for. Still wondering, she completed the frying of the old man's egg and scooped it on to a plate. She remembered playing in the yard when she and Bernadette were children, and Bernadette's doll being carried off to a hay-barn by one of the sheepdogs, and Bernadette crying. Sawdust had come out of the doll because the dog's tooth had pierced one of its legs. Peggy it had been called.

'Are you out in the fields, Hiney?' the old man enquired, returning from his travels through remembered time. 'Will I lend you a hand?'

'I'm weeding the mangolds.'

'I'll come out so.'

The old man cut his egg into quarters. He removed the centre of a slice of bread and soaked some of the fat on his plate into it. He spooned sugar into his tea.

'I'm at the bottom of the cliff field,' Hiney said.

'It's a fine day for the cliff field.'

No more was said about the priest's letter. No more was necessary. The silence it had been broken—that had been broken also by Bernadette's death—would knit together and be as it had been before. Nothing would be said to Father Brennan. The mass for Bernadette had been offered in the distant town, which was where she would now lie for ever, well separated from the family she had disgraced. No one outside the farmhouse had been told about her death. No one need know, and no one would ask. After Father Brenann had conveyed the message, he had gone quickly away, and they knew he would remain silent on the subject.

Hiney spread sugar on to a piece of buttered bread. He was five years older than the sister who had married Michael Lawless, and older by another three than Bernadette. When they were younger he had looked after them, once lying in wait for the two boys who had taken to following them along the road on their way home from school. While he'd cuffed the boys and threatened them with worse Maura Brigid had been demure but Bernadette had laughed. The boys would never have bothered them if Bernadette hadn't encouraged them in the first place.

Mrs Colleary wondered if Lawless had been as bad to Bernadette as he had been to Maura Brigid. That thought had just come into her mind, suggested somehow by the priest's letter. A man who'd desert a wife would have other sins up his sleeve, other punishments to mete out before he'd be finished. That had never occurred to her before, not even on the day of the funeral. God's anger had been assuaged was what she'd thought, wiping her eyes with a sleeve of her black mourning coat.

Maura Brigid wanted to read the letter again, but did not do so. Occasionally during her marriage she had woken up in the middle of the night to find her husband not beside her, and when she'd asked him the next morning he'd said he'd gone out for a walk because he couldn't sleep. When they'd watched television in the kitchen he usually sat next to Bernadette, though not in any noticeable way at the time. It was the brevity of the marriage, the way it was still something new, with people still coming up to both of them after mass to give them good wishes, that Maura Brigid hadn't been able to get out of her mind.

It was not Sunday, the old man was thinking. He knew it wasn't because she'd have reminded him, when she came into his bedroom, to put on different clothes. If it was a Sunday he'd be on the way to mass now, sitting in the back of the car with the girl.

'They say a man'd be fit for nothing,' he said, 'after a hunger strike.'

*

Four months later Michael Lawless returned. It was September then, the shortening days pleasantly mild, the smell of the season in the woods and the fields. In the twilight of an evening Maura Brigid's husband advanced cautiously up the avenue on a bicycle. He dismounted before he came within sight of the house and wheeled the bicycle on to the grass verge. He leaned it against the wire of the avenue fence and continued on foot.

In the yard the sheepdogs barked. They licked the hand he held out to them from the shadows where he stood. Ignoring their noise, Hiney emerged from an outhouse with a new shaft fitted into a spade. He passed through the yard, and the sheepdogs ran after him. Ten minutes later Mrs Colleary came out of the house and scattered feed for the fowls.

'Hullo, Maura Brigid,' Lawless whispered when his wife appeared later still that evening. 'Shh, don't call out,' he begged when her hand went up to her mouth to stifle a cry. 'I'm sorry I frightened you, Maura Brigid.'

He'd stepped out of the shadows and she'd seen the movement from the corner of her eye. She'd only recognised him when she turned her head and even then she had to peer. But when her eyes grew accustomed to the gloom she saw her husband clearly: the broad face and the reddish hair combed and parted, the collar and tie, the dark serge suit, its trouser ends held tidily in place with bicycle-clips.

'I've something I want to say to you, Maura Brigid.' He reached for her arm and gently guided her into the barn where the summer's hay was stacked. 'It wasn't my fault she died, Maura Brigid. She had an infection like anyone can have.'

'I don't want to talk to you. I don't know what you're doing here.'

'Maura Brigid—'

'Let go of my arm or I'll shout out.'

'Don't shout out, Maura Brigid. Please now. I'm sorry about everything that happened.'

'It's too late to be sorry now. You've no right to be here.'

'I only want to talk to you. I cycled the whole sixty miles of it.'

'We're troubled enough without you coming here.'

'I want to be with you, Maura Brigid.'

'What are you talking about?' She whispered, staring at him. She felt stupid, as though she had failed to comprehend what had been said to her, or had misunderstood it. She'd been on her way to the feed house to make sure the fire under the swill was damped down for the night, and the sudden presence of her husband both confused and alarmed her. She felt as she often did in a dream, plunged without warning into unreality, unable to escape.

'I want it to be like it was,' he said. 'I feel that way about you, Maura Brigid.'

'I'm going in now. Take your hand off of my arm and let me go. Don't ever come back here.'

'It was never right, Maura Brigid. We were never at ease, Bernadette and myself.' He paused, as though expecting a response. When none came he said: 'I wasn't the father.'

'Oh, my God!'

'Bernadette was that way. She led me a dance, Maura Brigid.'

Maura Brigid pulled her arm out of his grasp and ran across the yard. In the scullery passage she bolted the back door behind her. She didn't enter the kitchen but went straight up to her bedroom. She couldn't have faced her mother and Hiney, and they'd have known at once by the sight of her that something was the matter. They'd have asked her questions and she'd have told them in the end. Her mother would have sat there, tight-lipped. She knew, without even having to think, that the infection Bernadette had suffered had been due to an effort to prevent the birth. The nuns at the convent had called Bernadette wild.

'Dear Mother of God, help me,' Maura Brigid pleaded in her room, her voice distorted by agitation and tears she could no longer stifle. At the funeral she'd known he was trying to talk to her. She'd seen him looking at her, as though begging for mercy, but they'd driven straight off afterwards, not even stopping in a café for a cup of tea. Going away like that was what Hiney and her mother wanted. They'd hardly said thank you to the priest.

She mumbled through her rosary, sitting on the edge of the bed, the beads between her fingers. The first time she'd ever seen him he'd been a boy at the Christian Brothers', much quieter, more solitary, than the other boys. 'Who's that fellow with his eye on you?' Bernadette had said. He'd begun to turn up at the farm, asking Hiney for work, coming on a bicycle, as he had tonight. He'd done jobs for Hiney. He was better than Hiney at mending things.

Maura Brigid crossed to the window and slightly pulled aside the edge of the curtain. She had not yet turned on the light, fearful in case he was watching. Her room looked out over the gravel at the front of the house, and just for a moment she imagined she saw the movement of a figure on the avenue. 'Would you marry me?' was what he'd said. 'Am I good enough for you?'

She reached in among the curtains and pulled the blind down, separating herself further from what lay outside. She still did not light the room, but undressed in the darkness and crept into the bed she had shared with him. Her tears began again, a sobbing that was too soft for anyone passing by on the landing to hear.

*

The last of the potatoes were lifted. The old man and Maura Brigid and Mrs Colleary helped Hiney with them, and then Hiney ploughed the two potato fields. 'Is Lawless back?' the old man asked out of the blue, returning to the house with Maura Brigid and her mother.

When the old man walked he became bent, which made him seem even smaller. But he moved quickly, and would have been swifter over the stubble they crossed had he not slackened his pace in order to converse. His motion was a sideways one, the left shoulder hunched upwards and preceding the right, his grizzled head bent into his chest. 'Sure, a woman would want the man she has,' he remarked. 'Sure, why wouldn't she?'

Mrs Colleary ignored what he said, but Maura Brigid knew he must have seen her husband. He sometimes went wandering about the hill just before nightfall, setting snares. He would have looked down and recognised the familiar figure in the distance. His eyes were particularly sharp.

(183)

'Amn't I right, Maura Brigid?'

As though humouring him, she agreed that he was, and her mother paid no heed. Even if he'd stated that he'd spoken to her husband it wouldn't have mattered. Neither her mother nor Hiney would have placed any credence in the claim.

'He'll be a help for poor Hiney,' the old man said. 'It's hard going for Hiney sometimes.'

Maura Brigid knew she could write to the priest with a message for her husband. She could say she forgave him and was prepared to have him back. Whenever she thought about what he'd said concerning Bernadette, she had to repress her tears. When she'd known him well he'd never been untruthful. 'What d'you say that for?' Bernadette had crossly reprimanded her when she'd told Hiney that the boys who followed them on the road were a nuisance. Her sister's mood was quite different when she was scolded by the nuns: repentantly she would cast her eyes down. 'Sure, it was only a bit of fun, Sister,' she'd say, and probably she'd have made the same excuse to the man she'd led a dance. 'It won't happen again,' Maura Brigid could imagine her saying after she'd got pregnant with someone else. She had the ability to twist people round her little finger—their mother and Hiney and the old man, the nuns, someone in a shop she was bargaining with. She could wheedle her way with anyone.

'Leave off about him,' Mrs Colleary said snappishly when the old man again mentioned Michael Lawless. 'Don't speak that name, d'you hear?'

They reached the yard and for a moment Maura Brigid thought he might be there, hiding in the hay-barn until darkness came. She imagined his tidy hair and clothes. She remembered the strength of his arms when he put them around her, and the particular smell he had, a brackeny smell with a trace of tobacco in it. It had never occurred to her to say to herself that Bernadette wouldn't change just because she ran off with someone, just because she'd disgraced a whole family. She'd been the apple of their father's eye, and of their mother's until the scandal, and Hiney's favourite, and the old man's. She had been turned into a sinful woman by a man you couldn't mention: that was how they saw it.

Later that evening, when Maura Brigid crossed the yard to damp down the swill fire, no voice whispered her name. Later still, after she'd drawn down the blinds in her bedroom, she realised that her husband would not return unless she summoned him. He had come to make a case for his remorse; the priest had written from his conscience. Unless she chose to, she would hear no more from either of them.

*

Dear Father Mehegan, she wrote. *Thanks for writing to me. Would you tell Michael I will meet him halfway, in Cappoquin one Friday. Tell him I understand what he was saying to me.*

She addressed the envelope, but did not send the letter. She kept it in a drawer in her bedroom, saying she would post it the next Friday she went in to do the shopping. After that, she would be on the watch for a reply, ready to collect it from the scullery passage before Hiney found it. She'd drive on to Cappoquin on the Friday they arranged, making sure she put more petrol in the car, so that Hiney wouldn't notice how much had been used. They'd sit in the car in a car park.

'You'd need the fellow's assistance, Hiney,' the old man said. 'It's understandable you would.'

The old man sometimes sat in the dining-room, which was nowadays never used, under the impression that a land steward called Mahaffy was about to call to see him. Effortlessly he had created a world made up of random details from the past, and had peopled it as he wished. No one on the farm had ever heard of the land steward,

(185)

Mahaffy. Terence MacSwiney, Mayor of Cork, had died on his hunger strike sixty-seven years ago.

'Ah, don't be silly now,' Hiney said when the assistance of Michael Lawless was referred to, Hiney as keen as his mother that the name should not be mentioned. The scandal Maura Brigid had inflicted on the family by bringing a scoundrel to the farm was too recent and too painful to be permitted in an old man's silliness. 'That man didn't come back,' Hiney shouted in the kitchen. 'D'you understand that now? He's gone for good.'

But the old man insisted. Michael Lawless had come back up the avenue on a bicycle. The sheepdogs had barked when he walked into the yard. 'We'll ask him about it when we see him,' the old man said. 'We'll ask him wasn't I right.'

All of it was her fault, Maura Brigid could feel her mother and Hiney thinking. If she had not married the man Bernadette would not have been ruined. Bernadette would still be alive. It was her fault that a scoundrel had come and gone, doing the worst that could be done to two sisters, duping them.

'He did come back,' she said. 'A while after the funeral he came back.'

She was on her feet when she spoke, giving them their food, as so often she did. She had fried chops and mashed turnips, and tumbled a saucepan of potatoes on to a sheet of newspaper, which would become accumulated with peelings as the meal progressed. Chops or fried steak, fish or boiled bacon, frozen peas or turnips or cabbage, and potatoes: that was the food she cooked and served for the main meal they ate every day. At half-past twelve she placed the newspaper on the centre of the table. At a quarter-past one she made tea. She and her mother washed up afterwards.

'What are you talking about?' Hiney said. 'Lawless never came back here.'

'He came back and told me Bernadette was pregnant, only it wasn't his child. She tried to get rid of it.'

(186)

Mrs Colleary crossed herself. Hiney's solemn face was unusually animated. 'That's a bloody lie,' he said.

'He couldn't control her, Hiney. She was like she always was.'

The old man asked them what they were talking about, something he rarely did. Nobody answered him. Mrs Colleary said:

'He never told the truth.'

'Never in his life,' Hiney agreed with harsh vigour. 'We all know the kind Lawless is.'

'You were always taken in, Maura Brigid. You were always soft.'

She knew that if she began to cry she wouldn't be able to stop. But the tears she repressed kept making her blink and she turned her head away. They were the same kind, she and the man who had married her. They'd been companions the way he and her sister had never been, you could tell that from how he spoke of Bernadette. Bernadette had hurt him, too.

'It's bad enough the way things are,' Hiney insisted. 'Keep it to yourself he came back.'

When he'd first come to the farm to court her they used to walk in the woods and climb down the cliffs to the strand. He'd always been shy, only taking her hand and clumsily kissing her. After they were married there had never been any question about his not coming on to the farm: Hiney needed the assistance and Michael was employed on the roads, work he didn't like. She remembered how she had wondered about a baby being born, her own baby and his on the farm.

'There were girls at the convent,' she said, 'used call Bernadette a hooer.'

Again Mrs Colleary crossed herself. She drew her breath in and held it for a moment. Her eyes were closed.

'What's the matter with you, Maura Brigid?' Hiney asked quietly.

'On account of the way she enticed the Christian Brothers' boys. That's why they called her that.'

'If Lawless comes back here I'll take a gun to him,' Hiney said, still without raising his voice. He stood up, leaving his food untouched. He walked from the kitchen, and the sheepdogs who'd been lying under the table followed him.

'You shouldn't ever have married that man,' Mrs Colleary said, opening her eyes. Her face had gone pale. Her mouth was pulled down, as though in weariness, as though she couldn't be bothered arranging it differently any more. 'I told you at the time he was rotten to the core.'

Maura Brigid did not reply. It was not true to say the man she'd married had never told the truth in his life. He was weak, and she was weak herself: she didn't possess the courage to leave the farm, to run off with him as Bernadette had. She would be frightened, and she was well-behaved by nature. He hadn't come to the farm to ask her to run off, that wasn't his way; he'd come to the farm to tell her something, to see how she might feel about it. The priest had written to beg that there might be forgiveness.

'I'll go down and help them in the fields,' the old man said, finishing the cup of tea he'd poured himself. 'I think the pair of them are digging out ditches.'

The letter she had written would remain in her drawer. In the old man's senile fantasy her husband would continue to work on the cliff land, to cut timber in the woods, and help her with the Friday shopping, as he had once upon a time. In the old man's senile fantasy there was repentance, and forgiveness.

'Those are terrible things you said,' her mother whispered, still sitting at the table, her chop congealed in its fat. 'Enough has happened to us without that.'

When the old man died there would be no more talk of her husband, and when her mother died the task of making Hiney's bed would be hers, and there would only be Hiney and herself to cook for. Hiney would never marry because all Hiney was interested in was work. People would be sorry for her, but they would always say it was her foolishness that had dragged the family through disgrace, her fault for marrying a scoundrel. In the farmhouse and the neighbourhood that was the person she had become.

Children of the Headmaster

The greater part of the house was shabby from use. The white paintwork of the corridors and the rooms had been chipped and soiled. Generations of feet had clattered against skirting-boards; fingers had darkened an area around door-handles; shoulders had worn patches on walls. The part of the house known as 'Private Side' was in better decorative repair, this being the wing occupied by the Headmaster's family—six people in contrast to the hundred and twenty-odd boys who comprised the boarding-school. In the holidays the house regained its unity, and the Headmaster's children were together again. Jonathan returned to his own room from whichever dormitory he had occupied during the term, and was glad to do so. Margery, Georgina and Harriet explored the forbidden territory of the last few months.

Mr Arbuary, the children's father, had bought the house with money left to his wife in a will. On learning about the legacy, the Arbuarys returned to England from Hong Kong, where Mr Arbuary had been a police officer. The legacy allowed them the first chance in their married life to 'do something', as they put it privately to one another. In those days Mrs Arbuary was on for anything, but had since developed a nervous condition that drained her energy. Only the two older children were born before the family's return to England, Jonathan and Margery.

Mr Arbuary was a tall, bespectacled man with a sandy moustache, increasing in stoutness as the years advanced, and balding at about the same rate. His wife, once stout herself, was skin and bone due to her nervous complaint, with lank fair hair and eyes as darting as a rabbit's. Their combination had produced children who were physically like neither of them except that they were blue-eyed and were not sallow-skinned or black-haired. Yet among the children there was a distinct family resemblance: a longish face in which the features were cut with a precision that lent them an aristocratic air, a tendency to stare. Margery and Georgina, when they were ten and nine respectively, were pretty. Harriet, at eight, gave little indication of how she would be in the future. Jonathan, the oldest, had already been told by the Classics master, Old Mudger, that he was not without good looks.

The house that was both school and home was on the outskirts of a seaside town, at the end of a brief, hydrangea-laden drive. In purchasing it and deciding to start a boarding-school, Mr Arbuary did his homework carefully. He recalled his own schooldays and all that had gone with them in the name of education and 'older values'. He believed in older values. At a time when the country he returned to appeared to be in the hands of football hooligans and trade unionists such values surely needed to be re-established, and when he thought about them Mr Arbuary was glad he had decided to invest his wife's legacy in a preparatory school rather than an hotel, which had been an alternative. He sought the assistance of an old schoolfellow who had spent the intervening years in the preparatory-school world and was familiar with the ropes. This was the Classics master whom generations of boys came to know as Old Mudger when Mr Arbuary had enticed him to the new establishment. Mrs Arbuary—presenting in those days a motherly front—took on the responsibility of catering and care of the boys' health. The boarding-school began with three pupils, increasing its intake slowly at first, later accelerating.

'Now,' Georgina prompted on the first afternoon of the Easter holidays in 1988. 'Anything good?'

The furniture-room, in the attics above the private part of the house, was the children's secret place. They crouched among the stored furniture that, ten years ago, their mother had inherited with the legacy. That morning the boys had gone, by car mostly, a few by train. In contrast to the bustle and the rush there'd been, the house was as silent as a tomb.

'Nothing much,' Jonathan said. 'Really.'

'Must have been *something*,' Harriet insisted.

Jonathan said that the winter term in the other side of the house had been bitterly cold. Everyone had chilblains. He recounted the itching of his own, and the huddling around the day-room fire, and his poor showing at algebra, geometry and Latin. His sisters were not much impressed. He said:

'Half Starving got hauled up. He nearly got the sack.'

Three times a year Jonathan brought to his sisters the excitement of the world they were protected from, for it was one of the Headmaster's rules that family life and school life should in no way impinge upon one another. The girls heard the great waves of noise and silence that came whenever the whole school congregated, a burst of general laughter sometimes, a master's voice raised to address the ranks of boys at hand-inspection times in the hall, the chatter of milk-and-biscuits time. They saw, from the high windows of the house, the boys in their games clothes setting off for the playing-fields. Sometimes, when an emergency arose, a senior boy would cross to Private Side to summon their father. He would glance at the three girls with curiosity, and they at him. On Sundays the girls came closer to the school, walking to church with their mother and the undermatron, Miss Mainwaring, behind the long crocodile of boys, and sitting five pews behind them.

'Why did Half Starving get hauled up?' Georgina asked.

The junior master was called Half Starving because of his unhealthily pallid appearance. As such, he had been known to the girls ever since their brother had passed the nickname on. By now they'd forgotten his real name.

'Because of something he said to Haxby,' Jonathan said. At lunch one day Half Starving had asked Haxby what the joke was, since the whole table had begun to snigger. 'No joke, sir,' Haxby replied, and Half Starving said: 'What age are you, Haxby?' When Haxby said nine, Half Starving said he'd never seen a boy of nine with grey hair before.

Georgina giggled, and so did Harriet. Margery said: 'What happened then?'

'Another boy said that wasn't a very nice thing to say because Haxby couldn't help his hair. The boy—Temple, I think it was—said it was a personal remark, and Half Starving said he hadn't meant to make a personal remark. Then he asked Haxby if he'd ever heard of the Elephant Man.'

'The *what?*' Harriet stared at Jonathan with her mouth open, the way her father said she never in any circumstances whatsoever should.

'A man in a peepshow who looked like an elephant. Someone asked Half Starving if Haxby reminded him of this elephant person and Half Starving said the elephant person had had grey hair when he was a boy also. Then someone said Haxby might be good in a peepshow and Half Starving asked Haxby if travelling about sounded like a life he'd enjoy. Everyone laughed and afterwards Cuthbert hauled Half Starving up because of the noise.'

Cuthbert was the school's nickname for the children's father. Jonathan had felt embarrassed about using it to his sisters at first, but he'd got over that years ago. For his own part, Mr Arbuary liked simply to be known as 'the Headmaster'.

'I think I know which Haxby is,' Margery said. 'Funny-looking fish. All the same, I doubt anyone would pay to see him in a peepshow. Anything else?'

'Spence II puked in the dorm, first night of term. All the mint chocs he brought back and something that looked like turnips. Mange-coloured.'

'Ugh!' Harriet said.

Baddle, Thompson-Wright and Wardle had been caned for giving cheek. Thompson-Wright had blubbed, the others hadn't. The piano master had been seen on the promenade with one of the maids, Reene.

Jonathan's sisters were interested in that. The piano master's head sloped at an angle from his shoulders. He dressed like an undertaker and did not strike the girls as the kind to take women on to the promenade.

'Who saw them?' Georgina asked.

'Pomeroy when he was going for Old Mudger's tobacco.'

'I don't like to think of it,' Margery said. 'Isn't the piano master meant to smell?'

Jonathan said the piano master himself didn't smell: more likely it was his clothes. 'Something gets singed when it's ironed.'

'A vest,' Harriet suggested.

'I don't know what it is.'

'I think a vest probably.'

Soon after that the children left the furniture-room. There was tea in the dining-room then, a daily ritual in the holidays, the long mahogany table with curved ends laid for six. The Headmaster liked it to be so. He liked Mrs Arbuary to make sandwiches: sardine and egg in winter, in summer cucumber and tomato. The Headmaster's favourite cake was fruitcake, so there was fruitcake as well.

The dining-room was a darkish room, wallpaper in crimson and black stripes combining with two sets of curtains— velvet, in crimson also, and net—to set this sombre tone. The grained paintwork was the same deep brown as the curlicued sideboard, on which were arrayed the silver tea-pots and water-jugs, the gravy boats and loving cups, that

Mrs Arbuary had inherited at the same time as the furniture and her legacy. It was an aunt who had died.

The children took their places at the table. Mrs Arbuary poured tea. The maid who had been observed in the piano master's company brought in a plate of buttered toast. She and the other domestic staff—Monica and Mrs Hodge and Mrs Hodge's husband, who was the general handyman—continued to come daily to the school during the holidays, but for much shorter hours. That was the only way the Arbuarys could keep them.

'Thank you, Reene,' the Headmaster said, and the girls began to giggle, thinking about the piano master. He was a man who had never earned a nickname, and it was a tradition at the school not ever to employ his surname. Since Jonathan had passed that fact on to his sisters they had not, even in their thoughts, done so either.

'Well,' the Headmaster said next. 'We are *en famille*.'

Mrs Arbuary, who rarely instigated conversations and only occasionally contributed to them, did not do so now. She smeared raspberry jam on a finger of toast and raised it to her lips. The school was a triumph for her husband after a lustreless career in Hong Kong, but it had brought her low. Being answerable to often grumpy parents, organising a kitchen and taking responsibility during epidemics did not suit her nature. She had been happier before.

'A good term,' the Headmaster said. 'I think we might compliment ourselves on a successful term. Eh, Jonathan?'

'I suppose so.' The tone was less ungracious than the sentiment. Jonathan drummed as much cheeriness into it as he could muster, yet felt the opinion must be expressed honestly in those words. He had no idea if the term had been successful or not; he supposed so if his father claimed so.

'A single defeat on the hockey field,' the Headmaster reminded him. 'And your own report's not half bad, old chap.'

'Georgina got a frightful one,' Harriet said.

The girls attended a day school in the town, St Beatrice's. When the time came they would be sent away to boarding-school, but at the preparatory stage funds could not be stretched. Once, years ago, Mrs Arbuary had suggested that the girls might receive their preparatory education at her husband's school, but this was before she appreciated that the older values did not permit this.

'Georgina,' Mr Arbuary said, in his headmaster's rather than his father's voice, 'has much to mend this holidays. So, too, has Harriet.'

'My report wasn't too awful,' Harriet insisted in an unconvincing mutter meant mainly for herself.

'Speak clearly if you wish to be heard, Harriet. Reports are written to be assessed by parents. I would remind you of that.'

'I only meant—'

'You are a chatterbox, Harriet. What should be placed on chatterboxes?'

'Lids.'

'Precisely so.'

A silence fell around the table. Mrs Arbuary cut the fruitcake. The Headmaster passed his cup for more tea. Eventually he said:

'It is always a pity, I think, when Easter is as early as it is this year.'

He gave no reason for this view, but elicited nonetheless a general response—murmurs of agreement, nods. Neither Mrs Arbuary nor the children minded when Easter fell, but in the dining-room responses were required.

*

Increasingly, there was much that Jonathan did not pass on to his sisters. Mrs Arbuary's nickname, for instance, was the Hen because a boy called McAtters had said she was like a hen whose feathers had been drenched in a shower of rain—a reference to what McAtters, and others, considered to be a feeble manner. It had been noticed that Mrs Arbuary feared not just her husband, but Miss Mainwaring the undermatron and most of the assistant masters. It had been noticed that she played obsessively with one of her forefingers whenever parents engaged her in conversation. A boy called Windercrank said that once when she looked up from a flowerbed she was weeding there were soil-stained tears on her cheeks.

Jonathan had not passed on to his sisters the news that their father was generally despised. It had been easier to tell them about Old Mudger, how he sometimes came into the dorm if a boy had been sent to bed before prep because Miss Mainwaring thought he was looking peaky. 'Well, friendly, I suppose,' Jonathan had explained to Georgina and Harriet. 'Anyway, that's what we call it. Friendly.' Margery had an inkling: he'd seen it in her eyes. All three of them had laughed over the Mudger being friendly, Georgina and Harriet knowing it was funny because no one would particularly want to be friendly with their father's old schoolfellow. But they wouldn't laugh—nor would he—if he told them their mother was called the Hen. They wouldn't laugh if he told them their father was scorned for his pomposity, and mocked behind his back as a fearsome figure of fun.

And now—these Easter holidays—there was something else. A boy Jonathan did not like, who was a year older than he was, called Tottle, had sent a message to Margery. All term he had been bothering Jonathan with his messages, and Jonathan had explained that because of the Headmaster's rules he would have no opportunity to deliver one until the holidays. Tottle had doubted his trustworthiness in the matter, and two days before the term ended he pushed him into a corner in the lavatories and rammed his fist into Jonathan's stomach. He kept it there, pressing very hard, until Jonathan promised that he would deliver the message to Margery as soon as possible in the holidays. When Jonathan had first been a pupil in his father's school, when he was seven, no one had even seemed to notice his sisters, but during the last year or so—because they were older, he supposed—all that had changed. Boys he wasn't friends with asked questions about them, boys who'd never spoken to him before. Once, at lunch, Half Starving had warned a boy not to speak like that about the Headmaster's daughters. 'Fancy them yourself, sir?' someone else shouted down the table, and Half Starving went red, the way he always did when matters got out of hand.

'Tell her to meet me, first night of term,' Tottle's message was. 'Round by the carpentry hut. Seven.'

Tottle claimed that he had looked round and smiled at Margery in church. The third Sunday he'd done it she'd smiled back. Without any evidence to the contrary, Jonathan had denied that. 'You bloody little tit,' Tottle snapped, driving his fist further into Jonathan's stomach, hurting him considerably.

Tottle was due to leave at the end of next term, but Jonathan guessed that after Tottle there would be someone else, and that soon there would be messages for Georgina as well as Margery, and later for Harriet. He wouldn't have to be involved in that because he'd have left himself by then, but some other means of communication would be found, through Reene or Mrs Hodge or Hodge. Jonathan hated the thought of that; he hated his sisters being at the receiving end of dormitory coarseness. In the darkness there'd been guffaws when the unclothing of Reene by the piano master had been mooted—and sly tittering which he'd easily joined in himself. Not that he'd even believed Pomeroy when he said he'd seen them on the promenade. Pomeroy didn't often tell the truth.

But it wasn't the pursuit of his sisters that worried Jonathan most: it was what they would learn by the carpentry shed or in the seclusion of the hydrangeas. It stood to reason that their pursuers would let things slip. 'Cuthbert,' Tottle would say, and Margery would laugh, saying she knew her father was called Cuthbert. Then, bit by bit, on similar occasions, all the rest of it would tumble out. You giggled when the Hen was imitated, the stutter she'd developed, her agitated playing with a forefinger. Cuthbert's walk was imitated, his catchphrases concerning the older values repeated in self-important tones. 'Bad taste' another catchphrase was. When the pomposity was laid aside and severity took its place he punished ruthlessly, his own appointed source of justice. When the rules were broken he showed no mercy. Other people's fathers were businessmen or doctors, Bakinghouse's was a deep-sea salvage operator. No one mentioned what they were like; no one knew.

'Margery,' Jonathan said in the furniture-room when Georgina and Harriet were receiving tuition from their father. 'Margery, do you know what a boy called Tottle looks like?'

Margery went pink. 'Tottle?' she said.

'He's one of the first three leading into church. There's Reece and Greated, then usually Tottle.'

'Yes, I know Tottle,' Margery admitted, and Jonathan knew from her casual tone that what Tottle had said about Margery smiling back was true.

'Tottle sent you a message,' Jonathan said.

'What kind of a message?' She turned her head away, trying to get her face into the shadows.

'He said to meet him by the carpentry shed next term. Seven o'clock the first evening.'

'Blooming cheek!'

'You won't, will you, Margery? He made me promise I'd tell you, otherwise I wouldn't have.'

'Of course I won't.'

'Tottle's not all that nice.'

'He's not bad-looking if he's the one I'm thinking of.'

Jonathan didn't say anything. Bakinghouse's father

might turn into some kind of predator when he was at the bottom of the sea, quite different from the person Bakinghouse knew. A businessman mightn't be much liked by office people, but his family wouldn't know that either.

'Why d'you think Mummy's so nervy, Margery?'

'Nervy?'

'You know what I mean.'

Margery nodded. She didn't know why their mother was nervy, she said, sounding surprised. 'When did Tottle give you the message, Jonathan?'

'Two days before the end of term.'

Lying in bed the night before, he had made up his mind that he would pass the message on when Georgina and Harriet were occupied in one of the classrooms the next day. Best to get it over, he'd thought, and it was then that he began to wonder about their mother. He never had before, and clearly Margery hadn't either. He remembered someone saying that the Hen was probably the way she was because of Cuthbert. 'Poor old Hen,' a voice in the dorm had sympathised.

'Don't tell the others,' Margery pleaded. 'Please.'

'Of course not.'

Their mother overheard things in the laundry room when boys came for next week's sheet and clean pyjamas, and in the hall when she gave out the milk. As someone once said, it was easy to forget the poor old Hen was there.

'Don't meet him, Margery.'

'I told you I wouldn't.'

'Tottle's got a thing on you.'

Again Margery reddened. She told her brother not to be silly. Else why would Tottle want to meet her by the carpentry shed? he replied; it stood to reason. Tottle wasn't a prefect; he hadn't been made a prefect even though he was one of the oldest boys in the school. Had he been a prefect he wouldn't have been the third boy to enter the church on Sundays; he'd have led a battalion, as the five houses into which the school was divided were called. He wasn't a prefect because the Headmaster didn't consider him worthy and made no secret of the fact.

'It's nothing like that,' Margery persisted.

Jonathan didn't want to argue. He didn't even want to think about Tottle now that the message had been delivered. He changed the conversation; he asked Margery about Miss Mole, one of the mistresses who taught her, and about whom Margery was sometimes funny. But he hardly listened when she told him. It hadn't occurred to him before that Tottle was in some way attempting to avenge himself.

*

There was roast lamb for lunch. The Headmaster carved it. There was mint sauce, and carrots and mashed potatoes.

'I think we learned a thing or two this morning,' the Headmaster said. 'I hope we can compliment ourselves on that.'

Was he as bad as they said? Jonathan wondered. It was ridiculous to say he was like Mussolini, yet it had been said. 'Bully-boys are always a bit comic,' a boy called Piercey had suggested. 'Hitler. Mussolini. Cromwell. The Reverend Ian Paisley.'

'Jonathan.' His mother smiled at him, indicating that he should pass a dish to Harriet. By the end of the holidays she would be far less taut; that was always so. She and Mrs Hodge and Monica would launder blankets and clean the dormitory windows and polish the linoleum and wash down walls where it was necessary. Then all the beds had to be made and the dining-hall given a cleaning, the tables scrubbed and the serving range gone over with steel-wool. Hodge would clean the dining-hall windows because they were awkwardly placed. Crockery that had been broken during term would be replaced.

'Sorry,' Jonathan said, moving the dish of carrots towards

his youngest sister. By the end of the holidays, though still subdued and jumpy, Mrs Arbuary would be more inclined to take part in mealtime conversation. Her hands would not quiver so much.

'Mrs Salkind telephoned in the middle of our labours,' the Headmaster reported. 'Apparently the Salkinds are being posted abroad. Did you know this, Jonathan? Did Salkind say?'

Jonathan shook his head.

'Apparently to Egypt. Some business thing.'

'Did Mrs Salkind give notice?' The hopeful note in his mother's tone caught in Jonathan's imagination. With a bit of luck all the other parents might give notice also. Again and again, that very afternoon, the telephone might ring and the news would be that father after father had been posted to distant parts. The school would close.

'On the contrary,' the Headmaster replied. 'No, quite the contrary. Our Master Salkind will be flown back and forth at the expense of some manufacturing company. Heavy-duty vehicle springs, I believe it is, that pay the piper where Salkind senior is concerned. I recall correctly, Jonathan?'

'I'm afraid I don't know.'

'No cause for fear, old chap. Heavy-duty vehicle springs, if I am not wildly astray, once featured long in a conversation with the senior Salkind. Buses, lorries, military transports. Now, it seems, the good man is to instruct the Egyptians in their manufacture, or else to set up a factory, or generally to liaise. The good Mrs Salkind did not reveal.'

While speaking, the Headmaster cut the meat on his plate, adding potatoes and carrots to each forkful. He paused to eat between sentences, so that what he said came slowly from him. When the children were younger they had fidgeted during their father's mealtime dissertations. They had since learned not to.

'No, the reason for the good lady's telephone call was to enquire if Master Salkind might have extra French.'

Not wishing to listen, Jonathan thought of Tottle again. The older boy's rather big, handsome face appeared clearly in his mind, a smile slung lazily across it. He glanced at Margery, seated opposite him. Was she, too, thinking about her admirer, visualising him also? Was she wondering what it would be like to meet him as he'd suggested, what he'd say, how he'd act?

'French, apparently, is commercially *de rigueur* in Egypt, or at least in the Salkinds' corner of it.'

In the darkness of the dormitory there were confessions of desire. When one voice left off another began. Tales were told of what had been seen or heard. Intentions were declared, pretences aired.

'Though, truth to tell, I can hardly think of a reason why French should feature in any way whatsoever since the Egyptians have a perfectly good language of their own.'

The confessions of desire had to do with film stars usually, occasionally with Lady Di or Fergie, less often with Reene or Monica.

'Were you aware of that, old chap? French in Egypt?'

'No.'

'I think, you know, the good lady may have got it wrong.'

Tottle intended to try it on, and then to laugh in that way he had. He would put his big face close to Margery's, he'd put his big lips on to hers, and his hands would go all over her, just as though it wasn't real, just as though he was pretending. And later on, with someone else, it would be the same for Georgina, and for Harriet.

'But since Master Salkind's French is shaky an extra hour a week will hardly come amiss, eh?'

Everyone agreed.

*

The days of those Easter holidays went similarly by. The children of the Headmaster spent long afternoons on the grey sands that stretched beyond the shingle and the sea-front promenade. They sat in the Yew Tree Café sipping Coca-Cola and nibbling cheap biscuits. When their week's pocket-money ran out they crouched instead among the furniture of the furniture-room. Every morning Georgina and Harriet were given tuition by their father, and Jonathan and Margery read, alone in their rooms.

Tottle was not again mentioned, but as the weeks passed Jonathan found himself more and more dismayed by all that his imagination threw at him. It felt like that: as though heavy lumps of information were being lobbed in his direction, relentlessly and slowly. They dropped into the pond of his consciousness, creating little pictures. They nagged at him, and the intensity of colour in the pictures increased, and faces and expressions acquired greater distinctness.

Two nights before the holidays ended, restlessly awake, Jonathan arrived at a decision. The next afternoon he did not accompany his sisters to the sea-front and the Yew Tree Café, presenting them with the unlikely excuse that he had some history to read. He watched them set off from the window of his bedroom, delayed another twenty minutes, and then went slowly downstairs. He paused again, in doubt and trepidation, before he found the courage to knock on his father's study door. He had no idea how he might express himself.

'Yes?' the Headmaster responded.

Jonathan closed the door behind him. The study smelt, as always, of his father's pipe tobacco and a mustiness that could not be identified. Glass-paned cupboards were full of textbooks. There were supplies of chalk and geometrical instruments, globes of the world, cartridges for fountain-pens, stacks of new exercise-books, blotting-paper, pencils. His father sat behind his desk, a pipe in his mouth, the new term's time-tables spread out before him.

'Well, old chap? Come to lend a hand?'

Beyond the geniality lay the ghost of the Headmaster's

termtime self, of severity and suspicion. Pomposity wasn't what mattered most; talk of 'older values' and 'bad taste' was only tedious on its own. 'Bloody hypocrite,' some boy—neither Tottle nor Piercey—had said once. 'Nasty brute.'

'Always tricky, the summer time-tables.'

Jonathan nodded.

'Cricket's greedy,' the Headmaster said. 'Where time's concerned.'

'Yes, it is.'

His father knocked the ashes out of his pipe and drew a tin of tobacco towards him. All his life, Jonathan had been familiar with these tins: *Three Nuns* the tobacco was called, orange lettering on a creamy ground. He watched his father pressing the coiled shreds into the bowl of his pipe. His father knew: that was what Jonathan had at length deduced. His father had so determinedly separated Private Side from the school because he knew the girls must not be exposed to crudities. His father knew, but he didn't know enough. You couldn't insist there was a shutter that came down just because you pretended it did. You couldn't insist Old Mudger was a Mr Chips just because he looked like one.

'Girls out somewhere?' his father said.

'I think so.'

A match was struck, the tobacco caught. Jonathan watched it reddening, and smoke streaming from between his father's tightly clenched teeth. There was no conversation they could have. He could not mention the voices in the darkness of the dormitory, the confessions of desire, the declarations of intention. He could not tell his father he was despised for being the person he was, that boys were sorry for a woman they likened to a hen. He could not warn him of Tottle's revenge, nor suggest what lay ahead for Georgina and Harriet. Lying awake the night before, he had wanted to protect his sisters, and his mother also, because they were not to blame. And in a way he had even wanted to protect his father because he didn't know enough, because he blustered and was oppressive, and went about things stupidly.

'Well, I'd best get on, old chap,' his father said, applying himself once more to the sheets of paper that constituted the summer time-tables. The balding head was bent again. Smoke eddied about it complacently.

Jonathan went away, softly closing the study door behind him. He ran through the empty corridors of the school, and down the hydrangea drive. He ran along the sea-front, looking for his sisters.

August Saturday

'You don't remember me,' the man said.

His tone suggested a statement, not a question, but Grania did remember him. She had recognised him immediately, his face smiling above the glass he held. He was a man she had believed she would never see again. For sixteen years—since the summer of 1972—she had tried not to think about him, and for the most part had succeeded.

'Yes, I do remember you,' she said. 'Of course.'

A slice of lemon floated on the surface of what she guessed was gin and tonic; there were cubes of ice and the little bubbles that came from tonic when it was freshly poured. It wouldn't be tonic on its own; it hadn't been the other time. 'I've drunk a bit too much,' he'd said.

'I used to wonder,' he went on now, 'if ever we'd meet again. The kind of thing you wonder when you can't sleep.'

'I didn't think we would.'

'I know. But it doesn't matter, does it?'

'Of course not.'

She wondered why he had come back. She wondered how long he intended to stay. He'd be staying with the Prendergasts, she supposed, as he had been before. For sixteen years she had avoided the road on which the avenue that led to the Prendergasts' house was, the curve of the green iron railings on either side of the open gates, the unoccupied gate-lodge.

'You weren't aware that Hetty Prendergast died?' he said.

(207)

'No, I wasn't.'

'Well, she did. Two days ago.'

The conversation took place in the bar of the Tara Hotel, where Grania and her husband, Desmond, dined once a month with other couples from the tennis club—an arrangement devised by the husbands so that the wives, just for a change, wouldn't have to cook.

'You don't mind my talking to you?' the man said. 'I'm on my own again.'

'Of course I don't.'

'When I was told about the death I came on over. I've just come in from the house to have a meal with the Quiltys.'

'Tonight, you mean?'

'When they turn up.'

Quilty was a solicitor. He and his wife, Hazel, belonged to the tennis club and were usually present at the monthly dinners in the Rhett Butler Room of the Tara Hotel. The death of old Hetty Prendergast had clearly caught them unawares, and Grania could imagine Hazel Quilty sulkily refusing to cancel a long-booked babysitter in order to remain at home to cook a meal for the stranger who had arrived from England, with whom her husband presumably had business to discuss. 'We'll take him with us,' Quilty would have said in his soothing voice, and Hazel would have calmed down, as she always did when she got her way.

'Still playing tennis, Grania?'

'Pretty badly.'

'You've hardly aged, you know.'

This was so patently a lie that it wasn't worth protesting about. After the funeral of the old woman he would go away. He hadn't arrived for the other funeral, that of Mr Prendergast, which had taken place nearly ten years ago, and there wouldn't be another one because there was no other Prendergast left to die. She wondered what would happen to the house and to the couple who had looked after the old woman, driving in every Friday to shop for her. She didn't ask. She said:

'A group of us have dinner here now and again, the Quiltys too. I don't know if they told you that.'

'You mean tonight?'

'Yes.'

'No, that wasn't said.'

He smiled at her. He sipped a little gin. He had a long face, high cheekbones, greying hair brushed straight back from a sallow forehead. His blue-green eyes were steady, almost staring because he didn't blink much. She remembered the eyes particularly, now that she was again being scrutinised by them. She remembered asking who he was and being told a sort of nephew of the Prendergasts, an Englishman.

'I've often wondered about the tennis club, Grania.'

'It hasn't changed. Except that we've become the older generation.'

Desmond came up then and she introduced her companion, reminding Desmond that he'd met him before. She stumbled when she had to give him a name because she'd never known what it was. 'Prendergast,' she mumbled vaguely, not sure if he was called Prendergast or not. She'd never known that.

'Hetty died, I hear,' Desmond said.

'So I've been telling your wife. I've come over to do my stuff.'

'Well, of course.'

'The Quiltys have invited me to your dinner do.'

'You're very welcome.'

Desmond had a squashed pink face and receding hair that had years ago been reddish. As soon as he put his clothes on they became crumpled, no matter how carefully Grania ironed them. He was a man who never lost his temper, slow-moving except on a tennis court, where he was surprisingly subtle and cunning, quite unlike the person he otherwise was.

Grania moved away. Mavis Duddy insisted she owed her a drink from last time and led her to the bar, where she ordered two more Martinis. 'Who was that?' she asked, and Grania replied that the grey-haired man was someone from England, related to the Prendergasts, she wasn't entirely certain about his name. He'd come to the tennis club once, she said, an occasion when Mavis hadn't been there. 'Over for old Hetty's funeral, is he?' Mavis said and, accepting the drink, Grania agreed that that was so.

They were a set in the small town; since the time they'd been teenagers the tennis club had been the pivot of their social lives. In winter some of them played bridge or golf, others chose not to. But all of them on summer afternoons and evenings looked in at the tennis club even if, like Francie MacGuinness and the Haddons, they didn't play much any more. They shared memories, and likes and dis-likes, that had to do with the tennis club; there were photo-graphs that once in a blue moon were sentimentally mulled over; friendships had grown closer or apart. Billy Mac-Guinness had always been the same, determinedly a winner at fourteen and determinedly a winner at forty-five. Francie, who'd married him when it had seemed that he might marry Trish, was a winner also: Trish had made do with Tom Crosbie. There'd been quarrels at the tennis club: a great row in 1961 when Desmond's father had wanted to raise money for a hard court and resigned in a huff when no one agreed; and nearly ten years later there had been the quarrel between Laverty and Dr Timothy Sweeney which had resulted in both their resignations, all to do with a dispute about a roller. There were jealousies and gossip, occasionally both envy and resentment. The years had been less kind to some while favouring others; the children born to the couples of the tennis club were often compared, though rarely openly, in terms of achievement or promise. Tea was taken, supplied by the wives, on Saturday afternoons from May to September. The men supplied drinks on that one day of the week also, and even washed up the glasses. The children of the tennis club tasted their first cocktails there, Billy MacGuinness's White Ladies and Sidecars.

A handful of the tennis-club wives were best friends, and had been since their convent days: Grania and Mavis, Francie, Hazel, Trish. They trusted one another, doing so more easily now than they had when they'd been at the convent together or in the days when each of them might possibly have married one of the others' husbands. They told one another most things, confessing their errors and their blunders; they comforted and were a solace, jollying away feelings of inadequacy or guilt. Trish had worried at the convent because her breasts wouldn't grow, Hazel because her face was scrawny and her lips too thin. Francie had almost died when a lorry had knocked her off her bicycle. Mavis had agonised for months before she said yes to Oliver Duddy. As girls, they had united in their criticism of girls outside their circle; as wives they had not changed.

'I heard about that guy,' Mavis said. 'So that's what he looks like.'

That August Saturday in 1972 he'd come to the tennis club on a bicycle, in whites he had borrowed at the house where he was staying, a racquet tied with string to the crossbar. He'd told Grania afterwards that Hetty Prendergast had looked the whites out for him and had lent him the racquet as well. Hetty had mentioned the tennis club, to which she and her husband had years ago belonged themselves. 'Of course a different kind of lot these days,' she'd said. 'Like everywhere.' He'd pushed the bicycle through the gate and stood there watching a doubles game, not yet untying his racquet. 'Who on earth's that?' someone had said, and Grania approached him after about a quarter of an hour, since she was at that time the club's secretary and vaguely felt it to be her duty.

Sipping the Martini Mavis had claimed to owe her, Grania remembered the sudden turning of his profile in her direction when she spoke and then his smile. Nothing of what she subsequently planned had entered her head then; she would have been stunned by even the faintest inkling of it. 'I'm awfully sorry,' he'd said. 'I'm barging in.'

Grania had been twenty-seven then, married to Desmond for almost eight years. Now she was forty-three, and her cool brown eyes still strikingly complemented the lips that Desmond had once confessed he'd wanted to kiss ever since she was twelve. Her dark hair had been in plaits at twelve, later had been fashionably long, and now was short. She wasn't tall and had always wished she was, but at least she didn't have to slim. She hadn't become a mother yet, that Saturday afternoon when the stranger arrived at the tennis club. But she was happy, and in love with Desmond.

'Aisling's going out with some chartered accountant,' Mavis said, speaking about her daughter. 'Oliver's hopping mad.'

The Quiltys arrived. Grania watched while they joined Desmond and their dinner guest. Desmond moved to the bar to buy them drinks. Quilty—a small man who reminded Grania of a monkey—lit a cigarette. Politely, Grania transferred her attention to her friend. Why should Oliver be angry? she asked, genuinely not knowing. She could tell from Mavis's tone of voice that she was not displeased herself.

'Because he's nine years older. We had a letter from Aisling this morning. Oliver's talking about going up to have it out with her.'

'That might make it worse, actually.'

'If he mentions it will you tell him that? He listens to you, you know.'

Grania said she would. She knew Oliver Duddy would

mention it, since he always seemed to want to talk to her about things that upset him. Once upon a time, just before she'd become engaged to Desmond, he'd tried to persuade her he loved her.

'They earn a fortune,' Mavis said. 'Chartered accountants.'

Soon after that they all began to move into the Rhett Butler Room. Grania could just remember the time when the hotel had been called O'Hara's Commercial, in the days of Mr and Mrs O'Hara. It wasn't all that long ago that their sons, giving the place another face-lift as soon as they inherited it, had decided to change the name to the Tara and to give the previously numbered bedrooms titles such as Ashley's and Melanie's. The bar was known as Scarlett's Lounge. There were regular discos in Belle's Place.

'Who's that fellow with the Quiltys?' Francie Mac-Guinness asked, and Grania told her.

'He's come back for Hetty Prendergast's funeral.'

'God, I didn't know she died.'

As always, several tables had been pushed together to form a single long one in the centre of the dining-room. At it, the couples who'd been drinking in the bar sat as they wished: there was no formality. Una Carty-Carroll, Trish Crosbie's sister, was unmarried but was usually partnered on these Saturday occasions by the surveyor from the waterworks. This was so tonight. At one end of the table a place remained unoccupied: Angela, outside the circle of best friends, as Una Carty-Carroll and Mary Ann Haddon were, invariably came late. In a distant corner of the Rhett Butler Room one other couple were dining. Another table, recently occupied, was being tidied.

'I think it's Monday,' Grania said when Francie asked her when the funeral was.

She hoped he'd go away again immediately. That other Saturday he'd said he found it appallingly dull at the Prendergasts', a call of duty, no reason in the world why he should ever return. His reassurances had in a way been neither here nor there at the time, but afterwards of course she'd recalled them. Afterwards, many times, she'd strained to establish every single word of the conversation they'd had.

'D'you remember poor old Hetty,' Francie said, 'coming in to the club for a cup of tea once? Ages ago.'

'Yes, I remember her.'

A small woman, they remembered, a frail look about her face. There was another occasion Francie recalled: when the old woman became agitated because one of Wm. Cole's meal lorries had backed into her Morris Minor. 'I thought she'd passed on years ago,' Francie said.

They separated. Hazel was sitting next to him, Grania noticed, Quilty on his other side. Presumably they'd talk over whatever business there was, so that he wouldn't have to delay once the funeral had taken place.

'How're you doing, dear?' Oliver Duddy said, occupying the chair on her left. Desmond was on her right; he nearly always chose to sit next to her.

'I'm all right,' she replied. 'Are you O.K., Oliver?'

'Far from it, as a matter of fact.' He twisted backwards and stretched an arm out, preventing the waitress who was attempting to pass by from doing so. 'Bring me a Crested Ten, will you? Aisling's in the family way,' he muttered into Grania's ear. 'Jesus Christ, Grania!'

He was an architect, responsible for the least attractive bungalows in the county, possibly in the province. He and Mavis had once spent a protracted winter holiday in Spain, the time he'd been endeavouring to find himself. He hadn't done so, but that period of his life had ever since influenced the local landscape. Also, people said, his lavatories didn't work as well as they might have.

'Do you mean it, Oliver? Are you sure?'

'Some elderly Mr Bloody. I'll wring his damn neck for him.'

He was drunk to the extent that failing to listen to him wouldn't matter. No opportunity for comment would be offered. The advice sought, the plea for understanding, would not properly register in the brain that set in motion the requests. It was extremely unlikely that Aisling was pregnant.

'Old Hetty left him the house,' Desmond said on her other side. 'He's going to live in it. Nora,' he called out to the waitress, 'I need to order the wine.'

Oliver Duddy gripped her elbow, demanding the return of her attention. His face came close to hers: the small, snub nose, the tightly bunched, heated cheeks, droplets of perspiration on forehead and chin. Grania looked away. Across the table, Mavis was better-looking than her husband in all sorts of ways, her lips prettily parted as she listened to whatever it was Billy MacGuinness was telling her about, her blue eyes sparkling with Saturday-evening vivacity. Francie was listening to the surveyor. Mary Ann Haddon was nervously playing with her fork, the way she did when she felt she was being ignored: she had a complex about her looks, which were not her strong point. Hazel Quilty was talking to the man who'd come back for the funeral, her lean mouth swiftly opening and closing. Francie, who'd given up smoking a fortnight ago, lit a cigarette. Billy Mac-Guinness's round face crinkled with sudden laughter. Mavis laughed also.

The waitress hurried away with Desmond's wine order. Light caught one lens of Mary Ann's glasses. 'Oh, I don't *believe* you!' Francie cried, her voice for a single instant shrill above the buzz of conversation. The man who'd come back to attend the old woman's funeral still listened politely. Trish—the smallest, most demure of the wives—kept nodding while Kevy Haddon spoke in his dry voice, his features drily matching it.

There were other faces in the Rhett Butler Room, those of Clark Gable and Vivien Leigh reproduced on mirrored glass with bevelled edges, huge images that also included the shoulders of the film stars, the *décolletage* of one, the frilled evening shirt of the other. Clark Gable was subtly allowed the greater impact; in Scarlett's Lounge, together on a single mirror, the two appeared to be engaged in argument, he crossly pouting from a distance, she imperious in close-up.

'This man here, you mean?' Grania said to her husband when there was an opportunity. She knew he did; there was no one else he could mean. She didn't want to think about it, yet it had to be confirmed. She wanted to delay the knowledge, yet just as much she had to know quickly.

'So he's been saying,' Desmond said. 'You know, I'd forgotten who he was when you introduced us.'

'But what on earth does he want to come and live in that awful old house for?'

'He's on his uppers apparently.'

Often they talked together on these Saturday occasions, in much the same way as they did in their own kitchen while she finished cooking the dinner and he laid the table. In the kitchen they talked about people they'd run into during the day, the same people once a week or so, rarely strangers. When his father retired almost twenty years ago, Desmond had taken over the management of the town's laundry and later had inherited it. The Tara Hotel was his second most important customer, the Hospital of St Bernadette of Lourdes being his first. He brought back to Grania reports of demands for higher wages, and the domestic confidences of his staff. In return she passed on gossip, which both of them delighted in.

'How's Judith?' Oliver Duddy enquired, finger and thumb again tightening on her elbow. 'No Mr Bloody yet?'

'Judith's still at the convent, remember.'

'You never know these days.'

'I think you've got it wrong about Aisling being pregnant.'

'I pray to God I have, dear.'

Desmond said he intended to go to Hetty Prendergast's funeral, but she saw no reason why she should go herself. Desmond went to lots of funerals, often of people she didn't know, business acquaintances who'd lived miles away. Going to funerals was different when there was a business reason, not that the Prendergasts had ever made much use of the laundry.

'I have a soft spot for Judith,' Oliver Duddy said. 'She's getting to be a lovely girl.'

It was difficult to agree without sounding smug, yet it seemed disloyal to her daughter to deny what was claimed for her. Grania shrugged, a gesture that was vague enough to indicate whatever her companion wished to make of it. There was no one on Oliver Duddy's other side because the table ended there. Angela, widow of a German businessman, had just sat down in the empty place opposite him. The most glamorous of all the wives, tall and slim, her hair the colour of very pale sand, Angela was said to be on the look-out for a second marriage. Her husband had settled in the neighbourhood after the war and had successfully begun a cheese and pâté business, supplying restaurants and hotels all over the country. With a flair he had cultivated in her, Angela ran it now. 'How's Oliver?' She smiled seductively across the table, the way she'd smiled at men even in her husband's lifetime. Oliver Duddy said he was all right, but Grania knew that only a desultory conversation would begin between the two because Oliver Duddy didn't like Angela for some reason, or else was alarmed by her.

'Judith always has a word for you,' he said. 'Rare, God knows, in a young person these days.'

'Who's that?' Angela leaned forward, her eyes indicating the stranger.

She was told, and Grania watched her remembering him. Angela had been pregnant with the third of her sons that August afternoon. 'Uncomfortably warm,' she now recalled, nodding in recollection.

Oliver Duddy displayed no interest. He'd been at the club that afternoon and he remembered the arrival of the stranger, but an irritated expression passed over his tightly made face while Grania and Angela agreed about the details of the afternoon in question: he resented the interruption and wished to return to the subject of daughters.

'What I'm endeavouring to get at, Grania, is what would you say if Judith came back with some fellow old enough to be her father?'

'Mavis didn't say Aisling's friend was as old as that.'

'Aisling wrote us a letter, Grania. There are lines to read between.'

'Well, naturally I'd prefer Judith to marry someone of her own age. But of course it all depends on the man.'

'D'you find a daughter easy, Grania? There's no one thinks more of Aisling than myself. The fonder you are the more worry there is. Would you say that was right, Grania?'

'Probably.'

'You're lucky in Judith, though. She has a great way with her.'

Angela was talking to Tom Crosbie about dairy products. The Crosbies were an example of a marriage in which there was a considerable age difference, yet it appeared not to have had an adverse effect. Trish had had four children, two girls and two boys; they were a happy, jolly family, even though when Trish married it had been widely assumed that she was not in love, was if anything still yearning after Billy MacGuinness. It was even rumoured that Trish had married for money, since Tom Crosbie owned Boyd Motors, the main Ford franchise in the neighbourhood. Trish's family had once been well-to-do but had somehow become penurious.

'What's Judith going to do for herself? Nursing, is it, Grania?'

'If it is she's never mentioned it.'

'I only thought it might be.'

'There's talk about college. She's not bad at languages.'

'Don't send her to Dublin, dear. Keep the girl by you. D'you hear what I'm saying, Desmond?' Oliver Duddy raised his voice, shouting across Grania. He began all over again, saying he had a soft spot for Judith, explaining about the letter that had arrived from Aisling. Grania changed places with him. 'Oliver's had a few,' Angela said.

'He's upset about Aisling. She's going out with an older man.'

She shouldn't have said it with Tom Crosbie sitting there. She made a face to herself and leaned across the table to tell him he was looking perky. As soon as she'd spoken she felt she'd made matters worse, that her remark could be taken to imply he was looking young for his years.

'There's a new place,' Angela said when Grania asked her about her dress. ' "Pursestrings". D'you know it?'

Ever since she'd become a widow Angela had gone to Dublin to buy something during the week before each Saturday dinner. Angela liked to be first, though often Francie ran her close. Mavis tried to keep up with them but couldn't quite. Grania sometimes tried too; Hazel didn't mind what she wore.

'Is Desmond going to the funeral?' Tom Crosbie asked in his agreeable way—perhaps, Grania thought, to show that no offence had been taken.

'Yes, he is.'

'Desmond's very good.'

That was true. Desmond was good. He'd been the pick of the tennis club when she'd picked him herself, the pick of the town. Looking round the table—at Tom Crosbie's bald head and Kevy Haddon's joylessness, at the simian lines of Quilty's cheeks and Billy MacGuinness's tendency to glow, Oliver Duddy's knotted features—she was aware that, on top of everything else, Desmond had worn better than any of them. He had acquired authority in middle age;

the reticence of his youth had remained, but time had displayed that he was more often right than wrong, and his opinion was sought in a way it once had not been. Desmond was quietly obliging, a quality more appreciated in middle age than in youth. Mavis had called him a dear when he was still a bachelor.

They ate their prawn cocktails. The voices became louder. For a moment Grania's eye was held by the man who had said, at first, that she didn't remember him. A look was exchanged and persisted for a moment. Did he suspect that she had learnt already of his intention to live in the Prendergasts' house? Would he have told her himself if they hadn't been interrupted by Desmond?

'Hetty was a nice old thing,' Angela said. 'I feel I'd like to attend her funeral myself.'

She glanced again in the direction of the stranger. Tom Crosbie began to talk about a court case that was causing interest. Oliver Duddy got up and ambled out of the dining-room, and Desmond moved to where he'd been sitting so that he was next to his wife again. The waitresses were collecting the prawn-cocktail glasses. 'Oliver's being a bore about this Aisling business,' Desmond said.

'Desmond, did Prendergast mention being married now?'

He looked down the table, and across it. He shook his head. 'He hasn't the look of being married. Another thing is, I have a feeling he's called something else.'

'Angela says she's going to the funeral.'

One of the waitresses brought round plates of grilled salmon, the other offered vegetables. Oliver Duddy returned with a glass of something he'd picked up in the bar, whiskey on ice it looked like. He sat between Desmond and Una Carty-Carroll, not seeming to notice that it wasn't where he'd been sitting before.

Mavis's back was reflected in the Rhett Butler mirror, the V of her black dress plunging deeply down her spine Her movements, and those of Billy MacGuinness next to her, danced over the features of Clark Gable.

'He might suit Angela,' Desmond said. 'You never know.'

That August afternoon Billy MacGuinness, who was a doctor, had been called away from the club, some complication with a confinement. 'Damned woman,' he'd grumbled unfeelingly, predicting an all-night job. 'Come back to the house, Francie,' Grania had invited when the tennis came to an end, and it was then that Desmond had noticed the young man attaching his tennis racquet to the crossbar of his bicycle and had issued the same invitation. Desmond had said he'd drive him back to the Prendergasts' when they'd all had something to eat, and together they lifted his bicycle on to the boot of the car. 'I've something to confess,' Francie had said in the kitchen, cutting the rinds off rashers of bacon, and Grania knew what it would be because 'I've something to confess' was a kind of joke among the wives, a time-honoured way of announcing pregnancy. 'You're *not!*' Grania cried, disguising envy. 'Oh, Francie, how grand!' Desmond brought them drinks, but Francie didn't tell him, as Grania had guessed she wouldn't. 'February,' Francie said. 'Billy says it should be February.'

Billy telephoned while they were still in the kitchen, guessing where Francie was when there'd been no reply from his own number. He'd be late, as he'd predicted. 'Francie's pregnant,' Grania told Desmond while Francie was still on the phone. 'Don't tell her I said.'

In the sitting-room they had a few more drinks while in the kitchen the bacon cooked on a glimmer of heat. All of them were still in their tennis clothes and nobody was in a hurry. Francie wasn't because of the empty evening in front of her. Grania and Desmond weren't because they'd nothing to do that evening. The young man who was staying with the Prendergasts was like a schoolboy prolonging his leave. The sipping of their gin, the idle conversation—the young man told about the town and the tennis club, told who Angela was, and which the Duddys were: all of it took on the pleasurable feeling of a party happening by chance. Desmond picked up the telephone and rang the Crosbies but Trish said they wouldn't be able to get a babysitter or else of course they'd come over, love to. Eventually Desmond beat up eggs to scramble and Grania fried potato cakes and soda bread. 'We're none of us sober,' Desmond said, offering a choice of white or red wine as they sat down to eat. Eartha Kitt sang 'Just an Old-fashioned Girl'.

In the Rhett Butler Room Grania heard the tune again. '. . . and an old-fashioned millionaire,' lisped the cool, sensuous voice, each emphasis strangely accented. They'd danced to it among the furniture of the sitting-room, Francie and the young man mostly, she and Desmond. 'I'm sorry, darling,' Desmond whispered, but she shook her head, refusing to concede that blame came into it. If it did, she might as well say she was sorry herself. 'I have to get back,' Francie said. 'Cook something for Billy.' Desmond said he'd drop her off on his way to the Prendergasts, but then he changed the record to 'Love Grows', and fell asleep as soon as the music began.

Francie didn't want a lift. She wanted to walk because the air would do her good. 'D'you trust me?' Grania asked the young man, and he laughed and said he'd have to because he didn't have a lamp on his bicycle. She'd hardly spoken to him, had been less aware of him than of Desmond's apparent liking of him. With strangers Desmond was often like that. 'What do you do?' she asked in the car, suddenly shy in spite of all the gin and wine there'd been. He'd held her rather close when he'd danced with her, but she'd noticed he'd held Francie close too. Francie had kissed him goodbye. 'Well, actually I've been working in a pub,' he said. 'Before that I made toast in the Royal Hotel in Bournemouth.'

She drove slowly, with extreme caution, through the

narrow streets of the town. The public houses were closing;
gaggles of men loitered near each, smoking or just standing.
Youths thronged the pavement outside the Palm Grove
fish-and-chip shop. Beyond the last of its lamp-posts the
town straggled away to nothing, solitary cottages and bungalows gave way to fields. 'I haven't been to this house
before,' Grania said in a silence that had developed. Her
companion had vouchsafed no further information about
himself beyond the reference to a pub and making toast in
Bournemouth. 'They'll be in bed,' he said now. 'They go
to bed at nine.'

The headlights picked out trunks of trees on the avenue,
then urns, and steps leading up to a hall-door. White
wooden shutters flanked the downstairs windows, the paint
peeling, as it was on the iron balustrade of the steps. All of
it was swiftly there, then lost: the car lights isolated a rosebed and a seat on a lawn. 'I won't be a minute,' he said,
'unshackling this bike.'

She turned the lights off. The last of the August day
hadn't quite gone; a warm duskiness was scented with
honeysuckle she could not see when she stepped out of the
car. 'You've been awfully good to me,' he said, unknotting
the strings that held the bicycle in place. 'You and Desmond.'

In the Rhett Butler Room, now rowdy with laughter and
raised voices, she didn't want to look at him again, and yet
she couldn't help herself: waiting for her were the unblinking eyes, the hair brushed back from the sallow forehead,
the high cheekbones. Angela would stand at the graveside
and afterwards would offer him sympathy. Quilty would be
there, Hazel wouldn't bother. 'I'd say we all need a drink':
Grania could imagine Angela saying that, including Desmond in the invitation, gathering the three men around her.
In the dark the bicycle had been wheeled away and propped
against the steps. 'Come in for a minute,' he'd said, and
she'd begun to protest that it was late, even though it wasn't.

'Oh, don't be silly,' he'd said.

She remembered, in the garish hotel dining-room, the flash of his smile in the gloom, and how she'd felt his unblinking eyes caressing her. He reached out for her hand, and in a moment they were in a hall, the electric light turned on, a grandfather clock ticking at the bottom of the stairs. There was a hallstand, and square cream-and-terracotta tiles, brown engravings framed in oak, fish in glass cases. 'I shall offer you a nightcap,' he whispered, leading her into a flagged passage and then into a cavernous kitchen. 'Tullamore Dew is what they have,' he murmured. 'Give every man his dew.' She knew what he intended. She'd known it before they'd turned in at the avenue gates; she'd felt it in the car between them. He poured their drinks and then he kissed her, taking her into his arms as though that were simply a variation of their dancing together. 'Dearest,' he murmured, surprising her: she hadn't guessed that he intended, also, the delicacy of endearments.

Did she, before the car turned in at the avenue gates, decide herself what was to happen? Or was it later, even while still protesting that it was late? Or when he reached up to the high shelf of the dresser for the bottle? At some point she had said to herself: I am going to do this. She knew she had because the words still echoed. 'How extraordinary!' he murmured in the kitchen, all his talk as soft as that now. 'How extraordinary to find you at a tennis club in Ireland!' Her own arms held him to her; yet for some reason she didn't want to see his face, not that she found it unattractive.

The empty glasses laid down on the kitchen table, stairs without a carpet, a chest of drawers on a landing, towels in a pile on a chair, the door of his bedroom closing behind them: remembered images were like details from a dream. For a moment the light went on in his room: a pink china jug stood in a basin on a wash-stand, there was a wardrobe, a cigarette packet on the dressing-table, the shirt and trousers he'd changed from into his tennis clothes were thrown on to the floor. Then the light was extinguished and again he embraced her, his fingers already unbuttoning her tennis dress, which no one but Desmond had ever done in that particular way. Before her marriage she'd been kissed, twice, by Billy MacGuinness, and once by a boy who'd left the neighbourhood and gone to Canada. As all the tennis-club wives were when they married, she'd been a virgin. 'Oh God, Grania!' she heard him whispering, and her thoughts became worries when she lay, naked, on the covers of his bed. Her father's face was vivid in her mind, disposing of her with distaste. 'No, don't do that, dear,' her mother used to say, smacking with her tongue when Grania picked a scab on her knee or made a pattern on the raked gravel with a stick.

In the kitchen they ate raspberries and cream. She asked him again about himself but he hardly responded, questioning her instead and successfully extracting answers. The raspberries were delicious; he put a punnet on the seat beside the driving seat in the car. They were for Desmond, but he didn't say so. 'Don't feel awkward,' he said. 'I'm going back on Monday.'

A hare ran in front of the car on the avenue, bewildered by the lights. People would guess, she thought; they would see a solitary shadow in the car and they would know. It did not occur to her that if her expedition to the Prendergasts' house had been as innocent as its original purpose the people who observed her return would still have seen what they saw now. In fact, the streets were quite deserted when she came to them.

'God, I'm sorry,' Desmond said, sitting up on the sofa, his white clothes rumpled, the texture of a cushion-cover on his cheek, his hair untidy. She smiled, not trusting herself to speak or even to laugh, as in other circumstances she might have. She put the raspberries in the refrigerator and had a bath.

In the Rhett Butler Room they began to change places in the usual way, after the Black Forest gâteau. She sat by Francie and Mavis. 'Good for Aisling,' Francie insisted when Mavis described the chartered accountant; he did not seem old at all. 'I'll have it out with Oliver when we get back,' Mavis said. 'There's no chance whatsoever she's been naughty. I can assure you I'd be the first to know.' They lowered their voices to remark on Angela's interest in the stranger. 'The house would suit her rightly,' Mavis said.

All the rooms would be done up. The slatted shutters that flanked the windows would be repainted, and the balustrade by the steps. There'd be new curtains and carpets; a gardener would be employed. Angela had never cared for the house her well-to-do husband had built her, and since his death had made no secret of the fact.

'I'll never forget that night, Grania.' Francie giggled, embarrassedly groping for a cigarette. 'Dancing with your man and Desmond going to sleep. Wasn't it the same night I told you Maureen was on the way?'

'Yes, it was.'

The three women talked of other matters. That week in the town an elderly clerk had been accused of embezzlement. Mavis observed that the surveyor from the waterworks was limbering up to propose to Una Carty-Carroll. 'And doesn't she know it!' Francie said. Grania laughed.

Sometimes she'd wondered if he was still working in a pub and told herself that of course he wouldn't be, that he'd have married and settled down ages ago. But when she saw him tonight she'd guessed immediately that he hadn't. She wasn't surprised when Desmond had said he was on his uppers. 'I am going to do this': the echo of her resolve came back to her as she sat there. 'I am going to do this because I want a child.'

'God, I'm exhausted,' Mavis said. 'Is it age or what?'

'Oh, it's age, it's age.' Francie sighed, stubbing out her cigarette. 'Damn things,' she muttered.

Mavis reached for the packet and flicked it across the table. 'Present for you, Kevy,' she said, but Francie pleaded with her eyes and he flicked it back again. Grania smiled because they'd have noticed if she didn't.

In the intervening years he would never have wondered about a child being born. But if Angela married him he would think about it; being close by would cause him to. He would wonder, and in the middle of a night, while he lay beside Angela in bed, it would be borne in upon him that Desmond and Grania had one child only. Grania considered that: the untidiness of someone else knowing, her secret shared. There'd been perpetually, every instant of the day it sometimes seemed, the longing to share—with Desmond and with her friends, with the child that had been born. But this was different.

The evening came to an end. Cars were started in the yard of the hotel; there were warnings of ice on the roads. 'Goodnight, Grania,' the man who'd come for the funeral said. She buckled herself into her seat-belt. Desmond backed and then crawled forward into West Main Street. 'You're quiet,' he said, and immediately she began to talk about the possibility of Una Carty-Carroll being proposed to in case he connected her silence with the presence of the stranger. 'As a matter of fact,' he said when that subject was exhausted, 'I met that fellow of Aisling's once. He's only thirty-five.' She opened the garage door and he drove the car in. The air was refreshingly cold, sharper than it had been in the yard of the hotel.

They locked their house. Grania put things ready for the morning. It was a relief that a babysitter was no longer necessary, that she didn't have to wait with just a trace of anxiety while Desmond drove someone home. He'd gone upstairs and she knew that he'd done so in order to press open Judith's door and glance in at her while she slept. Whenever they came in at night he did that.

At the sink Grania poured glasses of water for him and

for herself, and carried them upstairs. When she had placed them on either side of their bed she, too, went to look in at her daughter—a mass of brown hair untidy on the pillow, eyes lightly closed. 'I might play golf tomorrow,' Desmond said, settling his trousers into his electric press. Almost as soon as he'd clambered into bed he fell asleep. She switched out his bedside light and went downstairs.

Alone in the kitchen, sitting over a cup of tea, she returned again to the August Saturday. Two of Trish's children had already been born then, and two of Mavis's, and Hazel's first. 'I wouldn't be surprised,' Billy Mac-Guinness had said, 'if Angela doesn't drop this one in a deckchair.' Mary Ann Haddon had just started her second. Older children were sitting on the clubhouse steps.

Grania forced her thoughts through all the rest of it, through the party that had happened by chance, the headlights picking out the rosebed. She savoured easily the solitude she had disguised during the years that had passed since then, the secret that had seemed so safe. In the quiet kitchen, when she had been over this familiar ground, she felt herself again possessed by the confusion that had come like a fog when she'd seen tonight the father of her child. Then slowly it lifted: she was incapable of regret.

Kathleen's Field

'I'm after a field of land, sir.'

Hagerty's tone was modest to the bank agent, careful and cautious. He was aware that Mr Ensor would know what was coming next. He was aware that he constituted a risk, a word Mr Ensor had used a couple of times when endeavouring to discuss the overdraft Hagerty already had with the bank.

'I was wondering, sir . . .' His voice trailed away when Mr Ensor's head began to shake. He'd like to say yes, the bank agent assured him. He would say yes this very instant, only what use would it be when Head Office wouldn't agree? 'They're bad times, Mr Hagerty.'

It was a Monday morning in 1948. Leaning on the counter, his right hand still grasping the stick he'd used to drive three bullocks the seven miles from his farm, Hagerty agreed that the times were as bad as ever he'd known them. He'd brought the bullocks in to see if he could get a price for them, but he hadn't been successful. All the way on his journey he'd been thinking about the field old Lally had spent his lifetime carting the rocks out of. The widow the old man had left behind had sold the nineteen acres on the other side of the hill, but the last of her fields was awkwardly placed for anyone except Hagerty. They both knew it would be convenient for him to have it; they both knew there'd be almost as much profit in that single pasture as there was in all the land he possessed already. Gently sloping, naturally drained, it was free of weeds and thistles, and

the grass it grew would do you good to look at. Old Lally
had known its value from the moment he'd inherited it. He
had kept it ditched, with its gates and stone walls always
cared for. And for miles around, no one had ever cleared
away rocks like old Lally had.

'I'd help you if I could, Mr Hagerty,' the bank agent
assured him. 'Only there's still a fair bit owing.'

'I know there is, sir.'

Every December Hagerty walked into the bank with a
plucked turkey as a seasonal statement of gratitude: the
overdraft had undramatically continued for seventeen years.
It was less than it had been, but Hagerty was no longer
young and he might yet be written off as a bad debt. He
hadn't had much hope when he'd raised the subject of the
field he coveted.

'I'm sorry, Mr Hagerty,' the bank agent said, stretching
his hand across the width of the counter. 'I know that field
well. I know you could make something of it, but there you
are.'

'Ah well, you gave it your consideration, sir.'

He said it because it was his way to make matters easier
for a man who had lent him money in the past: Hagerty
was a humble man. He had a tired look about him, his
spare figure stooped from the shoulders, a black hat always
on his head. He hadn't removed it in the bank, nor did he
in Shaughnessy's Provisions and Bar, where he sat in a
corner by himself, with a bottle of stout to console him. He
had left the bullocks in Cronin's yard in order to free himself for his business in the bank, and since Cronin made a
small charge for this fair-day service he'd thought he might
as well take full advantage of it by delaying a little longer.

He reflected as he drank that he hardly needed the bank
agent's reminder about the times being bad. Seven of his
ten children had emigrated, four to Canada and America,
the three others to England. Kathleen, the youngest, now
sixteen, was left, with Biddy, who wasn't herself, and Con,

who would inherit the farm. But without the Lallys' field it wouldn't be easy for Con to keep going. Sooner or later he would want to marry the Kilfedder girl, and there'd always have to be a home for Biddy on the farm, and for a while at least an elderly mother and father would have to be accommodated also. Sometimes one or other of the exiled children sent back a cheque and Hagerty never objected to accepting it. But none of them could afford the price of a field, and he wasn't going to ask them. Nor would Con accept these little presents when his time came to take over the farm entirely, for how could the oldest brother be beholden like that in the prime of his life? It wasn't the same for Hagerty himself: he'd been barefoot on the farm as a child, which was when his humility had been learned.

'Are you keeping yourself well, Mr Hagerty?' Mrs Shaughnessy enquired, crossing the small bar to where he sat. She'd been busy with customers on the grocery side since soon after he'd come in; she'd drawn the cork out of his bottle, apologising for her busyness when she gave it to him to pour himself.

'I am,' he said. 'And are you, Mrs Shaughnessy?'

'I have the winter rheumatism again. But thank God it's not severe.'

Mrs Shaughnessy was a tall, big-shouldered woman whom he remembered as a girl before she'd married into the shop. She wore a bit of make-up, and her clothes were more colourful than his wife's, although they were hidden now by her green shop overall. She had been flighty as a girl, so he remembered hearing, but in no way could you describe her as that in her late middle age; 'well-to-do' was the description that everything about Mrs Shaughnessy insisted upon.

'I was wanting to ask you, Mr Hagerty. I'm on the lookout for a country girl to assist me in the house. If they're any good they're like gold dust these days. Would you know of a country girl out your way?'

Hagerty began to shake his head and was at once reminded of the bank agent shaking his. It was then, while he
was still actually engaged in that motion, that he recalled a
fact which previously had been of no interest to him: Mrs
Shaughnessy's husband lent people money. Mr Shaughnessy was a considerable businessman. As well as the Provisions and Bar, he owned a barber's shop and was an agent
for the Property & Life Insurance Company; he had funds
to spare. Hagerty had heard of people mortgaging an area
of their land with Mr Shaughnessy, or maybe the farmhouse itself, and as a consequence being able to buy mach-
inery or stock. He'd never yet heard of any unfairness or
sharp practice on the part of Mr Shaughnessy after the deal
had been agreed upon and had gone into operation.

'Haven't you a daughter yourself, Mr Hagerty? Pardon
me now if I'm guilty of a presumption, but I always say if
you don't ask you won't know. Haven't you a daughter not
long left the nuns?'

Kathleen's round, open features came into his mind,
momentarily softening his own. His youngest daughter was
inclined to plumpness and to freckles, but her wide, un-
complicated smile often radiated moments of prettiness in
her face. She had always been his favourite, although Biddy,
of course, had a special place also.

'No, she's not long left the convent.'

Her face slipped away, darkening to nothing in his
imagination. He thought again of the Lallys' field, the curv-
ing shape of it like a tea-cloth thrown over a bush to dry.
A stream ran among the few little ash trees at the bottom,
the morning sun lingered on the heart of it.

'I'd never have another girl unless I knew the family, Mr
Hagerty. Or unless she'd be vouched for by someone the
like of yourself.'

'Are you thinking of Kathleen, Mrs Shaughnessy?'

'Well, I am. I'll be truthful with you, I am.'

At that moment someone rapped with a coin on the

counter of the grocery and Mrs Shaughnessy hurried away. If Kathleen came to work in the house above the Provisions and Bar, he might be able to bring up the possibility of a mortgage. And the grass was so rich in the field that it wouldn't be too many years before a mortgage could be paid off. Con would be left secure, Biddy would be provided for.

Hagerty savoured a slow mouthful of stout. He didn't want Kathleen to go to England. *I can get her fixed up*, her sister, Mary Florence, had written in a letter not long ago. 'I'd rather Kilburn than Chicago,' he'd heard Kathleen herself saying to Con, and at the time he'd been relieved because Kilburn was nearer. Only Biddy would always be with them, for you couldn't count on Con not being tempted by Kilburn or Chicago the way things were at the present time. 'Sure, what choice have we in any of it?' their mother had said, but enough of them had gone, he'd thought. His father had struggled for the farm and he'd struggled for it himself.

'God, the cheek of some people!' Mrs Shaughnessy exclaimed, re-entering the bar. 'Tinned pears and ham, and her book unpaid since January! Would you credit that, Mr Hagerty?'

He wagged his head in an appropriate manner, denoting amazement. He'd been thinking over what she'd put to him, he said. There was no girl out his way who might be suitable, only his own Kathleen. 'You were right enough to mention Kathleen, Mrs Shaughnessy.' The nuns had never been displeased with her, he said as well.

'Of course, she would be raw, Mr Hagerty. I'd have to train every inch of her. Well, I have experience in that, all right. You train them, Mr Hagerty, and the next thing is they go off to get married. There's no sign of that, is there?'

'Ah, no, no.'

'You'd maybe spend a year training them and then they'd be off. Sure, where's the sense in it? I often wonder I bother.'

(233)

'Kathleen wouldn't go running off, no fear of that, Mrs Shaughnessy.'

'It's best to know the family. It's best to know a father like yourself.'

As Mrs Shaughnessy spoke, her husband appeared behind the bar. He was a small man, with grey hair brushed into spikes, and a map of broken veins dictating a warm redness in his complexion. He wore a collar and tie, which Mr Hagerty did not, and the waistcoat and trousers of a dark-blue suit. He carried a number of papers in his right hand and a packet of Sweet Afton cigarettes in his left. He spread the papers out on the bar and, having lit a cigarette, proceeded to scrutinise them. While he listened to Mrs Shaughnessy's further exposition of her theme, Hagerty was unable to take his eyes off him.

'You get in a country girl and you wouldn't know was she clean or maybe would she take things. We had a queer one once, she used eat a raw onion. You'd go into the kitchen and she'd be at it. "What are you chewing, Kitty?" you might say to her politely. And she'd open her mouth and you'd see the onion in it.'

'Kathleen wouldn't eat onions.'

'Ah, I'm not saying she would. Des, will you bring Mr Hagerty another bottle of stout? He has a girl for us.'

Looking up from his papers but keeping a finger in place on them, her husband asked her what she was talking about.

'Kathleen Hagerty would come in and assist me, Des.'

Mr Shaughnessy asked who Kathleen Hagerty was, and when it was revealed that her father was sitting in the bar with a bottle of stout, and in need of another one, he bundled his papers into a pocket and drew the corks from two further bottles. His wife winked at Hagerty. He liked to have a maid about the house, she said. He pretended he didn't, but he liked the style of it.

All the way back to the farm, driving home the bullocks,

Hagerty reflected on that stroke of luck. In poor spirits he'd turned into Shaughnessy's, it being the nearest public house to the bank. If he hadn't done so, and if Mrs Shaughnessy hadn't mentioned her domestic needs, and if her husband hadn't come in when he had, there wouldn't have been one bit of good news to carry back. 'I'm after a field of land,' he'd said to Mr Shaughnessy, making no bones about it. They'd both listened to him, Mrs Shaughnessy only going away once, to pour herself half a glass of sherry. They'd understood immediately the thing about the field being valuable to him because of its position. 'Doesn't it sound a grand bit of land, Des?' Mrs Shaughnessy had remarked with enthusiasm. 'With a good hot sun on it?' He'd revealed the price old Lally's widow was asking; he'd laid every fact he knew down before them.

In the end, on top of four bottles of stout, he was poured a glass of Paddy, and then Mrs Shaughnessy made him a spreadable-cheese sandwich. He would send Kathleen in, he promised, and after that it would be up to Mrs Shaughnessy. 'But, sure, I think we'll do business,' she'd confidently predicted.

Biddy would see him coming, he said to himself as he urged the bullocks on. She'd see the bullocks and she'd run back into the house to say they hadn't been sold. There'd be long faces then, but he'd take it easy when he entered the kitchen and reached out for his tea. A bad old fair it had been, he'd report, which was nothing only the truth, and he'd go through the offers that had been made to him. He'd go through his conversation with Mr Ensor and then explain how he'd gone into Shaughnessy's to rest himself before the journey home.

On the road ahead he saw Biddy waving at him and then doing what he'd known she'd do: hurrying back to precede him with the news. As he murmured the words of a thanksgiving, his youngest daughter again filled Hagerty's mind. The day Kathleen was born it had rained from dawn till dusk. People said that was lucky for the family of an infant, and it might be they were right.

*

Kathleen was led from room to room and felt alarmed. She had never experienced a carpet beneath her feet before. There were boards or linoleum in the farmhouse, and linoleum in the Reverend Mother's room at the convent. She found the papered walls startling: flowers cascaded in the corners, and ran in a narrow band around the room, close to the ceiling. 'I see you admiring the frieze,' Mrs Shaughnessy said. 'I had the house redone a year ago.' She paused and then laughed, amused by the wonder in Kathleen's face. 'Those little borders,' she said. 'I think they call them friezes these days.'

When Mrs Shaughnessy laughed her chin became long and smooth, and the skin tightened on her forehead. Her very white false teeth—which Kathleen was later to learn she referred to as her 'delf'—shifted slightly behind her reddened lips. The laugh was a sedate whisper that quickly exhausted itself.

'You're a good riser, are you, Kathleen?'

'I'm used to getting up, ma'am.'

Always say ma'am, the Reverend Mother had adjured, for Kathleen had been summoned when it was known that Mrs Shaughnessy was interested in training her as a maid. The Reverend Mother liked to have a word with any girl who'd been to the convent when the question of local employment arose, or if emigration was mooted. The Reverend Mother liked to satisfy herself that a girl's future promised to be what she would herself have chosen for the girl; and she liked to point out certain hazards, feeling it her duty to do so. The Friday fast was not observed in Protestant households, where there would also be an absence of sacred reminders. Conditions met with after emigration left even more to be desired.

'Now, this would be your own room, Kathleen,' Mrs Shaughnessy said, leading her into a small bedroom at the top of the house. There was a white china wash-basin with a jug standing in it, and a bed with a mattress on it, and a cupboard. The stand the basin and the jug were on was painted white, and so was the cupboard. A net curtain covered the bottom half of a window and at the top there was a brown blind like the ones in the Reverend Mother's room. There wasn't a carpet on the floor and there wasn't linoleum either; but a rug stretched on the boards by the bed, and Kathleen couldn't help imagining her bare feet stepping on to its softness first thing every morning.

'There'll be the two uniforms the last girl had,' Mrs Shaughnessy said. 'They'd easily fit, although I'd say you were bigger on the chest. You wouldn't be be familiar with a uniform, Kathleen?'

'I didn't have one at the convent, ma'am.'

'You'll soon get used to the dresses.'

That was the first intimation that Mrs Shaughnessy considered her suitable for the post. The dresses were hanging in the cupboard, she said. There were sheets and blankets in the hot press.

'I'd rather call you Kitty,' Mrs Shaughnessy said. 'If you wouldn't object. The last girl was Kitty, and so was another we had.'

Kathleen said that was all right. She hadn't been called Kitty at the convent, and wasn't at home because it was the pet name of her eldest sister.

'Well, that's great,' Mrs Shaughnessy said, the tone of her voice implying that the arrangement had already been made.

*

'I was never better pleased with you,' her father said when Kathleen returned home. 'You're a great little girl.'

When she'd packed some of her clothes into a suitcase

that Mary Florence had left behind after a visit one time, he said it was hardly like going away at all because she was only going seven miles. She'd return every Sunday afternoon; it wasn't like Kilburn or Chicago. She sat beside him on the cart and he explained that the Shaughnessys had been generous to a degree. The wages he had agreed with them would be held back and set against the debt: it was that that made the whole thing possible, reducing his monthly repayments to a figure he was confident he could manage, even with the bank overdraft. 'It isn't everyone would agree to the convenience of that, Kathleen.'

She said she understood. There was a new sprightliness about her father; the fatigue in his face had given way to an excited pleasure. His gratitude to the Shaughnessys, and her mother's gratitude, had made the farmhouse a different place during the last couple of weeks. Biddy and Con had been affected by it, and so had Kathleen, even though she had no idea what life would be like in the house above the Shaughnessys' Provisions and Bar. Mrs Shaughnessy had not outlined her duties beyond saying that every night when she went up to bed she should carry with her the alarm clock from the kitchen dresser, and carry it down again every morning. The most important thing of all appeared to be that she should rise promptly from her bed.

'You'll listen well to what Mrs Shaughnessy says,' her father begged her. 'You'll attend properly to all the work, Kathleen?'

'I will of course.'

'It'll be great seeing you on Sundays, girl.'

'It'll be great coming home.'

A bicycle, left behind also by Mary Florence, lay in the back of the cart. Kathleen had wanted to tie the suitcase on to the carrier and cycle in herself with it, but her father wouldn't let her. It was dangerous, he said; a suitcase attached like that could easily unbalance you.

'Kathleen's field is what we call it,' her father said on

their journey together, and added after a moment: 'They're decent people, Kathleen. You're going to a decent house.'

'Oh, I know, I know.'

But after only half a day there Kathleen wished she was back in the farmhouse. She knew at once how much she was going to miss the comfort of the kitchen she had known all her life, and the room along the passage she shared with Biddy, where Mary Florence had slept also, and the dogs nosing up to her in the yard. She knew how much she would miss Con, and her father and her mother, and how she'd miss looking after Biddy.

'Now, I'll show you how to set a table,' Mrs Shaughnessy said. 'Listen to this carefully, Kitty.'

Cork mats were put down on the tablecloth so that the heat of the dishes wouldn't penetrate to the polished surface beneath. Small plates were placed on the left of each mat, to put the skins of potatoes on. A knife and a fork were arranged on each side of the mats and a spoon and a fork across the top. The pepper and salt were placed so that Mr Shaughnessy could easily reach them. Serving spoons were placed by the bigger mats in the middle. The breakfast table was set the night before, with the cups upside down on the saucers so that they wouldn't catch the dust when the ashes were taken from the fire-place.

'Can you cut kindling, Kitty? I'll show you how to do it with the little hatchet.'

She showed her, as well, how to sweep the carpet on the stairs with a stiff hand-brush, and how to use the dust-pan. She explained that every mantelpiece in the house had to be dusted every morning, and all the places where grime would gather. She showed her where saucepans and dishes were kept, and instructed her in how to light the range, the first task of the day. The backyard required brushing once a week, on Saturday between four o'clock and five. And every morning after breakfast water had to be pumped from the tank in the yard, fifteen minutes' work with the hand lever.

'That's the W.C. you'd use, Kitty,' Mrs Shaughnessy indicated, leading her to a privy in another part of the back-yard. 'The maids always use this one.'

The dresses of the uniforms didn't fit. She looked at her-self in the blue one and then in the black. The mirror on the dressing-table was tarnished, but she could tell that neither uniform enhanced her in any way whatsoever. She looked as fat as a fool, she thought, with the hems all crooked, and the sleeves too tight on her forearms. 'Oh now, that's really very good,' Mrs Shaughnessy said when Kathleen emerged from her bedroom in the black one. She demonstrated how the bodice of the apron was kept in place and how the afternoon cap should be worn.

'Is your father fit?' Mr Shaughnessy enquired when he came upstairs for his six o'clock tea.

'He is, sir.' Suddenly Kathleen had to choke back tears because without any warning the reference to her father had made her want to cry.

'He was shook the day I saw him,' Mr Shaughnessy said, 'on account he couldn't sell the bullocks.'

'He's all right now, sir.'

The Shaughnessys' son reappeared then too, a narrow-faced youth who hadn't addressed her when he'd arrived in the dining-room in the middle of the day and didn't address her now. There were just the three of them, two younger children having grown up and gone away. During the day Mrs Shaughnessy had often referred to her other son and her daughter, the son in business in Limerick, the daughter married to a county surveyor. The narrow-faced son would inherit the businesses, she'd said, the barber's shop and the Provisions and Bar, maybe even the insurances. With a bout of wretchedness, Kathleen was reminded of Con inheriting the farm. Before that he'd marry Angie Kilfedder, who wouldn't hesitate to accept him now that the farm was improved.

Kathleen finished laying the table and went back to the

kitchen, where Mrs Shaughnessy was frying rashers and
eggs and slices of soda bread. When they were ready she
scooped them on to three plates and Kathleen carried the
tray, with a tea-pot on it as well, into the dining-room. Her
instructions were to return to the kitchen when she'd done
so and to fry her own rasher and eggs, and soda bread if she
wanted it. 'I don't know will we make much of that one,'
she heard Mrs Shaughnessy saying as she closed the dining-
room door.

That night she lay awake in the strange bed, not wanting
to sleep because sleep would too swiftly bring the morning,
and another day like the day there'd been. She couldn't
stay here: she'd say that on Sunday. If they knew what it
was like they wouldn't want her to. She sobbed, thinking
again of the warm kitchen she had left behind, the sheepdogs lying by the fire and Biddy turning the wheel of the
bellows, the only household task she could do. She thought
of her mother and father sitting at the table as they always
did, her mother knitting, her father pondering, with his hat
still on his head. If they could see her in the dresses they'd
understand. If they could see her standing there pumping
up the water they'd surely be sorry for the way she felt. 'I
haven't the time to tell you twice, Kitty,' Mrs Shaughnessy
said over and over again, her long, painted face not smiling
in the least way whatsoever. If anything was broken, she'd
said, the cost of it would have to be stopped out of the
wages, and she'd spoken as though the wages would actually
change hands. In Kathleen's dreams Mrs Shaughnessy kept
laughing, her chin going long and smooth and her large
white teeth moving in her mouth. The dresses belonged to
one of the King of England's daughters, she explained,
which was why they didn't fit. And then Mary Florence
came into the kitchen and said she was just back from Kilburn with a pair of shoes that belonged to someone else.
The price of them could be stopped out of the wages, she
suggested, and Mrs Shaughnessy agreed.

When Kathleen opened her eyes, roused by the alarm clock at half-past six, she didn't know where she was. Then one after another the details of the previous day impinged on her waking consciousness: the cork mats, the shed where the kindling was cut, the narrow face of the Shaughnessys' son, the greasy doorknobs in the kitchen, the impatience in Mrs Shaughnessy's voice. The reality was worse than the confusion of her dreams, and there was nothing magical about the softness of the rug beneath her bare feet: she didn't even notice it. She lifted her nightdress over her head and for a moment caught a glimpse of her nakedness in the tarnished looking-glass—plumply rounded thighs and knees, the dimple in her stomach. She drew on stockings and underclothes, feeling even more lost than she had when she'd tried not to go to sleep. She knelt by her bed, and when she'd offered her usual prayers she asked that she might be taken away from the Shaughnessys' house. She asked that her father would understand when she told him.

'The master's waiting on his breakfast, Kitty.'

'I lit the range the minute I was down, ma'am.'

'If you don't get it going by twenty to seven it won't be hot in time. I told you that yesterday. Didn't you pull the dampers out?'

'The paper wouldn't catch, ma'am.'

'If the paper wouldn't catch you'll have used a damp bit. Or maybe paper out of a magazine. You can't light a fire with paper out of a magazine, Kitty.'

'If I'd had a drop of paraffin, ma'am—'

'My God, are you mad, child?'

'At home we'd throw on a half cup of paraffin if the fire was slow, ma'am.'

'Never bring paraffin near the range. If the master heard you he'd jump out of his skin.'

'I only thought it would hurry it, ma'am.'

'Set the alarm for six if you're going to be slow with the fire. If the breakfast's not on the table by a quarter to eight he'll raise the roof. Have you the plates in the bottom oven?'

When Kathleen opened the door of the bottom oven a black kitten darted out, scratching the back of her hand in its agitation.

'Great God Almighty!' exclaimed Mrs Shaughnessy. 'Are you trying to roast the poor cat?'

'I didn't know it was in there, ma'am.'

'You lit the fire with the poor creature inside there! What were you thinking of to do that, Kitty?'

'I didn't know, ma'am—'

'Always look in the two ovens before you light the range, child. Didn't you hear me telling you?'

After breakfast, when Kathleen went into the dining-room to clear the table, Mrs Shaughnessy was telling her son about the kitten in the oven. 'Haven't they brains like turnips?' she said, even though Kathleen was in the room. The son released a half-hearted smile, but when Kathleen asked him if he'd finished with the jam he didn't reply. 'Try and speak a bit more clearly, Kitty,' Mrs Shaughnessy said later. 'It's not everyone can understand a country accent.'

The day was similar to the day before except that at eleven o'clock Mrs Shaughnessy said:

'Go upstairs and take off your cap. Put on your coat and go down the street to Crawley's. A half pound of round steak, and suet. Take the book off the dresser. He'll know who you are when he sees it.'

So far, that was the pleasantest chore she had been asked to do. She had to wait in the shop because there were two other people before her, both of whom held the butcher in conversation. 'I know your father,' Mr Crawley said when he'd asked her name, and he held her in conversation also, wanting to know if her father was in good health and asking about her brothers and sisters. He'd heard about the buying of the Lallys' field. She was the last uniformed maid in the town, he said, now that Nellie Broderick at O'Mara's had had to give up because of her legs.

'Are you mad?' Mrs Shaughnessy shouted at her on her return. 'I should be down in the shop and not waiting to put that meat on. Didn't I tell you yesterday not to be loitering in the mornings?'

'I'm sorry, ma'am, only Mr Crawley—'

'Go down to the shop and tell the master I'm delayed over cooking the dinner and can you assist him for ten minutes.'

But when Kathleen appeared in the grocery Mr Shaughnessy asked her if she'd got lost. The son was weighing sugar into grey paper-bags and tying string round each of them. A murmur of voices came from the bar.

'Mrs Shaughnessy is delayed over cooking the dinner,' Kathleen said. 'She was thinking I could assist you for ten minutes.'

'Well, that's a good one!' Mr Shaughnessy threw back his head, exploding into laughter. A little shower of spittle damped Kathleen's face. The son gave his half-hearted smile. 'Can you make a spill, Kitty? D'you know what I mean by a spill?' Mr Shaughnessy demonstrated with a piece of brown paper on the counter. Kathleen shook her head. 'Would you know what to charge for a quarter pound of tea, Kitty? Can you weigh out sugar, Kitty? Go back to the missus, will you, and tell her to have sense.'

In the kitchen Kathleen put it differently, simply saying that Mr Shaughnessy hadn't required her services. 'Bring a scuttle of coal up to the dining-room,' Mrs Shaughnessy commanded. 'And get out the mustard. Can you make up mustard?'

Kathleen had never tasted mustard in her life; she had heard of it but did not precisely know what it was. She began to say she wasn't sure about making some, but even before she spoke Mrs Shaughnessy sighed and told her to wash down the front steps instead.

*

'I don't want to go back there,' Kathleen said on Sunday. 'I can't understand what she says to me. It's lonesome the entire time.'

Her mother was sympathetic, but even so she shook her head. 'There's people I used to know,' she said. 'People placed like ourselves whose farms failed on them. They're walking the roads now, no better than tinkers. I have ten children, Kathleen, and seven are gone from me. There's five of them I'll maybe never see again. It's that you have to think of, pet.'

'I cried the first night. I was that lonesome when I got into bed.'

'But isn't it a clean room you're in, pet? And aren't you given food to eat that's better than you'd get here? And don't the dresses she supplies save us an expense again? Wouldn't you think of all that, pet?'

A bargain had been struck, her mother also reminded her, and a bargain was a bargain. Biddy said it sounded great, going out into the town for messages. She'd give anything to see a house like that, Biddy said, with the coal fires and the stairs.

'I'd say they were well pleased with you,' Kathleen's father said when he came in from the yard later on. 'You'd have been back here inside a day if they weren't.'

She'd done her best, she thought as she rode away from the farmhouse on Mary Florence's bicycle; if she'd done everything badly she would have obtained her release. She wept because she wouldn't see Biddy and Con and her father and mother for another week. She dreaded the return to the desolate bedroom which her mother had reminded her was clean, and the kitchen where there was no one to keep her company in the evenings. She felt as if she could not bear it, more counting of the days until Sunday and when Sunday came the few hours passing so swiftly. But she knew, by now, that she would remain in the Shaughnessys' house for as long as was necessary.

'I must have you back by half six, Kitty,' Mrs Shaughnessy said when she saw her. 'It's closer to seven now.'

Kathleen said she was sorry. She'd had to stop to pump the back tyre of her bicycle, she said, although in fact this was not true: what she'd stopped for was to wipe away the signs of her crying and to blow her nose. In the short time she had been part of Mrs Shaughnessy's household she had developed the habit of making excuses, and of obscuring her inadequacies beneath lies that were easier than the truth.

'Fry the bread like I showed you, Kitty. Get it brown on both sides. The master likes it crisp.'

There was something Mr Shaughnessy liked also, which Kathleen discovered when seven of her free Sunday afternoons had gone by. She was dusting the dining-room mantelpiece one morning when he came and stood very close to her. She thought she was in his way, and moved out of it, but a week or so later he stood close to her again, his breath warm on her cheek. When it happened the third time she felt herself blushing.

It was in this manner that Mr Shaughnessy rather than his wife came to occupy, for Kathleen, the central role in the household. The narrow-faced son remained as he had been since the day of her arrival, a dour presence, contributing little in the way of conversation and never revealing the fruits of his brooding silence. Mrs Shaughnessy, having instructed, had apparently played out the part she'd set herself. She came into the kitchen at midday to cook meat and potatoes and one of the milk puddings her husband was addicted to, but otherwise the kitchen was Kathleen's province now and it was she who was responsible for the frying of the food for breakfast and for the six o'clock tea. Mrs Shaughnessy preferred to be in the shop. She enjoyed the social side of that, she told Kathleen; and she enjoyed the occasional half glass of sherry in the bar. 'That's me all over, Kitty. I never took to housework.' She was more amiable in her manner, and confessed that she always found training a country girl an exhausting and irksome task and might therefore have been a little impatient. 'Kitty's settled in grand,' she informed Kathleen's father when he looked into the bar one fair day to make a mortgage payment. He'd been delighted to hear that, he told Kathleen the following Sunday.

Mr Shaughnessy never said anything when he came to stand close to her, although on other occasions he addressed her pleasantly enough, even complimenting her on her frying. He had an easy way with him, quite different from his son's. He was more like his two other children, the married daughter and the son who was in Limerick, both of whom Kathleen had met when they had returned to the house for an uncle's funeral. He occasionally repeated a joke he'd been told, and Mrs Shaughnessy would laugh, her chin becoming lengthy and the skin tightening on her forehead. On the occasion of the uncle's funeral his other son and his daughter laughed at the jokes also, but the son who'd remained at home only smiled. 'Wait till I tell you this one, Kitty,' he'd sometimes say, alone with her in the dining-room. He would tell her something Bob Crowe, who ran the barber's shop for him, had heard from a customer, making the most of the anecdote in a way that suggested he was anxious to entertain her. His manner and his tone of voice denied that it had ever been necessary for him to stand close to her, or else that his practice of doing so had been erased from his memory.

But the scarlet complexion of Mr Shaughnessy's face and the spiky grey hair, the odour of cigarette smoke that emanated from his clothes, could not be so easily forgotten by Kathleen. She no longer wept from loneliness in her bedroom, yet she was aware that the behaviour of Mr Shaughnessy lent the feeling of isolation an extra, vivid dimension, for in the farmhouse kitchen on Sundays the behaviour could not be mentioned.

Every evening Kathleen sat by the range, thinking about it. The black kitten that had darted out of the oven on her second morning had grown into a cat and sat blinking beside her chair. The alarm clock ticked loudly on the dresser. Was it something she should confess? Was it a sin to be as silent as she was when he came to stand beside her? Was it a sin to be unable to find the courage to tell him to leave her alone? Once, in the village where the convent was, another girl in her class had pointed out a boy who was loitering with some other boys by the 1798 statue. That boy was always trying to kiss you, the girl said; he would follow you about the place, whispering to you. But although Kathleen often went home alone the boy never came near her. He wasn't a bad-looking boy, she'd thought, she wouldn't have minded much. She'd wondered if she'd mind the boys her sisters had complained about, who tried to kiss you when they were dancing with you. Pests, her sisters had called them, but Kathleen thought it was nice that they wanted to.

Mr Shaughnessy was different. When he stood close to her his breathing would become loud and unsteady. He always moved away quite quickly, when she wasn't expecting him to. He walked off, never looking back, soundlessly almost.

Then one day, when Mrs Shaughnessy was buying a new skirt and the son was in the shop, he came into the kitchen, where she was scrubbing the draining-boards. He came straight to where she was, as if between them there was some understanding that he should do so. He stood in a slightly different position from usual, behind her rather than at her side, and she felt for the first time his hands passing over her clothes.

'Mr Shaughnessy!' she whispered. 'Mr Shaughnessy, now.'

He took no notice. Some part of his face was touching her hair. The rhythm of his breathing changed.

'Mr Shaughnessy, I don't like it.'

He seemed not to hear her; she sensed that his eyes were closed. As suddenly, and as quickly as always, he went away.

'Well, Bob Crowe told me a queer one this evening,' he said that same evening, while she was placing their plates of fried food in front of them in the dining-room. 'It seems there's a woman asleep in Clery's shop window above in Dublin.'

His wife expressed disbelief. Bob Crowe would tell you anything, she said.

'In a hypnotic trance, it seems. Advertising Odearest Mattresses.'

'Ah, go on now! He's pulling your leg, Des.'

'Not a bit of him. She'll stop there a week, it seems. The Guards have to move the crowds on.'

Kathleen closed the dining-room door behind her. He had turned to look at her when he'd said there was a woman asleep in Clery's window, in an effort to include her in what he was retailing. His eyes had betrayed nothing of their surreptitious relationship, but Kathleen hadn't been able to meet them.

'We ploughed the field,' her father said the following Sunday. 'I've never turned up earth as good.'

She almost told him then. She longed to so much she could hardly prevent herself. She longed to let her tears come and to hear his voice consoling her. When she was a child she'd loved that.

'You're a great girl,' he said.

Mr Shaughnessy took to attending an earlier mass than his wife and son, and when they were out at theirs he would come into the kitchen. When she hid in her bedroom he followed her there. She'd have locked herself in the outside W.C. if there'd been a latch on the door.

'Well, Kitty and myself were quiet enough here,' he'd say in the dining-room later on, when the three of them were eating their midday dinner. She couldn't understand how he could bring himself to speak like that, or how he

could so hungrily eat his food, as though nothing had
occurred. She couldn't understand how he could act normally with his son or with his other children when they came
on a visit. It was extraordinary to hear Mrs Shaughnessy
humming her songs about the house and calling him by his
Christian name.

'The Kenny girl's getting married,' Mrs Shaughnessy
said on one of these mealtime occasions. 'Tyson from the
hardware.'

'I didn't know she was doing a line with him.'

'Oh, that's been going on a long time.'

'Is it the middle girl? The one with the peroxide?'

'Enid she's called.'

'I wonder Bob Crowe didn't hear that. There's not much
Bob misses.'

'I never thought much of Tyson. But, sure, maybe
they're well matched.'

'Did you hear that, Kitty? Enid Kenny's getting married.
Don't go taking ideas from her.' He laughed, and Mrs
Shaughnessy laughed, and the son smiled. There wasn't
much chance of that, Kathleen thought. 'Are you going
dancing tonight?' Mr Crawley often asked her on a Friday,
and she would reply that she might, but she never did because it wasn't easy to go alone. In the shops and at mass
no one displayed any interest in her whatsoever, no one
eyed her the way Mary Florence had been eyed, and she
supposed it was because her looks weren't up to much. But
they were good enough for Mr Shaughnessy, with his
quivering breath and his face in her hair. Bitterly, she dwelt
on that; bitterly, she imagined herself turning on him in the
dining-room, accusing him to his wife and son.

'Did you forget to sweep the yard this week?' Mrs
Shaughnessy asked her. 'Only it's looking poor.'

She explained that the wind had blown in papers and
debris from a knocked-over dustbin. She'd sweep it again,
she said.

'I hate a dirty backyard, Kitty.'

Was this why the other girls had left, she wondered, the girls whom Mrs Shaughnessy had trained, and who'd then gone off? Those girls, whoever they were, would see her, or would know about her. They'd imagine her in one uniform or the other, obedient to him because she enjoyed his attentions. That was how they'd think of her.

'Leave me alone, sir,' she said when she saw him approaching her the next time, but he took no notice. She could see him guessing she wouldn't scream.

'Please, sir,' she said. 'Please, sir. I don't like it.'

But after a time she ceased to make any protestation and remained as silent as she had been at first. Twelve years or maybe fourteen, she said to herself, lying awake in her bedroom: as long as that, or longer. In her two different uniforms she would continue to be the outward sign of Mrs Shaughnessy's well-to-do status, and her ordinary looks would continue to attract the attentions of a grey-haired man. Because of the field, the nature of the farm her father had once been barefoot on would change. 'Kathleen's field,' her father would often repeat, and her mother would say again that a bargain was a bargain.